ATHENS
A PICTORIAL HISTORY

By James K. Reap

ATHENS
A PICTORIAL HISTORY

By James K. Reap

Design by Jamie Backus Raynor
Donning Company/Publishers
Norfolk/Virginia Beach

Copyright © 1985 by James K. Reap

All rights reserved, including the right to reproduce this book in any form whatsoever without permission in writing from the publisher, except for brief passages in connection with a review. For information write:
The Donning Company/Publishers
5659 Virginia Beach Boulevard,
Norfolk, Virginia 23502.

Library of Congress Cataloging in Publication Data

Reap, James K.
Athens, a pictorial history.
Bibliography: p
Includes index.
1. Athens, Ga.—Description—Views.
2. Athens, Ga.—History—Pictorial works. I. Title.
F294.A7R4   975.8′18   80-28133
ISBN 0-89865-110-7 (pbk.)   AACR1

Printed in the United States of America

CONTENTS

Foreword 7
Preface 9
Chapter One
    1801-1860 11
Chapter Two
    1861-1900 43
Chapter Three
    1901-1940 97
Chapter Four
    1941-1985 159
Bibliography 203
Index 204

This book is dedicated to the historians, raconteurs, artists, and photographers who have chronicled Athens's intriguing history for future generations.

FOREWORD

It is a great pleasure for the Athens-Clarke Heritage Foundation to take part in the re-publication of James Reap's splendid book on our city, *Athens: A Pictorial History*.

The ample text provided by Mr. Reap for the wonderful photographs certainly makes this volume much more than just a picture book; rather, as one follows section by section the chronology of our city, it becomes apparent that a more thorough history of Athens could hardly be found.

I have recommended to citizens and visitors alike: "If you can buy just one book about Athens, this is the one!"

Athenians will always be indebted to James Reap for finding and preserving in photographs so much of our city that is gone; we will be equally indebted to him for spurring the interest of his readers to save what we still have.

Part of the purchase price of this volume will go to the Heritage Foundation for the furtherance of our goals in historic preservation. We hope you enjoy and learn from this book. It should encourage us all to strive to live by the ancient Athenian oath: To leave our city a more beautiful place than we found it.

Thank you for your support of historic preservation.

Sincerely,

L. Milton Leathers III
President

PREFACE

The city of Athens has a fascinating history, stretching back more than 180 years. From its earliest days it has occupied a prominent place among the cities of Georgia, and many of its residents have played significant roles in the history of the city, state, and nation. Athens has served as the commercial and industrial hub of Northeast Georgia and, most importantly, as the seat of the University of Georgia. The history of city and university are so interrelated that it is impossible to consider them separately. This relationship was described by Georgia historian E. Merton Coulter in his *College Life in the Old South:* "Those in authority who made the University also made the town, and the life of one was peculiarly and inseparably entwined and enmeshed with the other. No town was ever more completely the creature of an educational institution than was Athens and the character of no town ever more deeply partook of its creator." The two have grown up together and have shared progress and growth, in spite of the vicissitudes of war and depression, politics and natural disaster. The rough frontier settlement of 1801 has developed into a city of nearly 50,000 with a diversified economy and a bright outlook for the future. The city is also one of beauty and tradition. Writing in 1942, Hal Steed said, "Here in Athens the tourist can say: 'This is the South I have read about.'" Those unique qualities were in danger of being lost during the 1960s, when Athens for a time rushed to "modernize" because it was the thing to do. Urban renewal and unregulated growth threatened both the city's appearance and a way of life. By the 1970s, however, the city had begun to rediscover its unique identity in its historic structures and rich traditions. Today it is possible for Athenians to enjoy the best of both: progress and the preservation of their heritage. The townspeople have begun to learn that the two can be synonymous. Nevertheless, without legal protection, Athens landmarks remain subject to capricious development, and otherwise avoidable losses will continue to occur.

This book does not attempt to cover all aspects of Athens's 180-year-history, but to present people, places, and events that have been recorded in photographs, paintings, drawings, and documents. These vivid images help capture the flavor and character of the past in a way not possible with the written word alone. Brief introductions to each chapter and captions accompanying the photographs form an historical framework in which the images can be viewed. The narrative is based on information obtained from the materials cited in the accompanying bibliography and from personal interviews conducted by the author.

This book would not have been possible without the help of a great many persons, and I am deeply grateful to all of them. I would like to express my appreciation to the following: all of the individuals who searched personal collections to provide me with photographs and documentary information; Susan Barrow Tate for her guidance and suggestions, for identifying photographs, and for reading the manuscript; Larry Gulley and the staff of the University of Georgia Libraries Special Collections for help in locating photographs and documents in their collections; Dr. John Edwards for assistance with materials in the University Archives; the staff of the library's Photographic Services section for careful reproduction of many of the images used in the book; Walker Montgomery of the University of Georgia Office of Public Relations for providing photographs.

I would also like to thank Gail Miller of the Georgia Department of Archives and History and Anne Harman of the Georgia College Library for help in obtaining photographs from their collections; Robert Chambers, Conoly Hester, Masie Underwood, and the staffs of Athens Newspapers, Incorporated for their advice, encouragement, and access to photographic files; Gene Blythe of Associated Press for permission to reproduce photographs; Dr. James E. Kibler for his invaluable suggestions and patient reading of the manuscript; Ann Hammond Dure for many hours of editorial and creative design assistance with the second edition; and the board of the Athens-Clarke Heritage Foundation, particularly Milton Leathers and Carol Yoder, for their interest and cooperation.

—James K. Reap

Abraham Baldwin, the man properly regarded as the father of the University of Georgia, was born in Connecticut on November 22, 1754. Graduating from Yale in 1772, he studied for the ministry and was licensed to preach in 1775. He returned to Yale as a tutor but resigned in 1775 to serve as a chaplain in the Revolutionary army. After the hostilities, Baldwin entered a new profession, being admitted to the bar in 1783. In that same year he migrated to Georgia and soon received a land grant in Wilkes County.

When the General Assembly set aside 40,000 acres of land in February of 1784 for the endowment of a college or seminary, Baldwin was appointed one of the trustees. The following year the people of Wilkes County sent him to the General Assembly where he drafted and secured the passage of the charter of the University of Georgia. He was appropriately chosen to be the first president of the new institution.

Soon thereafter, Baldwin achieved national prominence as a member of the Continental Congress and the Constitutional Convention and was one of Georgia's signers of the Federal Constitution. He was immediately elected to the United States House of Representatives, serving there until he entered the Senate in 1799, where he served until his death.

Although his political duties demanded much of his time, he never lost interest in the university he had created. He resigned as president of the university in 1801 in favor of his former pupil at Yale, Josiah Meigs, but he continued to serve on the board of trustees. He was also appointed a member of the committee which selected the site of the university in 1801. Baldwin, who never married, devoted his life to serving his adopted state and became one of its greatest statesmen. He died in Washington, D.C. on March 4, 1807 and is buried there beside his colleague from Georgia, James Jackson.

Baldwin County, site of Georgia's Antebellum capital, Milledgeville, is named in his honor. This illustration was engraved by J. B. Forrest from a drawing by E. G. Leutz, after an original sketch by R. Fulton. Photograph courtesy of the University of Georgia Libraries Special Collections

Chapter One
1801-1860

The story of Athens begins on February 25, 1784, only months after the signing of the treaty which ended the Revolutionary War. The General Assembly, in laying out the new counties of Washington and Franklin, set aside 40,000 acres of land to endow "a college or seminary of learning." Georgia, which had a small and scattered population and few financial resources, had been devastated by the war and faced the problems of organizing a state government and establishing control over a vast and rapidly expanding frontier.

Planning for an institution of higher learning might have been easily postponed in these circumstances but for the vision of a group of prominent Georgians, largely New England educated, living primarily in Savannah and the coastal region. Leadership of this group fell to Abraham Baldwin, a native of Connecticut and a graduate of Yale University, who had moved to Georgia in 1783. Working with John Milledge and Nathan Brownson, Baldwin quickly drew up a charter for a university and presented it to the legislature, which approved it on January 27, 1785. Georgia thus became the first state to charter a state university. A governing body, called the Senatus Academicus of the University of Georgia, was established, and Abraham Baldwin was elected first president of the educational establishment, which embraced elementary schools and academies as well as the university.

Several years of inactivity followed, but by 1798 it was discovered that about $6,000 had accumulated from the sale and rental of the lands granted in 1784. With enough money to start a university, the Senatus Academicus began bickering over a location for the institution. The issue was finally settled in 1801 when Jackson County, which had been created out of the original Franklin County, was chosen, and a committee composed of Abraham Baldwin, John Milledge, John Twiggs, Hugh Lawson, and George Walton was appointed to locate a site and contract for the construction of an appropriate building. While scouting Jackson County in the summer of 1801, the committee came upon a place called Cedar Shoals on the north fork of the Oconee River where Daniel Easley, a speculator and shrewd entrepreneur, had purchased 1,000 acres of land and established a small mill. Easley convinced the committee that 633 acres of his land on a high hill on the west bank of the river was ideal for the new seat of learning. Although the university owned 5,000 acres nearby, John Milledge purchased the land from Easley and gave it to the trustees, and the committee named the place "Athens." The site was a particularly beautiful one with large forest trees and cool, clear water. Josiah Meigs, who had replaced Abraham Baldwin as president of the university, gave a glowing description of the place with its several good springs, pleasant breezes, and extended horizon. He concluded, "If there is a healthy and beautiful spot in Georgia this is one."

President Meigs, an outstanding educator who had been a student of Baldwin's at Yale, set out with vigor to create a university in the wilderness. He contracted with Easley for construction of a president's house and a frame schoolhouse and supervised the laying of the foundation for a permanent brick college building patterned after Connecticut Hall at Yale. The first class of the new institution had graduated in 1804 before the work on the building, now known as Old College, was completed in 1806. The college was christened Franklin College in honor of Benjamin Franklin, who had served as Georgia's colonial agent in London.

Lots were laid out for a town along Front Street (now Broad Street), and the income from the sale and rental of these lots and the other lands owned by the university provided the bulk of the institution's income. During their first decade, both university and nascent town increased in size as interest in the college grew. In 1801 they were included in a new county, Clarke, and in 1806, when Athens was incorporated by the General Assembly, the town boasted an estimated seventeen families, ten frame houses, and four stores. The first lots were within the parallelogram formed by Foundry, Broad, Hull, and Hancock streets, but prior

AUGUSTA, *July* 25.

THE UNIVERSITY.

OF an institution deeply interesting to the present age, and still more so to an encreasing posterity, every information respecting its establishment and progress should be known to the people at large; and for which purpose we are assured, that, from time to time, suitable communications will be made through the medium of this Gazette.

The Senatus Academicus, having designated the county in which the University should be established, named a committee to select the site and contract for a building.

The committee accordingly, on the 29th of the same month, repaired to the county of Jackson, and proceeded with attention and deliberation, to examine a number of situations, as well upon the tracts belonging to the University, as upon others of private individuals. The committee having completed their views, and estimated their respective advantages, proceeded by ballot to make the choice; when the vote was unanimous in favour of a place belonging to Mr. Daniel Easley, at the Cedar Shoals, upon the north fork of the Oconee river; and the same was resolved to be selected and chosen for the Seat of the University of Georgia, accordingly.

For this purpose the tract, containing six hundred and thirty three acres, was purchased of Mr. Easley, by Mr. Milledge, one of the committee, and made a donation of to the Trustees; and it was called *Athens*.

It lies, of course, in the county of Jackson, and is distant from Augusta, a west course, and by the post road, ninety miles; and is adjacent to a tract of five thousand acres belonging to the trust.

The river at Athens is about one hundred and fifty feet broad; its waters rapid in their descent: and has no low grounds.

The site of the University is on the south side, and half a mile from the river. On one side the land is cleared; the other is wood-land. On the cleared side are two ample orchards of apple and peach trees; forming artificial copses, between the site and the river, preferable to the common under growth of nature.

What little vapour rises at any time from the river is always attracted by the opposite hills, towards the rising sun.

About two hundred yards from the site, and at least three hundred feet above the level of the river, in the midst of an extensive bed of rock, issues a copious spring of excellent water; and, in its meanderings to the river, several others are discovered.

On the place is a new well built framed dwelling house; entirely equal to the accommodation of the President and his family. There is also another new house, equal to a temporary school room.

The square of the University, containing thirty-six acres and an half, is laid off so as to comprehend the site, the houses, the orchards and the spring, together with a due proportion of the wood-land.

The first report that a site had been chosen for the location of the University of Georgia appeared in the Augusta Chronicle on July 25, 1801. This column recounted the actions of the selection committee, the gift of the land by John Milledge, and the naming of the location "Athens." The Chronicle praised the site selected and over the following weeks and months continued to print descriptions of the locale and stories of the university's progress. Photograph courtesy of the University of Georgia Libraries Special Collections

to 1820 only the area to the east of Lumpkin Street was developed. In its first decade, Athens gained a female seminary, its first hotel, and a weekly newspaper, *The Georgia Express*. The town, however, retained much of a frontier character. Indians often visited to trade or to shoot arrows for the entertainment of the university students, and during the War of 1812, a small Indian raid in the lower part of the county caused a brief panic.

The university and town languished during their second decade, but the 1820s saw a general revitalization under President Moses Waddel. Economic conditions improved, new residents arrived, additional schools and stores opened, the town's first churches were built, and Georgia's first major textile mill was established. With an eye to future development, the university trustees had a large section of their land to the west of the town surveyed in 1833, and in July of the following year, John A. Cobb advertised the sale of eighty lots which adjoined the town on the northwest, and which lay on both sides of the main road (now Prince Avenue) "leading through Jefferson and Gainesville to the Gold Region." This development, Athens's first "suburb," was christened the Village of Cobbham.

In the decades that followed, Athens became the commercial and industrial center of Northeast Georgia. George White reported in his *Statistics of the State of Georgia*, published in 1849, that Athens was the market for Clarke, Jackson, Habersham, Rabun, Elbert, Union, Madison, Oglethorpe, and Lumpkin counties, and parts of North Carolina, South Carolina, and Tennessee. Several large cotton factories, as well as a number of smaller manufacturers, were responsible for placing Clarke County, by 1840, second only to Savannah and Chatham County in capital invested in manufacturing. The founding of the Georgia Railroad in Athens in 1833 and the beginning of rail service in

On December 5, 1801 a new county was created by the General Assembly out of the part of Jackson County in which Athens and the University of Georgia were located. It was named after Elijah Clarke, a Revolutionary War hero and adventurer. Clarke, who was born in South Carolina, was living in Wilkes County, Georgia when the Revolution broke out. He served in many skirmishes and battles in the South and became a brigadier general in 1781-1783. He shared the credit for the decisive battle at Kettle Creek in Wilkes County in 1779. In recognition for his outstanding service, the legislature granted him a large estate.

After the war, Clarke became involved in many adventures on the frontier. He defeated the Indians at Jack's Creek in Walton County in 1787 and became involved in 1793 with French officials in a scheme to enlist Georgia Creeks and Cherokees in a campaign against the Spanish. Along with other land-hungry Georgians he created the Trans-Oconee Republic, which set up forts and laid out towns in Creek territory. President Washington ordered the state, which had been tolerant of the development, to break it up. Faced with a blockade by Georgia troops and the desertion of many of his followers, Clarke surrendered. In spite of his many adventures, his general reputation remained high in the state.

The Daughters of the American Revolution in Athens created an Elijah Clarke chapter in his honor and erected a monument to his memory which stands in the middle of Broad Street across from the university. Photograph courtesy of the University of Georgia Libraries Special Collections

---

1841 also contributed to Athens's superior trading position.

Antebellum Athens was an attractive, prosperous, and cultured town. In 1849 White reported that the population had reached 3,000, and that the amount of business done per annum was in excess of $400,000. He declared that "the health of Athens is unsurpassed by that of any town of the same size in the United States. The citizens are noted for refinement and taste. Many of the private residences are beautiful and furnished in a costly manner. The gardens are laid out with much taste." English writer and traveler James Silk Buckingham also found Athens "picturesque and romantic," and had high praise for the citizens' appearance, intelligence, and manners. After attending a commencement party given for the senior class at the university by President Alonzo Church, Buckingham wrote, "I doubt whether any town in England or France, containing a population of little more than a thousand persons—for that is the extent of the white inhabitants here—could furnish a party of two hundred, among whom should be seen so much ease, frankness, and even elegance of manners." The accommodations at the Planter's Hotel were also to his liking except for the incessant noise of the dogs, cows, and hogs which roamed the streets at night.

Athens supported a wide variety of commercial establishments by the 1840s and 1850s. Drugstores, confectionary shops, bookstores, clothing stores, barber shops, jewelry stores, beauty shops, ice cream shops, a paint store, a gun store, and general merchandise stores were among the establishments seeking the patronage of university students, townspeople, and visitors alike. An Athens branch of the Bank of the State of Georgia was established along with the Georgia Railroad Bank, which later moved to Augusta. In 1856 the Bank of Athens was incorporated and showed a profit of $11,904 by the end of the first year. It was little affected by the financial panic of 1857. Several insurance companies were also organized during this period, the best known of which was the Southern Mutual Insurance Company, chartered in Griffin in 1847 and moved to Athens in 1848. It has remained one of Athens's most important and enduring institutions.

The town was governed by a board of commissioners which appropriated $1,000 in 1845 to build a town hall and market house. Located in the middle of Market Street (now Washington), the new facility housed a meeting room on the second floor, with the market and calaboose on the ground floor. The only other public building constructed during this period was a powder magazine which was completed in 1850. In 1848 the town received a new charter which changed the form of government to an intendant and warden system. The people elected wardens from each of the town's three wards, who in turn chose one of their number as intendant with the same powers as the old commission chairman. The intendant and warden selected a town marshal to collect taxes, attend the market, superintend the working of the streets, and patrol the town. By the end of the decade a clerk was appointed to attend to the marshal's non-police duties, and the marshal was elected by the people.

Fire was a major concern of the citizens of Athens, but little action was taken until after New College was destroyed by fire in 1830. A volunteer company was formed, but without a supply of water or a fire engine little could be done. As the Antebellum period drew to a close, a number of volunteer companies were formed, and the town constructed cisterns and a reservoir to assure a sufficient water supply. These groups, in addition to providing valuable civic service, became important social organizations which offered parties,

If it had not been for the generosity of John Milledge, the little settlement at Cedar Shoals on the Oconee River might never have been made the seat of the University of Georgia, and the town of Athens might not have risen on the wooded hills above the river. As a member of the committee appointed to select a site for the university in 1801, Milledge purchased 633 acres from Daniel Easley and gave it to the trustees of the university. It was on this land that the college rose and the town of Athens began.

A man of little formal education, John Milledge was one of Georgia's leading patriots and statesmen in the period that stretched from the Revolution to the War of 1812. Beginning his career at the bar by studying law in the office of the King's Attorney, young Milledge joined the Revolutionary cause in the exciting days following the news of Lexington and Concord. He served with distinction at the seiges of Augusta and Savannah and became attorney general of the state in 1780. He served in the Georgia General Assembly and as a member of Congress, from which he resigned in 1802 to become governor. After two terms in that office he was sent to the United States Senate in 1806 where he became president pro tempore before retiring in 1809. After a distinguished career, he died on February 8, 1818, at the age of sixty-one, in his home in Augusta.

The state honored Milledge by christening its Antebellum capital "Milledgeville." Milledge Avenue, one of Athens's major thoroughfares, reminds local citizens of his role in the founding of their city. The portrait illustrated here was painted in 1800 by Robert Field. It was rediscovered in recent years in a New York art gallery and purchased by Fulton Federal Savings and Loan Association. Haines Hargrett, president of Fulton Federal, presented it to the Georgia College Foundation, and it hangs in Georgia's Antebellum governor's mansion in Milledgeville, now home of the president of Georgia College. Photograph courtesy of Georgia College Library

picnics, and most importantly, competitions between companies for the entertainment of their members and the townspeople.

By the late 1850s there was an increased interest in community planning. In 1859 a committee was appointed to name the streets, which had no official names prior to this time, and some had no names at all. In 1860 the trustees of Oconee Hill Cemetery were incorporated, culminating an effort begun in 1855 to locate a new burying ground. By 1856 lots were being sold in the new cemetery, which replaced the crowded old burying ground on Jackson Street.

One of the most exciting developments of the time was the advent of gas lights and the incorporation of the Athens Gas Light Company in 1856. The supply was often irregular, however, and occasionally the lights would flicker out, plunging houses or other buildings into darkness. Referring to this situation, the preacher of the Methodist church once amused the town by announcing that at the next service, "there will be plenty of gas." The inconvenience deterred few people from installing the new lights, and the city contracted for lamps on College and Broad streets in 1859.

The university remained the single most important institution in the community during the entire Antebellum period. The fortunes of the college rose and fell with the vicissitudes of the economy, the whims of the legislature, and the policies of the president and trustees. President Meigs resigned in 1810 amidst declining enrollment at the college and political disagreements with the trustees. After the intervening presidencies of John Brown and Robert Finley, during which the decline continued, Moses Waddel, one of the most respected educators in the South, once again brought stability and growth. During his term of office, which lasted from 1819 to 1829, the campus was expanded with the construction of New College,

Demosthenian Hall, and a large building for a grammar school. Upon his resignation to return to the ministry, he was succeeded by Alonzo Church, a native of Vermont and a professor of mathematics at the university since 1819. Serving until 1859, the austere and conservative Church dominated the remainder of the Antebellum period. During his tenure, the Chapel, Philosophical Hall, Phi Kappa Hall, and the Ivy Building were constructed, and New College was rebuilt after a disastrous fire. The faculty was enlarged, and the famous botanical garden was begun. Although the college remained small, in the period from 1821 to 1844, according to Robert Preston Brooks in his chronicle of the university, it graduated an associate justice of the United States Supreme Court, eleven justices of the Supreme Court in Georgia and other states, two United States senators, eleven members of Congress, a speaker of the United States House of Representatives, one cabinet member, seven governors of Georgia and other states, six college or university presidents, four ministers to other countries, four Confederate generals, three noteworthy authors, two prominent theologians, and a great doctor. These achievements were made in spite of lack of state support, competition from sectarian institutions, and a conservative attitude toward curriculum and university affairs in general. The university was reorganized in 1859, and a new law school was begun that year. By 1860 the university had a new outlook and a new head, Andrew Lipscomb, with the new title of Chancellor.

Student life was somewhat different from what it is today. It was difficult to get admitted, and prospective students were expected to know Greek, Latin, and arithmetic. The curriculum was inflexible and contained more Greek, Latin, and mathematics, with additional courses in grammar, geography, astronomy, natural and experimental philosophy, chemistry, botany, history, rhetoric, composition, moral philosophy, and government. Literary societies provided a diversion from classes, as well as an opportunity to practice public speaking. Entertainments were few and discipline was strict. Many students were reprimanded or expelled for card playing, drinking, dancing, swearing, attending the circus, and a wide variety of other infractions of the rules.

One of the high points of the year, both among students and the population of the state at large, was commencement. Families of the students, politicians, alumni, and townspeople came for the graduation and for the round of parties, speeches, and declamations. The gala atmosphere prevailed for weeks throughout the town. Another outlet for the students' energy was provided through military companies. Although outlawed by the administration from time to time, these were always popular with the students, giving them an opportunity to drill and parade on the campus and in the town.

The academic atmosphere created by the university encouraged the growth of other academies and schools in Athens. From the first decade of the town's existence, a private education was offered to young men and women, and a system of "poor schools" operated throughout much of the Antebellum period. Among the best known of the academies was the Center Hill School, operated by A. M. Scudder first in Cobbham and later behind his house on the corner of Hancock and Lumpkin streets. The most famous girls school was Lucy Cobb Institute, founded in 1858 by Thomas R. R. Cobb and other prominent Athenians. It immediately became an important part of community life and enjoyed a reputation for excellence until it closed in the 1930s.

Society in Antebellum Athens was composed of wealthy planters, merchants and industrialists, middle

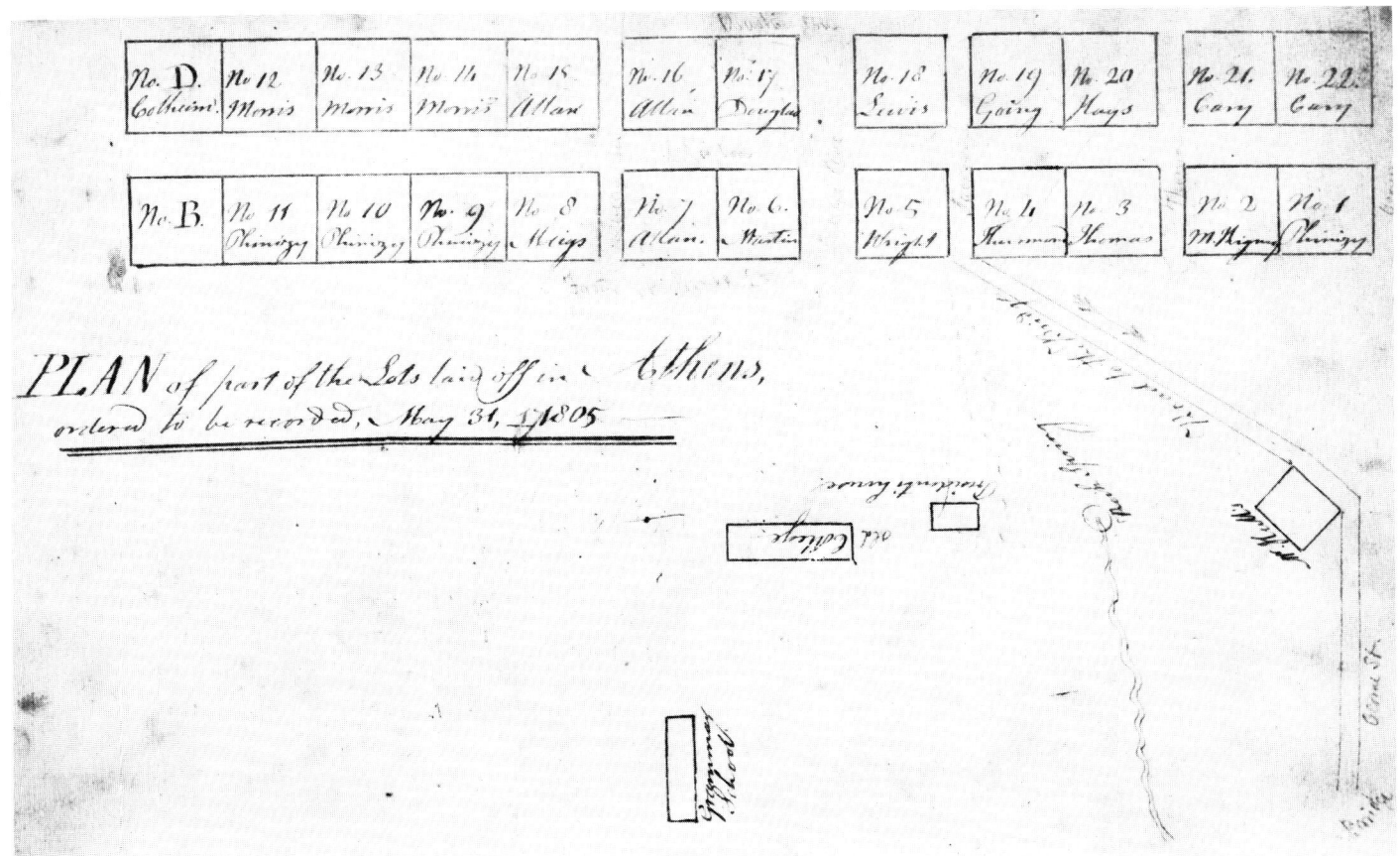

In 1803 the General Assembly authorized the university to lay out lots in Athens for sale or lease, retaining thirty-seven acres for a college yard. This map, drawn in 1804 and recorded in 1805, appears in the minutes of the trustees. It is the first known map of the town and college. Shown are the spring, the wooden grammar school, the President's House, and the brick College building, then under construction. The note that this was "Old" College was added at a later date.

The Road to the Bridge is the present Oconee Street, and the lots are laid out along what became Front (now Broad) and Clayton streets. Among the purchasers of the lots were: John Cary, owner of the town's first hotel (lots no. 21 and 22); Stevens Thomas, an early merchant (lot no. 3); and Ferdinand Phinizy, a prominent entrepreneur (lots no. 1, 9, 10, and 11). President Meigs purchased lot no. 8 for himself. Photograph courtesy of University Archives

class whites, poor whites, free blacks, and slaves. Living conditions were, of course, determined by the family's economic status. Most middle class citizens built comfortable houses, and many of the wealthy built large Federal or Greek Revival mansions in the fashion of the day. Town lots had to be big enough to accomodate the many outbuildings necessary to maintain a household: smoke house, carriage house, stable or barn, kitchen, privy, and the like. Most houses had vegetable and flower gardens, and yards were fenced to keep out roaming animals. Furnishings were simple, particularly in the early days, but as people's tastes became more refined and their prosperity increased, the more elaborate trappings of the Victorian era replaced the plantation-made furniture and homespun clothing. The biggest social events of the time were commencement, the Fourth of July, and militia muster day; but circuses, concerts, Washington's Birthday celebrations, theater performances, and lectures were also popular with all classes of citizens. Many shared a deep religious committment, and periodic revivals swelled the membership rolls of local churches—Methodist, Baptist, Presbyterian, Episcopal, and Disciples of Christ—which provided a social outlet as well as strength and consolation in time of distress and sorrow.

The currents which were sweeping the South and the nation toward the War Between the States intruded into the quiet college community and drew many of its citizens into the mainstream of the debates on abolitionism, free soil, states' rights, and secession. Howell and Thomas Cobb, Asbury Hull, Jefferson Jennings, and Wilson Lumpkin played important roles in the debate and political maneuvering locally and statewide. As the election of 1860 approached, there was marked dissension among local voters. The Democratic *Southern Banner* supported John Breckenridge, nominee of the Southern Democrats, while the *Southern Watchman*, an old Whig paper, endorsed John Bell, candidate of the Constitutional Union Party. When the votes were counted, John Bell led with 383 votes. Breckenridge garnered 334 votes, and even Stephen Douglas, nominee of the Northern Democrats, received 40 votes. On one issue the voters agreed: the Republican candidate, Abraham Lincoln, received no votes. When Lincoln

emerged victorious nationally, the community was confronted directly with the question of secession. Meetings were called and debates were held that led toward secession and war. A way of life for the town and the university, which had its beginnings in the exciting times following the War of Independence, was drawing to a close.

This photograph shows Old College, the oldest standing building in Athens, as it appeared in 1875. Although work was begun in 1803, it took contractor John Billups until 1806 to complete the structure. Labor was unreliable, lime and nails were expensive and had to be hauled overland from Augusta by wagon, and bricks had to be made from clay found over two miles from the campus.

In the early years, Old College housed students, faculty, tutors, servants, and classrooms. There were twenty-four principal rooms, forty-eight bedrooms, but only twenty-four fireplaces. During the War Between the States, Old College housed refugee families until the Confederate government seized the building to use it as a hospital for ill and wounded soldiers. When the college reopened after the war, it was once again used to house students.

Edward B. Mell recalled that during his father's tenure as chancellor (1878-1888), Old College was known as Summey House for the family that lived there and operated it like a boarding house. The trustees proposed to substitute proctors for the families in Old College and New College, but Chancellor Mell believed that they helped make it "home-like" for the students. The low cost of board meant cheap food; and "Summey House biscuits" were described as "a dyspeptic germ when fresh and a dangerous projectile when stale" (Hull, Annals).

By the turn of the century the building was vacant, deteriorated, and threatened with demolition, but funds were raised to rehabilitate the old landmark. It now houses administrative offices of the university. Photograph from Davis' Souvenir Album; courtesy of the University of Georgia Libraries Special Collections

The man responsible for translating the dream of a University of Georgia into a reality was Josiah Meigs, another native of Connecticut and a graduate of Yale. Upon his appointment as president of the new institution in 1801 at a salary of $1,500 a year and an allotment of $400 for moving, Meigs moved his family to Athens and began the task of creating a college in the wilderness. He cleared the campus, laid out a street which is now Broad Street, staked out town lots, and contracted for the erection of college buildings. While the latter were under construction, he conducted classes under an arbor.

By 1803 President Meigs could report that "three dwelling houses, three stores and a number of other valuable buildings have been erected on Front Street (now Broad)," and that the thirty students and the townspeople had been healthy during the year. Meigs was the only teacher for several years; then a professor of French and a tutor were added. He established a grammar school for students who were not prepared to enter college.

The institution progressed well until about 1808 when Meigs, a Jeffersonian, got into a conflict with Federalist trustees. Enrollment also began to decline, and Meigs resigned as president in 1810, remaining for one year as professor of mathematics. In 1812 he received a presidential appointment as surveyor-general in Cincinnati. Two years later he moved to Washington where he lived until his death in 1822.

Although Meigs received much criticism for the low state of the university at the time of his resignation in 1810, it was his perserverance that brought the college and town into existence. Meigs Hall formerly LeConte Hall on the Old North Campus of the university, is named in his honor. This portrait by Lewis Gregg is in the collection of the Georgia Museum of Art on the university campus. Photograph courtesy of the University of Georgia Libraries Special Collections

In February 1803, students at the university organized a society "for the promotion of extemporizing, or extemporary speaking" which became known as the Demosthenian Society. It became a popular activity, and provided for the students one of the few diversions which were approved by the administration. Interest was heightened further by the formation of a rival society, Phi Kappa, in 1820. This photograph, taken about 1875, shows the building that the society constructed for its hall in 1824 at a cost of $4,000. It is still being used by the Demosthenian Society.

The structure is unquestionably the finest and most attractive of the surviving Antebellum campus buildings. It has Federal detailing throughout, including the Palladian window above the entrance, the mantels, and the ornate plaster ceiling of the meeting room on the second floor. In 1979 the society initiated efforts to restore the lower chamber. The work was completed in 1981, and the hall was furnished with period furnishings provided by Athenian, Albert Sams, Sr. Photograph courtesy of the University of Georgia Libraries Special Collections

Moses Waddel was the first Southerner to become president of the university. During his tenure, 1819-1829, he rescued the young institution from near extinction. He was born in North Carolina in 1770, but moved with his parents to Greene County, Georgia in 1788. He was educated for the ministry in Virginia and preached for a time in Charleston, South Carolina. He soon moved to the upcountry, establishing academies first at Appling, Georgia and then at Vienna and Willington, South Carolina. These academies established his reputation as one of the most respected and popular educators in the South. Among his students were John C. Calhoun, William H. Crawford, George R. Gilmer, Augustus Baldwin Longstreet, and many other men who had large roles in shaping the history and character of the Antebellum South.

When Waddel arrived in Athens, the university and town were at a low ebb. His leadership and popularity helped restore vitality to the university. In addition, he established the Presbyterian Church in Athens in 1820 and continued to preach as long as he remained in town. During his tenure, a second major building, New College, was constructed, along with Phi Kappa and Demosthenian halls, and a new grammar school. He retired in 1829 and returned to South Carolina to preach. In 1836 illness forced him to return again to Athens where he lived with his son until his death in 1840. This portrait of Waddel hangs in the university library's Special Collections. Photograph courtesy of University of Georgia Libraries Special Collections

Philosophical Hall is the second oldest building still standing on the university campus. Since its completion in 1821, it has seen a wide variety of uses. Originally built as a classroom and laboratory building, it had become a gymnasium by the time this photograph was made in the 1890s. From 1903 to 1908 it was used by the college of agriculture and was called Agricultural Hall. For thirty-six years it was the home of Thomas Reed, registrar and treasurer of the university, and was known as Reed House. In 1953 the Campus Grill was moved here from New College, and the building was once again renovated for a new use.

In recent years it was rechristened Waddel Hall and has been used by a speech therapy center, the Institute of Government, and the University Press. The building now houses the Rusk Center for International Law. Over the years, additions were made to the rear of the building, but these have been removed. Except for a coat of white paint and the removal of the shutters, old Philosophical Hall appears today much as it did when this photograph was made. Photograph by McDannel Studios; courtesy of University of Georgia Libraries Special Collections

Commencement balls were one of the most important social events of the year in Athens, and the lady who received the invitation on the facing page in 1829 was honored indeed. The ball was held at Captain Samuel Brown's Assembly Room, which was located on the northeast corner of Broad and Thomas streets. It had been the hotel of John Cary, Athens's first innkeeper. Captain Brown took over the management of it when he married Mrs. McKigney, widow of the previous owner.

To prepare for the annual ball, many ladies and gentlemen would take instruction from itinerant dancing masters who would arrive in Athens in the spring. By August, the "amateurs of refined pleasure" were ready to enjoy themselves at Captain Brown's. Photograph courtesy of University of Georgia Libraries Special Collections

As the university's enrollment increased under the administration of President Waddel, it became apparent that a new large college building was needed to house the additional students. The foundations of New College were laid in 1822, and the work was completed the next year. Juniors and seniors were housed there until a fire gutted the building in 1830, destroying the college library and all of the mathematical and scientific apparatus. Money was finally raised to reconstruct the building in 1832, and the work was undertaken by James Carlton and Ross Crane. Crane became the principal builder in Athens during the Antebellum period.

Like Old College, New College was filled with refugees during the War Between the States and housed Federal troops for a brief period after the war. After the soldiers were removed, it once again became a dormitory. Mrs. George Richardson ran a student boarding house in the building until 1886 when the W. R. Stillwells took over the operation. It was known as Richardson House during most of this period.

The building was later converted to classrooms, and during its use by the School of Pharmacy in 1950, the building was evacuated for fear that it would collapse. Iron tie rods were installed and the building was renovated. The following year, the student co-op and bookstore, which occupied the basement, were moved to Philosophical Hall. Upon completion of the new Pharmacy Building in 1964, New College was used by the psychology department and in 1970 was converted into administrative offices. It houses the campus planning office and the dean of arts and sciences. Photograph (circa 1875) from Davis's Souvenir Album; courtesy of University of Georgia Libraries Special Collections

The university's first chapel, a gift from the Reverend Hope Hull, was completed in 1808 for less than $1,000. By the 1820s it was too small for the college's needs and looked "as if the chips of the College buildings had been gotten together at the close, and a chapel trumpt up by the carpenter's apprentice." Another critic labeled it an "execrable little coop" (Coulter, College Life). The state finally yielded to the pleas for a new building and the Chapel shown in the photograph was constructed in 1832 at a cost of $15,000.

A beautiful and well proportioned building, it was one of the first Greek Revival structures in Athens and undoubtedly influenced the planters and merchants who were soon building homes in this style. By 1860, the trustees regarded the structure as too small, but were unable to persuade the legislature to provide funds for a new one. The bell which signaled class periods and summoned students to chapel hung in the square cupola until 1913 when Registrar Reed pursuaded Chancellor Barrow to take both cupola and bell down. The bell was moved to a wooden tower behind the building where the tradition developed of ringing it to celebrate athletic victories. After many football games the bell has rung all night. The present bell is, in fact, a replacement, the original having been cracked by constant ringing.

According to the legend, Robert Toombs, who had been expelled from the college for gambling, stood under this tree outside of the Chapel during commencement and began to speak. His burning oratory, it is said, brought those in the audience outside, leaving the speakers alone on the podium. Augustus Hull labeled the story a fabrication, attributing it to the creative imagination of Henry Grady (Hull, Annals). Toombs's reputation for eloquence, earned as a politician and advocate for secession, is so strong that the story has persisted. The tree was struck by lightning on July 4, 1884, and the stump finally fell in 1908. A sundial was erected to mark the spot. Today the Chapel is used for lectures, concerts, and meetings. Photograph courtesy of University of Georgia Libraries Special Collections

This view of the interior of St. Peter's in Rome which hangs in the Chapel has become familiar to generations of university students and Athens residents. The huge painting (17 ft. x 23½ ft.) was presented to the university by Alabama industrialist Daniel Pratt in 1867. Pratt had commissioned the painting from George Cooke, a well-known nineteenth-century artist who lived and traveled in the South and who spent some time in Athens. Cooke was known particularly for his paintings of cities, including West Point, Richmond, Washington, and Charleston. He painted the view of Athens in 1842 which hangs in the university library.

After Cooke's death in 1849, his widow married an Athenian, Asbury Hull. She was instrumental in persuading Pratt, who had lived for many years in Milledgeville and Clinton, Georgia, to donate the painting to the university when he dispersed his art collection. The painting was touched-up by Jennie Smith, an art teacher at Lucy Cobb Institute, after it had begun to flake slightly. It was again touched-up by P. H. Baumgarten of the O'Brien Gallery in Chicago in 1936.

In 1955 the painting was damaged by fire and required extensive restoration. Artist Walter Frobos of the Athens Lumber Company repaired the damaged canvas, remounted it on masonite, and framed it in redwood. After removing the paint that had been added by Smith and Baumgarten, Frobos and his daughter spent eighteen months restoring the painting.

Dean Tate once asked university astronomy students to determine the best time of day to view the painting. After a study they concluded that between eleven in the morning and noon the sun is aligned with the rays coming through the windows. The painting may then be seen to the best advantage. Photograph courtesy of University of Georgia Office of Public Relations

The exterior of Phi Kappa Hall, shown here in 1875, appears today much as it did on the day it was dedicated, July 5, 1836. The Phi Kappa Literary Society was founded in 1820 as a rival to the older Demosthenian Society and met in various locations on campus until the completion of their hall. The guiding force behind the organization of the society was Joseph Henry Lumpkin, who later became Georgia's first supreme court chief justice.

Phi Kappa's were meticulous in their care of the building, once requesting local planters not to stack their cotton too near the building because of the danger of fire. Members developed secret signs and a system of diplomatic language and procedure. They particularly guarded against disclosure of their proceedings to the rival Demosthenians. This legendary rivalry is fully recounted by Dr. E. M. Coulter in College Life.

The college's first real gymnasium was installed on the first floor of Phi Kappa in 1888. The equipment was purchased with a gift from Hoke Smith, an Atlanta attorney who later became governor, United States senator, and member of President Cleveland's cabinet. In recent years, the lower floor of the hall was used by the late Dr. Coulter as an office and library. The upper hall, which has lost much of its detailing, is used periodically as a meeting room. Photograph from Davis's Souvenir Album; courtesy of University of Georgia Libraries Special Collections

The Dr. Eustace Speer House stood on the southwest corner of College Avenue and Washington Street until about 1920 when it was replaced by a range of stores. The stores in turn fell to the wrecker's ball after a disastrous fire in 1968 and the new Palace Theatre was constructed.

The house is said to have been built by a Major Walker about 1830 and was lived in successively by Colonel T. N. Hamilton and John H. Newton. Dr. Speer acquired the house from Newton after 1875. Photograph (circa 1890) courtesy of University of Georgia Libraries Special Collections

This illustration of the old campus appeared in Gleason's Magazine in the 1850s. Its original source is unknown, but it appeared on a clock manufactured in the 1830s. The view is from Broad Street across the Old College quadrangle. On the left is Phi Kappa Hall (1836). The identity of the building second from the left is not certain. It is believed to represent Philosophical Hall, although the proportions of the building as drawn are not accurate.

In the center is Old College (1806), followed by New College (1832), the Chapel (1833), Demosthenian Hall (1824), and the Ivy Building (1831), now incorporated into the Academic Building. The portion of a building with the pointed-arch window shown on the far right was the old Presbyterian church. It was replaced in 1859 by the old Library Building which, after the turn of the century, was incorporated with the Ivy Building, into the Academic Building.

The college yard was fenced to keep out livestock. The illustration shows the stiles which were used to cross the fence. This wooden fence was replaced in the 1850s by the present cast iron fence with proceeds from the sale of the old botanical garden. Illustration courtesy of University of Georgia Libraries Special Collections

This fascinating old house once stood on the north side of Oconee Street about where Armstrong and Dobbs's Warehouse Number Ten is now located. It is popularly believed to have been the house of Daniel Easley, the man who sold John Milledge the university's original 633 acres. Recent research by Patricia Cooper tends to disprove this tradition. It was once owned by E. R. Hodgson and seems to have been confused with another house owned by Hodgson on the south side of the street closer to Broad Street. That house, shown as the house of Hope Hull on the 1805 map of Athens, may indeed have been built by Daniel Easley.

The house in this photograph was probably built by Sterling Lane as early as 1807. The cedar trees in the front yard were, according to A. L. Hull, planted in front of the house by Lane's father after the young lawyer died of typhus in 1820. E. R. Hodgson bought the house for his mother, Elizabeth Preston Hodgson, who came to Athens in 1840. The house remained in the family until after the turn of the century when Hugh Hodgson removed the fine entrance with a fanlight and installed it in his house on Springdale Street, now the home of Mr. and Mrs. Edgar Cook.

One interesting feature of the photograph is the joggling board on which the woman and child are seated at the left of the cedar trees. This Carolina low country import was used as a stimulant to digestion or, with only one support, as a see-saw. Photograph courtesy of Mr. and Mrs. Edward R. Hodgson, III

The Mary Hardin Home, which once stood on the north side of Hancock Avenue between Hull and Pulaski streets, was the scene of one of Athens's favorite romantic stories which has been told and retold, and undoubtedly exaggerated. As the story goes, John Howard Payne, a dramatist and poet, stopped in Athens at the home of General Hardin while on the way to visit John Ross, chief of the Cherokees.

A friendship and romance developed between Payne and Hardin's daughter Mary. The father, however, did not regard the peripatetic writer as a suitable son-in-law, so Payne did not remain long in Athens. When he left he was said to have given the original of his poem, "Home, Sweet Home," to Miss Mary. John Howard Payne did, in fact, visit Athens, as reported in the Athens Banner in October 1835. He may also have given Miss Mary a copy of his poem, but it was unlikely that it was the original, which had been published some fifteen years before his visit.

Miss Hardin also received a letter from Payne after his departure in which he expressed his undying devotion in the flowery manner of the period. This is the extent of the evidence. The house was still standing at the turn of the century but was soon demolished. It is now the site of Griffith Brothers Tire Company. Photograph by David Earnest; courtesy of University of Georgia Special Collections

It is believed that the Church-Waddel-Brumby House was begun in 1820 by university faculty member and later president, Alonzo Church. Before its completion it was sold to another university president, Moses Waddel, who is said to have preferred the quiet of Hancock Avenue to the noisy campus. In 1860, Mrs. Sarah H. Harris acquired the house from the Waddel family. Her descendants, the Brumbys, lived in the house until 1964.

The two-story frame house with Federal detailing was erected, according to Augustus Longstreet Hull, by "a Yankee named Peck," who had come to Athens with his sons and other relatives. Over the years, additions were made to accommodate the needs of growing families, in time almost doubling the space in the house. This photograph shows the house with these additions as it appeared when the Brumby family lived there early in this century. The house has since been moved to Dougherty Street and restored for the city's Welcome Center. Photograph courtesy of University of Georgia Libraries Special Collections

The Lucas House, shown in this photograph taken near the turn of the century, stood on a hill at the end of Jackson Street and had a wide lawn extending down to Baldwin Street. The entire old campus lay above Baldwin, and as late as 1920 a row of modest houses stretched along the south side of the street. Although the house's massive Doric portico is indicative of 1840s and 1850s construction, the delicate Federal moldings and fanlights above the entrance and balcony doorway point to an earlier date for the house.

The F. W. Lucas family was living there in the early 1870s at the time of Sylvanus Morris's strolls. "It was one of the most popular houses in the place," he recalled, "and the young ladies were the belles of the day" (Morris, Strolls). Lucas owned a dry goods and clothing store on the north side of Broad Street between Wall and Jackson. It was said that when he went North after the Civil War to buy new stock, that he paid all of his debts for goods shipped to him four years before. The house was moved before 1912 nearer Memorial Hall and was demolished in the early 1950s, after serving for some years as an athletic dormitory. Reed Hall now occupies that site. Photograph courtesy of University of Georgia Libraries Special Collections

Little is known of the history of the Golding-Gerdine House which once stood on the northeast corner of Dougherty and Lumpkin streets. It is believed to have been built about 1836 by Thomas Golding and after his death inherited by his daughter Susan Golding, wife of Dr. John Gerdine. The Gerdines later moved to another house on the corner of Hancock and Lumpkin (where Athens Federal Savings Bank is today).

When photographed by the Historic American Building Survey in 1936, it was owned by Linton Gerdine and was rental property. The house was demolished and replaced by a grocery store in the 1950s. The site is currently the location of Thrifcity Grocery. The house, showing a transition between the Federal and Greek Revival styles, was illustrated in Nichols's Early Architecture of Georgia. Photograph by L. D. Andrew, HABS, Library of Congress

James Carlton, one of Athens's most prominent Antebellum contractors, built this substantial brick structure on the northwest corner of Hull and Dougherty streets for his own residence in the late 1830s. Carlton had made his reputation by constructing the University Chapel with Ross Crane in 1832 and continued to receive lucrative commissions for another thirty years.

Among the important buildings which he constructed were the Georgia Railroad depot (1856) and the Baptist church (1860), both now destroyed. In the late nineteenth century, the house was owned by the Mandeville family, who probably added the Victorian porch. It was demolished before 1950, and after the area was cleared by urban renewal in the late 1960s, the Jessie B. Denney Tower was erected on the site. Photograph courtesy of University of Georgia Libraries Special Collections

The fetching young lady seated on the horse in this photograph is in the side yard of the house on Cobb Street now popularly known as Moss-Side. Construction of the house has been attributed to Hiram Hayes. Deed records point to a date of 1846, but some interior Federal or transitional details may indicate an earlier date. The property was acquired in 1861 by R. L. Moss, who served on the staff of General Howell Cobb during the war. Afterwards he was a director and promoter of the Northeastern Railroad which provided Athens with rail links to the northern part of the state.

R. L. Moss and A. K. Childs owned a good deal of property at Tallulah Falls, a popular resort with Athenians, and Sylvanus Morris recalled staying in the Moss Cottage there (Morris, Strolls). Dr. William Lorenzo Moss, who discovered the technique of blood typing while doing research at Johns Hopkins Hospital, was born in 1876 in this house. A 1921 survey showed that his system of blood-typing was used in 95 percent of all hospitals. The house once occupied the entire block bounded by Cobb, Billups, Hill, and Franklin streets, but the LaFayette Square Apartments have been built on the rear of the lot. The old Grove School (not pictured) formerly stood on the east side of the house. The house looks today much as it did in this photograph, and it is still owned by the Moss family. Photograph courtesy of Mrs. James T. Heery, Jr.

The Camak House, located on the block surrounded by Hancock, Newton, Meigs, and Finley streets, was one of the first houses constructed in the Prince Avenue area of Athens. It was built circa 1834 by James Camak, one of the state's most important early industrialists, who had come to Athens to teach mathematics at the university in 1817. He was involved in numerous enterprises, the most important of which was the founding of the Georgia Railroad. He was elected the first president of the railroad and later served as cashier. Tradition places the organizational meeting of the corporation at this house in 1834. In that same year he became a director of the Branch Bank of the State of Georgia and served as president of the Georgia Railroad Bank when it was organized. He had a major role in the founding of Princeton Factory in 1833.

Camak was also interested in agriculture, experimenting with the introduction of new varieties of grasses, grapes and plums. He was even head of the editorial department of the Southern Cultivator for a time. He served on the vestry of Emmanuel Episcopal Church, and it is said that his financial support was crucial to the church's survival.

After Camak's death in 1847, the house remained in his family until it was purchased by the Mount Vernon Lodge No. 22, F. & A. M. in August 1949. A state historical marker recognizing the importance of the house in the history of the Georgia Railroad was dedicated by the Athens Historical Society on May 31, 1963, and the site was listed in the National Register of Historic Places in 1975. It is now owned by the Athens Coca-Cola Bottling Company, which has constructed a parking lot along Newton Street and has restored the exterior of the building. Photograph (circa 1940) courtesy of University of Georgia Libraries Special Collections

This view of Athens from Carr's Hill was painted in the 1840s by George Cooke. It now hangs in the University of Georgia Library. In the background are the town and university on the high hills west of the Oconee River. The middle ground shows the bridge across the river and the buildings of Athens Factory. In the foreground are the cars of the Georgia Railroad.

Tradition has it that the Georgia Railroad was founded in response to frustrations suffered by James Camak, William Williams, and William Dearing. It is said that they lost months of construction time when the machinery for their new factory, being sent overland from Augusta by wagon, was mired in the mud all one winter long near Union Point. The story does illustrate the difficulty suffered by travelers and merchants in that day.

The Georgia Railroad was chartered by the General Assembly on December 21, 1833. On March 10, 1834 the organizational meeting was held in Athens, where Camak was elected president. Work soon began, but the railroad did not reach Athens from Augusta until 1841. The first cars were drawn by mule over the branch from Union Point to Athens, but were soon replaced with steam engines, as indicated in the painting.

In 1841 an Augustan, John P. King, was elected president of the company, and the headquarters were moved there the following year, although Athenians continued to play an important part in the company. To the consternation of both travelers and merchants, the railroad terminated on the east side of the Oconee River. Hack drivers and freight haulers made a handsome profit until competition by other railroads in the late nineteenth century finally forced the Georgia Railroad to relocate its tracks and terminal from Carr's Hill to the west side of the river near Broad Street. Photograph courtesy of University of Georgia Libraries Special Collections

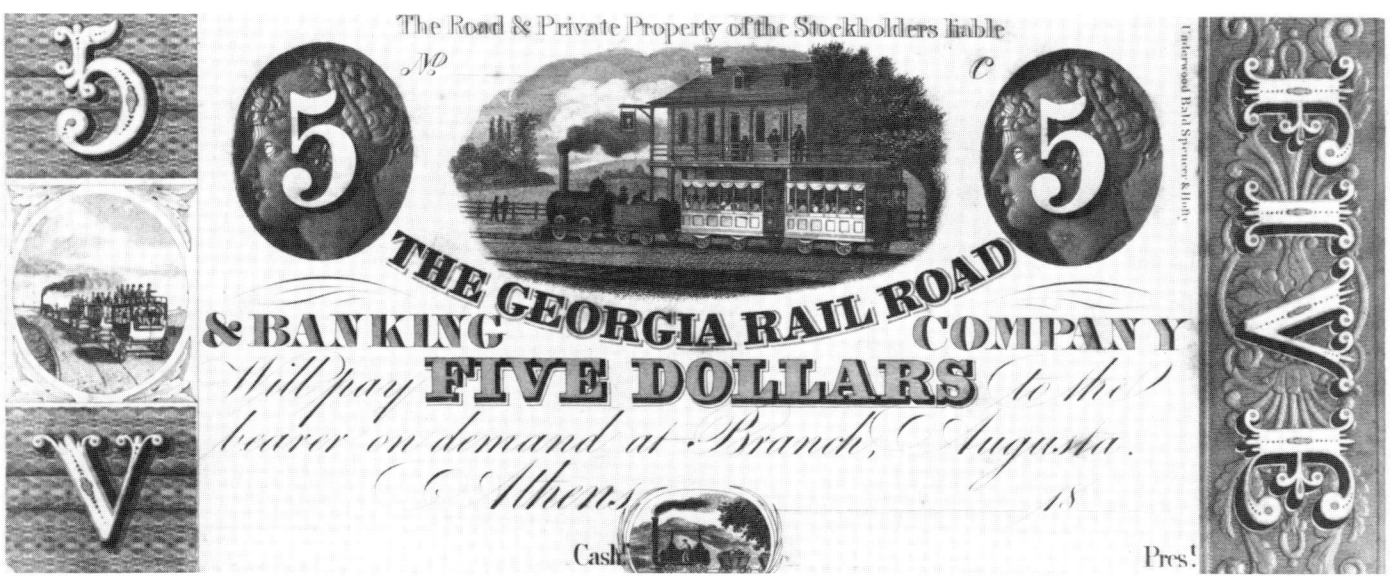

In 1835 the General Assembly amended the charter of the Georgia Railroad, conferring on it banking powers and privileges. The following year the action was ratified by the stockholders who voted to open a bank in Athens and a branch in Augusta. The financial panic of 1837 caused problems for both branches, but each survived the crisis. When the Georgia Railroad and Banking Company, as it was then called, moved its headquarters to Augusta in 1842, the Athens bank closed its doors. The Georgia Railroad Bank, as was the custom of banks at that time, issued its own currency.

The banknote shown above is a proof of a five dollar note issued by the bank before the move to Augusta. As a proof, it does not bear the validating signatures of the president and the cashier of the company. This proof is extremely rare; only two examples are known. Note courtesy of Gary Doster

Athens's old Town Hall stood in the center of Market Street (now Washington Street) between Lumpkin and Hull from 1847 until it was destroyed by fire in 1893. The entrance, which faced Lumpkin Street, was flanked by a double row of China trees, and there was a well to one side. The lower floor served the dual purpose of town market and calaboose. The sanitary conditions in this "malodorous" facility were long a topic of conversation among townspeople. The hall was on the second floor.

Over the years it was used for political debates, concerts and recitals, minstrel shows, dramatic performances, suppers, public meetings, school commencements, and trials. After the county seat was moved to Athens from Watkinsville in 1872, it served as the courthouse until a new one could be built. During the Civil War it even served as a place of refuge.

One Sunday morning, when the women were in church and the men at home, several pranksters set off the double-barrel cannon in front of the hall. This was a pre-arranged signal for the women to get inside the hall and the men to form a circle around it and fight. "After the excitement subsided," according to Sylvanus Morris, "the hall was found packed with men, not a woman could get inside. The number wounded in the scuffle to get inside has never been reported" (Morris, Strolls). When city offices moved, the building became a livery stable and burned in 1893. Conjectural sketch courtesy of Athens Newspapers, Incorporated

This sketch, entitled Palace of King John Lackland, was inscribed on the back "To Annie Smith, the bewitching, from her venerable cousin Arthur Huger. Christmas 1865." Nothing further is known of the parties mentioned, but the drawing is of one of the five dwellings constructed by the university to house its faculty. This house was named the Strahan House after one of its occupants, Professor Charles Morton Strahan, a graduate (1883) of the university who remained for sixty-two years teaching primarily civil engineering and mathematics, but serving also the departments of English, ancient languages, modern languages, chemistry, and history.

Strahan initiated the state's road improvement program in 1918 and became the first chairman of the State Highway Department. He is responsible for the design of many buildings in Athens, among them Academic Building, which he created by joining the Ivy Building with the old library. His book, Clarke County (1893) provides helpful insight into institutions, businesses, and industries of the day.

Other notable residents of the Strahan House include Richard Malcolm Johnston, professor of belles letters and rhetoric (1857-1861) and author of Dukesborough Tales. In recent years the house served as the Institute of Law and Government and as a student center before being demolished in the late 1960s to make way for an addition to the law school. Drawing courtesy of University of Georgia Libraries Special Collections

Crawford W. Long, one of Georgia's notable citizens, came to Athens from his home in Danielsville at the age of fourteen to enter the university. During his stay he shared a room in Old College with Alexander Stephens, who later became vice president of the Confederacy. Long was a member of the Demosthenian Society and was fined several times for "sleeping in the hall," "loitering on the steps," "going out without permission," and "neglect of duty as treasurer" (Coulter, College Life).

After graduating in 1835, he attended medical school at the University of Pennsylvania. He practiced surgery briefly in New York before returning to Georgia to set up his practice in Jefferson. While living there, his friends pursuaded him to give a "nitrous oxide frolic," in which participants became exhilarated by inhaling laughing gas. Being out of nitrous oxide, Long substituted sulfuric ether. He noticed that those inhaling it became euphoric, and a number suffered bruises but felt no pain.

On March 30, 1842 he administered ether to a patient, James Venable, and removed a tumor from the back of his neck. This was the first operation performed under a general anesthetic. The account of his discovery was not published until 1849, after another doctor had claimed the first use of ether in an operation. "Long was modest almost to timidity," recalled A. L. Hull, "and for that reason never took the place in the community to which he was entitled," and made no claim to any credit for discovering the anesthetic effect of ether.

Dr. Long moved to Athens in 1850, where he continued to practice medicine and opened a drugstore on Broad Street in the middle of the block between Jackson and College streets. During the War Between the States he served as a surgeon. Dr. Long's medical discovery has been widely recognized since his death in 1878, and he was one of the two Georgians honored by having a statue erected in his honor in the United States Capitol. The silhouette of Crawford Long on the facing page belonged to Judge Howell Cobb of Athens and was given by his daughter Sarah Cobb Baxter to Long's daughters for exhibition in the Chicago World's Fair. Courtesy of Univerity of Georgia Libraries Special Collections

This photograph is of Crawford Long's home, which was located on Prince Avenue near the intersection with Chase Street. After the turn of the century it was turned to face Chase Street. It has since been demolished for a parking lot. Photograph courtesy of University of Georgia Libraries Special Collections

The wooden statue in this photograph was a prominent feature on Broad Street, where it stood before the Long Drug Store. Carved from hickory wood by Charles Oliver in the 1850s, the statue was dubbed "Tom Long." It disappeared in the late nineteenth century, but was found in Elberton by Dr. A. B. Long, Crawford Long's son, who had it refurbished. It disappeared again after this photograph was made and its location is no longer known. Photograph courtesy of University of Georgia Libraries Special Collections

The Hull-Morton-Snelling House, located at 198 South Hull Street, is believed to have been built by John Hope Hull in 1842. The house was later occupied by Asbury Hull who was secretary and treasurer of the university for almost a half century (1819-1866). He participated in the founding of the Georgia Railroad and served as president of the Southern Mutual Insurance Company. The Morton family acquired the property from the Hulls, and in this century it was the residence of Mrs. Morton's daughter and son-in-law, the Charles M. Snellings. Charles Snelling was dean of the university and was appointed chancellor in 1926.

When Dean William Tate was a college freshmen, he took refuge on the wide Victorian porch shown in the photograph to escape some pursuing sophomores who were running freshmen out of the picture show. "I scooted into the Snelling yard, eased on the porch, and lay down," he recalled. "At the gate the chasers with their paddles stopped, not willing to raid the dean's house for a worthless freshman" (Tate, Strolls). The house is now owned by the Christian College of Georgia. The commodious front porch has been removed. Photograph courtesy of University of Georgia Libraries Special Collections

A university parking lot marks the site of the house in the photograph on the left which faced Waddell Street in the block between Hull Street and Florida Avenue. Reputed to have been built for Moses Dobbins by the prominent builder/architect Ross Crane, it was owned by Mr. and Mrs. Jones, parents of Dr. William L. Jones, at the time of Sylvanus Morris's strolls in the 1870s. By the turn of century it was occupied by the H. R. Bernard family. Often called the Long House, it is said that this Antebellum dwelling was once the home of Dr. Crawford W. Long.

Dean William Tate remembered once using the house as a 4-H cooperative dormitory during his tenure at the university and regretted its demolition (Tate, Strolls). The photograph was taken about 1940 when the house was the 4-H Club Home, as indicated by the sign over the door. The site has been chosen for the new Georgia Museum of Art. Photograph courtesy of University of Georgia Libraries Special Collections

This broadside advertises the stage coach service from Athens to Gainesville offered by Edward R. and W. V. P. Hodgson in early 1845. The Hodgson brothers were carriage and buggy makers by trade and carried on an extensive blacksmith business until after the Civil War. As the advertisement noted, the Hodgsons also supplied private horses and carriages for hire. Other firms offering stage service during the Antebellum period included J. W. Martin, to Clarkesville; Bradford and Shaw, to Helicon Springs; H. N. Wilson, to Union Point; and W. P. Smith, also to Gainesville.

Roads during the period were often impassable in wet weather, and rough and dusty in dry. Bridges were frequently washed away by periodic floods. Even those who did little traveling were affected by the bad roads because the mail was transported over them. The road to Gainesville, over which the Hodgson's stage traveled, was improved in the early 1830s because it provided both a link with the gold country near Dahlonega and a route for carrying the mail. Prince Avenue today follows the first stretch of that road. Broadside courtesy of Mr. and Mrs. Paul Hodgson

Joseph Henry Lumpkin was one of the outstanding jurists of the nineteenth century. Except for two terms in the state legislature, he spent all of his adult life practicing law or serving on the bench. When the Supreme Court of Georgia was created in 1845, Lumpkin was appointed to the court along with Hiram Warner and Eugenius Nisbet, who elected him Chief Justice. He held that position until his death in 1867. An accomplished economist, Judge Lumpkin advocated (beginning in the early 1850s) the industrialization and commercial development of the South.

It can be safely said that without the landmark decisions that he and his colleagues handed down in the areas of debtor-creditor rights, banking and contract, and fiduciary cases, much of the Postbellum commercial development of Georgia, Henry Grady's New South, would not have been possible. Many legal authorities regard Judge Lumpkin as one of the nation's greatest chancellors, who adapted English equitable principles to American commercial institutions. Lumpkin is also credited with the establishment, along with Thomas R. R. Cobb and William Hope Hull, of the University of Georgia law school, which bears his name. Photograph courtesy of the Joseph Henry Lumpkin Foundation, Incorporated

Joseph Henry Lumpkin built this Greek Revival mansion on Prince Avenue in 1843. Although by no means a small house, the unusual T-shaped plan and imposing front facade make it appear larger than it actually is. Judge Lumpkin lived here until his death in 1867. A. K. Childs purchased the house about 1876. The house was rented for nearly thirteen years to Madame Sophie and Miss Callie Sosnowski, who operated the celebrated Home School for young ladies there. About 1906, the house was moved forward on the lot, closer to the street.

In 1919 the Athens Woman's Club bought the house in what was one of the city's first preservation efforts. Until the club gave it to the Joseph Henry Lumpkin Foundation in 1975, the structure was used as a club house, a furniture showroom, and an interior decorator's office. Both the Phi Mu sorority and the Delta Tau Delta fraternity rented the house at times during those years.

The Lumpkin Foundation is restoring the house for use by the university law school, state and local bar associations, and the public as a place for entertaining, small meetings, and seminars. The house was photographed by the Historic American Buildings Survey in the 1930s and was listed in the National Register of Historic Places in 1975.

The exterior restoration, completed in 1981, and the interior restoration, completed in 1985, were funded in part through a matching grant from the United States Department of the Interior. The photograph was taken before the house was moved. Courtesy of Susan Barrow Tate

This classic Greek Revival house with a monumental Doric portico was built by Colonel Stevens Thomas in 1848 on Pulaski Street at the corner of Hancock. In the nineteenth century it was acquired by Dr. Isham H. Goss, who opened the Everleila Sanitorium, named for his wife, in the house. The Banner described the building at the turn of the century as a ten room structure with the two front rooms being used for a parlor and an office. To the rear were dining and bedrooms. The second floor contained more bedrooms and an operating room with "all the necessary glass enameled tables and a most perfect line of the latest and best operating implements." Trained nurses were employed, and electric bells and lights were arranged "to give great convenience."

This photograph was taken before 1911, when the building was purchased by the Y.W.C.A. and was turned to face Hancock Avenue. Two years later a gymnasium was completed along Pulaski Street. The house is now the law offices of Howard Scott, who has also converted the gymnasium to office space. The photograph was made before the house was moved. Courtesy of Marguerite Thomas Hodgson

When Stevens Thomas built his mansion on Pulaski Street he also gave thought to the appearance of the grounds. The design of its formal garden is attributed to John Bishop, an English landscape gardener who was in charge of the university botanical garden. The plan was dominated by a formal boxwood garden in a palm and crescent plan accented by Southern magnolias. Large oak trees shaded the expansive lawn. The house was surrounded with vines, shrubs, and flowers. The rear service yard and outbuildings were separated from the lawn by a fence and a row of shrubs. A similar fence was placed along the street. Fruit and vegetable gardens occupied the rear of the lot (Garden History of Georgia).

Part of the formal gardens are visible in the turn-of-the-century photograph above. The gardens were destroyed when the house was turned to face Hancock. Drawing by P. Thornton Marye; courtesy of the Georgia Department of Archives and History

The Newton House, located at the corner of Broad Street and College Avenue, was one of the best known of the hotels operating in Athens in the 1850s. Among the others were the Central, Hancock, Lanier, Lumpkin, Athens hotels and the Franklin House. In 1854 the university commencement ball was held in the Newton House Saloon, where "fashion displayed her beauteous wand, mirth and hilarity beat high in every bosom, and a sound of revelry was heard" (Coulter, College Life).

The builder, Elizur L. Newton, was a prosperous merchant not given to much frivolity. According to Augustus L. Hull, "He said he was never tempted to spend five cents just because he had it, and he never did spend it except for something he needed." During the War Between the States, Newton served with other men too old for regular service in the local Thunderbolts company.

In the late nineteenth century, the building became the Commercial Hotel. It was during this time that this engraving was made for stationery letterhead by J. H. Warner of New York. In the 1920s the building was substantially remodeled, and the exterior was refaced with new brick. It was at that time called the Colonial Hotel. The Varsity restaurant occupied the corner storefront for many years. The building has been rehabilitated for commercial and office space. Engraving courtesy of University of Georgia Libraries Special Collections

Joe Keno, a Frenchman whose real name was Joseph Zebenee, was one of Athens's colorful characters in the last century. A butcher by trade, he was known to take meat to a cook, saying her master had ordered it. When it was cooked and eaten, the master had to pay for it. "He slaughtered goat, kid, and dog," said A. L. Hull, "and it all became lamb in his skillful hands" (Hull, Annals).

Before the Civil War he ran a restaurant on Jackson Street and had contracts with all the merchants to feed their cats. The rush of hungry cats at feeding time gave the name "Cat-Alley" to the stretch of Jackson between Broad and Clayton.

Keno was a mild mannered man and his wife often beat him. He escaped her by enlisting in General Cobb's regiment during the war. When Sylvanus Morris knew him, he was a night watchman with lantern, stick, and three-legged dog (Morris, Strolls). Others also recalled him as the town's lamplighter. Photograph courtesy of University of Georgia Libraries Special Collections

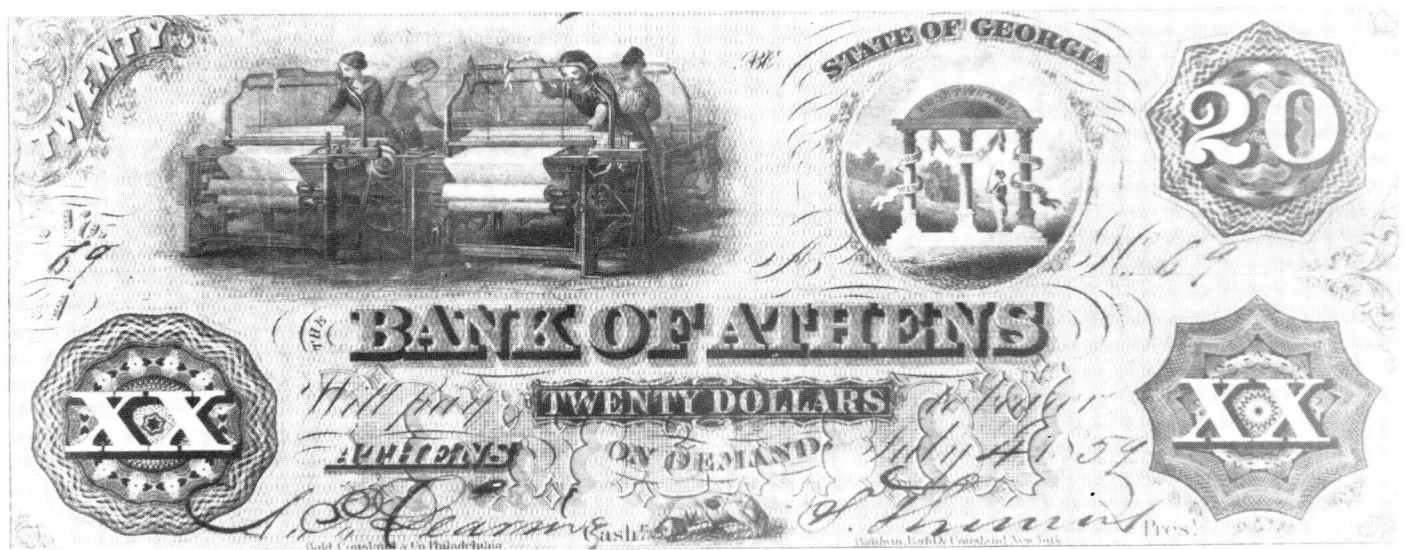

After the Georgia Railroad Bank moved to Augusta in 1842, Athens had only one bank (the branch Bank of the State of Georgia) until the Bank of Athens was incorporated in 1856. The new bank immediately faced a crisis in the panic of 1857, but the Southern Banner reported in the fall of that year that it was the only upcountry bank in South Carolina or Georgia with notes which stood on an equal footing with the best of the South.

In 1857 the bank moved into a building on the northwest corner of Jackson and Broad streets with the Southern Mutual Insurance Company. Although the bank did not survive the Civil War, the building remains today on that Broad Street corner.

The banknote illustrated here was issued on July 4, 1859 and was signed by William Dearing and Stevens Thomas, prominent local merchants and bankers. The choice of the illustration in the upper left of the note, weavers at their looms, was an appropriate one for an Athens bank, as textile manufacturing was an important part of the local economy. Banknote courtesy of Gary Doster

This photograph shows the Athens Factory on the Oconee River as it appeared in the late nineteenth century. Organized first as the Athens Cotton & Wool Factory in 1832 by William Dearing, John Nisbet, Augustin S. Clayton, and Abraham Walker, on land purchased from William Carr, the first buildings were probably of frame construction. In 1834 the mill burned and was rebuilt. It lost one wing in the Harrison freshet of 1840 and again burned in 1857. It was after this fire that the buildings in the photograph were built.

During the Antebellum period, the factory produced osnaburgs, stripes, bed-ticking, and linsey-woolsey. The company prospered during the War Between the States, during which time it sold some of its land up the river on the east bank to Cook and Brother who constructed an armory. After the war, the company purchased the property back and moved its weaving operations there. The Athens Factory buildings were then used exclusively for spinning.

During the 1880s, Robert L. Bloomfield became president of the company. He had many houses constructed for his factory workers and built St. Mary's Chapel (Episcopal) which still stands, though changed and quite deteriorated, on Oconee Street. In 1897 Athens Manufacturing Company suffered a financial collapse and was reorganized by A. H. Hodgson.

After the turn of the century the work of Athens Factory diminished and the buildings, used only for storage, fell into decay. By 1977 only two buildings of the complex remained, the wool building with the stone foundation next to the river, and the cotton building at right angles to it. They had been modified around the turn of the century; the clerestory windows on the roof had been replaced by a full top story and an elevator shaft had been added. O'Mally's Tavern now occupies the wool building. Photograph courtesy of University of Georgia Libraries Special Collections

By the 1850s the old common burial ground on Jackson Street had been nearly filled by a half century or more of burials. In 1853 a committee was appointed to select a site for a new cemetery, and in 1855 a tract was purchased along the Oconee River south of the Athens Factory. The plan for the cemetery, called Oconee Hill, was drawn by Dr. James Camak.

Lots were divided into three classes: first, second, and third, and sold for fifty dollars, thirty dollars, and ten dollars respectively. Free spaces were set aside for those who could not pay. Trustees were chosen to administer the cemetery, and Thomas R. R. Cobb was elected chairman. The trustees were incorporated in 1860 and continue to administer the cemetery today.

By the turn of the century it became obvious that more space was required, so additional land was purchased on the east side of the river, and an iron truss-bridge was built to connect the two parts. The bridge still remains today, and burials occur in both parts of the cemetery. The photograph shows an impressive group of nineteenth-century grave markers in the old part of the cemetery. Photograph by Richard Fowlkes; courtesy of Athens Newspapers, Incorporated

The mill building in this photograph was located across the river and slightly downstream from Athens Factory on land owned by the Athens Manufacturing Company. Little is known about the history of this mill, but it probably dates from the rebuilding of Athens Factory in 1858. The mansard roof may be a later addition.

The building was not in use when the photograph was taken about the turn of the century. The building, located on the Boys Club property, was demolished in the winter of 1976-1977. Photograph by David Earnest; courtesy of University of Georgia Special Collections

Alonzo Church, president of the University of Georgia from 1829 to 1859, was a Vermont Yankee and Middlebury College graduate who migrated to Georgia about 1816. He settled first in Eatonton where he became head of an academy and married Sarah J. Trippe, daughter of a Putnam County planter. His success as a teacher helped secure his election as professor of mathematics at the university in 1819. A deeply religious man, Church was licensed to preach by the Presbyterian Church in 1820 and was ordained an evangelist four years later. Upon the resignation of President Waddel in 1829, he was elected president in spite of opposition from many Methodists and Baptists who resented control of the university by a Presbyterian.

As president, he was a strict disciplinarian and a strong advocate of classical learning, with particular emphasis on the ancient languages. These conservative views led to conflict with younger and more liberal members of the faculty in the 1850s. Such men as John and Joseph LeConte (later founders of the University of California), Charles McCay, Charles Venable, and William Broun sought to reform the curriculum by placing a greater emphasis on scientific thought and methods. Furthermore, they refused to spy on students in their rooms and enforce discipline as President Church required. In 1855 John LeConte resigned, and in 1856 Church pursuaded the trustees to call for the resignation of all faculty members, including himself. When the faculty was reorganized, Joseph LeConte, Venable, and Broun were not reelected. Joseph LeConte described Church in his autobiography as "a bigoted, dogmatic, and imperious old man."

President Church was, however, highly respected by the citizens of Athens who, to a great degree, supported him in his conflict with the dissident faculty members and presented him with a silver service as a token of their affection and esteem in 1856. Tired and ill, he resigned from the presidency in 1859 and moved to his country home where he died on May 18, 1862. Photograph courtesy of the University of Georgia Libraries Special Collections

This locally-made silver service was presented to University of Georgia President Alonzo Church in 1856. The inscription on the tray reads: "A token of affectionate remembrance from the citizens of Athens to the Rev. Alonzo Church, D.D., 1856." It was crafted by Asaph King Childs, a local silversmith and banker. Childs, who was born in Springfield, Massachusetts in 1820, was one of the founders of the National Bank of Athens in 1866 and served as its president from 1881 to 1900. He also served as president of the Northeastern Railroad and was an early supporter of Lucy Cobb Institute. Many local families still cherish heirloom silver marked "A. K. Childs."

The silver service presented to Dr. Church passed to his descendants, who had exact duplicates cast of the pieces to create two sets. The set illustrated here was owned by Alonzo Church, III, of Mattoon, Illinois, who left it in his will to the Athens-Clarke Heritage Foundation in 1978. The tray and teapot are known to be part of the original set cast by A. K. Childs. Photograph by Karekin Goekjian; courtesy of Athens Newspaper, Incorporated

The Lyle House is said to have been built about 1850 by a man named Anderson. It was owned for most of the Postbellum period by the Lyle family. James R. Lyle, a prominent Athens attorney, grew up in the house. At the turn of the century, it was the home of Professor Alfred Ackerman. From 1916 to 1936 it was run as a boarding house by Mrs. W. E. Shehee and was owned in 1936 by Deupree Hunnicutt. The house has been considered a classic of the Greek Revival style and has appeared in several books on architecture which have received national circulation. The house stood on the southwest corner of Lumpkin and Wray streets and has been replaced by a fraternity house. Photograph by L. D. Andrew, HABS, Library of Congress

This photograph shows the interior of the John Thomas Grant House, now known as the University of Georgia President's House, as it appeared early in this century. The double parlors, with their arched marble mantels, and elaborate floral plaster moldings, are furnished in typical Victorian era fashion. Photograph courtesy of University of Georgia Libraries Special Collections

The Grant House/University President's House was built on Prince Avenue in 1856. Perhaps Athens's most elaborate Greek Revival mansion, the house stands a full two stories above a daylight basement and has a monumental Corinthian colonnade. A formal boxwood garden with large magnolias separates the house from the sidewalk.

This photograph, taken after the turn of the century, shows the house and garden much as they are today, except the garden is now better maintained and the front steps have been re-designed. Its builder, John Grant, sold the house after the Civil War to Benjamin Harvey Hill, a university alumnus who had married an Athens lady, Caroline Holt, in 1845.

Hill, a Whig and Know-Nothing who opposed secession, supported the Confederacy during the war and opposed Reconstruction. He became the first powerful voice of the New South when he delivered an address to the Georgia Alumni Society in 1871, calling on Georgia to cast off the past tradition of plantation slavery and look toward modernization and industrialization. He was elected to the United States House of Representatives in 1873 and to the Senate in 1877. Hill died in 1882, and the following year his property on Prince Avenue was sold to Athens broker and industrialist James White.

The house was acquired from the estate of White's daughter, Mrs. W. F. Bradshaw, in 1949 by the Bradley Foundation of Columbus, Georgia. The house was presented to the university and restored to museum quality. It is used for official university functions. Photograph courtesy of University of Georgia Libraries Special Collections

The A. K. Childs House was built by John Billups in 1856 on the northeast corner of Clayton and Thomas streets. The Childs family acquired the property soon thereafter, and their daughter, Frances Ingle Childs, was born in the house in 1859. She recalled, as a small child, looking out of the windows and seeing near the river the campfires of the mountain people who came by wagon to Athens with apples and other farm products. About 1876 Reuben Nickerson bought the house and lived there until his death at the turn of the century. The house remained standing until the 1920s but was demolished to make way for a filling station. The site is now a parking lot. Photograph (circa 1890) courtesy of Susan Barrow Tate

The Thurmond House, shown here about 1940, was one of the few Italianate mansions in Athens to have a cupola on the roof. Because of the house's situation on a high hill, the view from the cupola must have been spectacular. Samuel P. Thurmond, a local attorney, purchased the large lot bounded by Dearing, Church, Waddell, and Harris streets from John Linton in February 1860 and constructed the house facing Dearing Street. Bought in 1943 by H. L. Cofer, the Thurmond House was sold and demolished in 1965. The Dearing Garden Apartments were built on the site. Photograph courtesy of University of Georgia Libraries Special Collections

The striking Treanor House, combining the features of the pervasive Southern Greek Revival style with more decorative and delicate Gothic Revival elements, has long been a landmark on Lumpkin Street. Whether the house was built by John Addison Cobb as a wedding present for his daughter Laura, who married Professor Williams Rutherford in 1841, or whether Professor Rutherford bought the house from Mrs. Rebecca Hillyer and repaired it for his residence remains a mystery. Both Cobbs and Rutherfords, however, were living together in the house in 1850.

John A. Cobb, who brought his wife Sarah Rootes to Athens from Jefferson County in 1818, played an important role in the early development of the town. He served on the first board of directors of the Georgia Railroad and developed Athens's first "suburb," Cobbham, in the 1830s on land he owned along Prince Avenue. He suffered heavy losses during the financial panic of 1837, including most of his Cobbham land. Among John and Sarah Cobb's seven children were Governor Howell Cobb and General Thomas R. R. Cobb.

Professor Williams Rutherford, whose father was in the university's first graduating class in 1804, was born in Milledgeville in 1818 and graduated from the university in 1838. He taught in several academies, organizing the Cobbham Academy in 1855, and was appointed professor of mathematics at the university in 1865, holding that position for thirty-three years.

Two daughters born in the house, Mildred Lewis Rutherford and Mary Rutherford Lipscomb, achieved wide recognition as head mistresses of Lucy Cobb Institute. Henry L. Brittain purchased the house in the late 1850s when Professor Rutherford moved his family to one of the faculty houses on the university campus. The house, still known to many as the Brittain Place, remained in his family until 1905. In 1912 a wealthy Watkinsville merchant, Alexander Woodson Ashford, acquired the property for a private family "dormitory," where his four sons lived while attending the university. Mrs. Kate McKinley Treanor bought the house in 1935, and it remains the home of her daughters.

The house is largely intact today, with only minor additions and changes in details, and retains much of its characteristic nineteenth-century landscaping. The house is listed in the National Register of Historic Places. Photograph courtesy of University of Georgia Libraries Special Collections

The Mell House, built on Jackson Street by Lewis J. Lampkin, was one of Athens's most unusual Antebellum dwellings. The Gothic columns with the lyre-like capitals give the house a light, airy feeling. This type of column, which can also be found on the Treanor House, was, along with the brackets under the cornice and above the windows, characteristic of the eclecticism of the 1850s. If the house was built about 1840, as tradition holds, the portico may have been added in the following decade.

The house was later occupied by Colonel L. H. Charbonnier and William C. Ashe. About 1910 John D. Mell purchased the house and moved it to the corner of Milledge and Rutherford. It was demolished during the 1960s. The Zeta Tau Alpha sorority is now located on the site of the Mell House. Photograph courtesy of University of Georgia Libraries Special Collections

The Phinizy-Segrest House was begun by Thomas N. Hamilton in 1857 and finished by his widow, Sarah Hamilton, the following year. Mrs. Hamilton moved to the newly opened section along Milledge Avenue from the once-fashionable Lickskillet section of town on Thomas Street near Hancock. Her son, James S. Hamilton, owned the house adjoining hers on the north, and her daughter, Eugenia Hamilton Dearing, lived immediately to the south.

After Mrs. Hamilton's death in 1876, the house was rented to Dr. and Mrs. H. C. White whose Northern visitors shocked the locals "from center to circumference." One lady, wearing divided skirts, had the audacity to ride a horse astride, and near pandemonium broke out in the town when another lady guest rode a bicycle in bloomers.

After the death of Dr. James Hamilton, the house was sold to the widow of Ferdinand Phinizy in 1890. Mrs. Phinizy remodeled the house in the Victorian manner, adding stained glass windows, golden oak paneling, damask wall coverings, gas chandeliers, and marble mantels. Mrs. R. T. Segrest, granddaughter of Mrs. Phinizy, sold the house to the Phi Mu sorority. The Phi Mu's have removed some of the Victorian trappings and added wings to the house for additional space. This view shows the house before it was sold to Phi Mu. Photograph courtesy of University of Georgia Libraries Special Collections

In 1854 an article by an anonymous mother appeared in the Southern Banner under the title "Female Education in Athens." The author, later discovered to be Laura Cobb Rutherford, pleaded for the establishment of a high school for young ladies in the community. Asserting that "the female mind is susceptible to the highest state of cultivation," she appealed to patriotism of Athenians and deprecated the necessity of sending Southern girls North for an education. Many responded to her call, including her brother, Thomas R. R. Cobb. His energies were largely responsible for turning the dream into a reality.

According to A. L. Hull, "He canvassed the town, enthused the people, got subscriptions and organized the Trustees. Some subscribed money, some merchandise, some materials. He sold the merchandise, used the materials and collected the money. When a citizen was backward in subscribing he subscribed for him and said, "if you don't pay it I will" (Hull, Annals). In 1856 the trustees were able to buy eight acres on the Watkinsville Road (now Milledge Avenue) and by 1858 had completed the building shown in the photograph.

Classes began in January of the following year with thirty-seven pupils. Originally called Athens Female High School, it was renamed Lucy Cobb Institute in honor of T. R. R. Cobb's daughter, Lucy, who had died of scarlet fever in 1858. The first class developed a reputation for charm and beauty that was the hallmark of the Lucy Cobb girl until the institution closed its doors in 1931. William Hope Hull wrote to Mrs. Howell Cobb in 1859: "Tom is worrying because the boys will gather in front of the church to see the Lucy Cobb girls come out."

Although it had a short Antebellum history, the Lucy Cobb Institute became one of Athens's most important social and cultural institutions and was regarded as one of the finest girls' schools in the nation. Photograph (1866) courtesy of University of Georgia Libraries Special Collections

This portrait shows Lucy Cobb in 1858, the year of her death. She was thirteen years of age. Photograph courtesy of University of Georgia Libraries Special Collections

The building shown in this 1875 photograph figured prominently in the educational history of Athens. Known widely as Rock College, it was constructed in 1859 of crushed stone and cement, without reinforcement. It was originally intended for university freshmen and sophomores, but they would not go there, saying that they would sooner stay at home.

It was decided to make it a preparatory school for the university, and it was dedicated as University High School on April 29, 1862, with Benjamin R. Carroll of Charleston as principal and L. H. Charbonnier as his assistant. The School remained open during the war and proved extremely popular. Professor Charbonnier, a French soldier and graduate of St. Cyr, formed the boys into companies and drilled them for local defense.

After the war, the state provided aid for the education of Confederate soldiers, and the school prospered. When the aid ended, the school was discontinued by the state and a private school, conducted by B. T. Hunter and W. W. Lumpkin, was conducted there for several years. The building also served at other times as a student boarding house and as the university farm.

When the State Normal School was organized in 1891 it was located on the Rock College property. The building was rechristened Gilmer Hall in honor of Governor George R. Gilmer and used as a girls' dormitory. When the university again took control of the building as part of Co-ordinate Campus in 1932, it continued to be used as a dormitory. After the United States Navy Supply Corps acquired the property in 1954, the building was demolished. Photograph from Davis's Souvenir Album; courtesy of University of Georgia Libraries Special Collections

This photograph, taken about 1875, shows the old university Library which was begun in 1859 and completed in 1862. It was the first building encountered on the campus when entering through the arch from Broad Street. About 1878 Henry Tuck described the interior as having a large hall which would seat 300 people on the first floor near the entrance. Here the chancellor would deliver his Sunday afternoon sermons to the students. At the rear of the first floor was a recitation room, used by Professor Williams Rutherford. Above this there was a second recitation room. The balance of the second floor was given over to the library.

After the library was moved to the new building in 1904, the old Library was joined with the Ivy Building to create Academic Building.

The cast iron arch seen in the center of the photograph, has long been a symbol of the university. The arch was patterned after the Georgia State Seal and, along with the iron fence, was cast during the 1850s with funds provided by the sale of the botanical garden. Note the stone stile used for crossing the fence and the missing broken pickets. The arch is still the main entrance to the university. Photograph from Davis's Souvenir Album; courtesy of University of Georgia Libraries Special Collections

On the third floor of the Library the museum collections of the university were housed: "Hundreds of skeletons of bedraggled birds, peacocks, cranes, wild ducks, wild cats, snakes, and so forth, entomological specimens, and all species of fauna, covered with dust and spider webs, which all presented a sad reminder of more ambitious if not more prosperous days in the history of the College" (Tuck, Four Years).

The skeletons in this photograph were part of the university's collection of fauna and flora that was once housed in the old library, here shown and displayed in a more organized fashion than that described by Mr. Tuck. Photograph courtesy of University of Georgia Libraries Special Collections

Thomas R. R. Cobb was one of Athens's favorite sons. He was a lawyer, writer, statesman, soldier, and philanthropist. When he died on the battlefield at Fredericksburg during the War Between the States, the whole community mourned his passing. He was admitted to the bar in 1842, and from 1849 to 1857 he served as reporter for the Georgia Supreme Court under his father-in-law, Chief Justice Joseph Henry Lumpkin. These two men, along with fellow Athenian William Hope Hull, founded the University of Georgia law school in the closing days of the Antebellum period.

Cobb was a prolific writer on legal topics and authored some of the definitive works on the laws of slavery. His most important contribution to Georgia law, however, was the Cobb Code. This codification of Georgia's statutes into one body of law was a first in the English law world. When Lincoln was elected, Cobb led the forces that advocated secession for Georgia.

"One figure in particular took the imagination and ruled the spirits of that susceptible people," wrote Woodrow Wilson years later, "the figure of Thomas R. R. Cobb. The manly beauty of his tall, athletic person; his frank eyes on fire; his ardor...given over to a cause not less sacred, not less fraught with the issues of life and death than religion itself; his voice...musical and sure to find its way to the heart...made his words pass like flame from countryside to countryside" (Stegeman, These Men She Gave).

He was elected a delegate to the Secession Convention that took Georgia out of the Union and sent Thomas and his brother Howell to represent the state at the convention in Montgomery which organized the Confederacy. In Montgomery, Thomas was appointed to the committee which formulated a permanent constitution and had the major hand in drafting that document. Although he had no formal military training, Cobb soon left the political arena and organized Cobb's Legion. He was promoted to brigadier general and was leading his troops at the battle of Fredericksburg in December 1862 when he was killed.

His body was returned to Athens for a funeral at First Presbyterian Church and burial in Oconee Hill Cemetery. He is remembered with affection in Athens for his many charities and his civic leadership, particularly his roll in the founding of Lucy Cobb Institute. The portrait reproduced here hangs in the rotunda of the University of Georgia law school. Photograph courtesy of University of Georgia Libraries Special Collections

Chapter Two
1861-1900

On January 2, 1861, the citizens of Clarke County chose Thomas R. R. Cobb, Jefferson Jennings, and Asbury Hull, the pro-secessionist slate, to represent them at the Milledgeville convention. There, a decision would be made as to whether Georgia would leave the Union. Georgia's political leaders assembled at the capitol, and after several days of hot debate, voted for secession. When the news reached Athens, a torchlight parade was led by the college students who hung Union General Winfield Scott in effigy, houses were illuminated with candles in the windows, the Troup Artillery fired a 100 gun salute, and a balloon was launched with the names of the seceded states. Although there were still some dissenters, most Athenians quickly pulled together to support the action taken by their state. Two of Athens's favorite sons, Howell and Thomas R. R. Cobb, were sent to the convention of seceding states which assembled in Montgomery, Alabama in February. Howell was elected president of the convention and Thomas was architect of the constitution of the new Confederate States of America.

Until April 12, when the batteries at Charleston opened fire on Fort Sumter and Lincoln called for volunteers, most people believed, or wanted to believe, that war could be avoided. Now preparations for the conflict began in earnest as men rushed to join the military units and ladies sewed flags and uniforms and gathered provisions to send with the new troops. The Troup Artillery was the first company to leave Athens, just twelve days after Fort Sumter. Most of the town turned out to give them an enthusiastic send-off at the Georgia Railroad depot. This scene was repeated each time a new company left for the fighting. Almost every family was affected. By May 1, 1861, the *Banner* reported that Judge Lumpkin had four sons, two son-in-laws, two grandsons, and six nephews in the service of the Confederacy.

As the hard fighting began on the front, the euphoria at home began to fade, and the people of Athens got down to the difficult task of supplying the troops and providing for themselves as well. There were shortages of just about every product that was not produced locally. Substitutes had to be found for those that were unavailable: chicory and parched okra seeds for coffee, sorghum syrup for sugar, and sassafras for tea. Inflation ran wild; prices skyrocketed. Bacon was seven dollars per pound, onions fifty dollars a bushel. A ham cost forty dollars. Since many merchants would not accept the devalued Confederate currency and refused to give credit, people had to resort to barter. To help relieve the suffering, public meetings and benefits were held to raise money for the needy.

The paper mill burned, throwing many people out of work, and the university was forced to close because of dwindling attendance. The college buildings were used to house refugees and served as hospitals later in the war. The University High School and Lucy Cobb Institute continued to operate, however, and a new company, Cook and Brother, moved from New Orleans to the safety of Athens to manufacture guns for the Confederacy.

As the war ground on month after month and the casualty list continued to mount, the optimism at home faded and was replaced with quiet resignation and determination. As Sherman advanced into Georgia, Athenians began to be alarmed. In August 1864 it was learned that a troop of Union cavalry was coming towards Athens from Watkinsville. The local home guards quickly manned the fortifications near the paper mill on Barber's Creek and fired shells into the midst of the approaching forces as they neared the bridge. The Union troops turned away and Confederates soon captured about 300 of them. The tired, ragged prisoners were marched into Athens and held on the college campus before being dispatched to the Confederate prison at Andersonville. These were the only Federal troops seen in Athens during the war.

When the surrender came in April of 1865 at Appomattox, the community breathed a sigh of relief. As the soldiers began to return home, the *Banner* wrote,

It is appropriate that the Confederate Constitution should have found its way to the town of its principal author, Thomas R. R. Cobb. In April 1865 a newspaper correspondent, Felix G. DeFontaine, was in Chester, South Carolina, when he heard that a train carrying members of the Confederate government fleeing from Richmond had been abandoned and was being looted. He went to the depot and retrieved a number of documents including the permanent and provisional Confederate constitutions. Through a New York agent, he later sold the permanent constitution to Mrs. George Wymberley Jones DeRenne.

The DeRenne papers and the Confederate Constitution were purchased by the state of Georgia in the early 1930s and were placed in the University of Georgia Libraries. The constitution, which is written on a roll of parchment twelve feet long, is stored in a copper tube. On Confederate Memorial Day, April 26 of each year, it is put on display by the library. Photograph courtesy of University of Georgia Librarires Special Collections

When Fort Sumter fell, everyone in Athens began preparing for war. The men organized themselves into military companies, and the ladies were busy making clothes and getting the men ready to be sent away. The state announced that it would furnish soldiers with "one coat, two handkerchiefs, two pairs pants, one black necktie, one cap, two flannel shirts, two pairs drawers, three pairs of socks, one pocket knife, one tin cup, one spoon, one knife, one fork, two pairs boots, and one flannel band to tie around the stomach when exposed to the damp" (Hull, Annals).

This was a sharp contrast with the condition the soldiers would find themselves in four years later, often barefooted and clothed in tatters. As the troops began to leave town on the train there were speeches and parades. The ladies presented the companies with flags, and the girls of Lucy Cobb and the townspeople escorted them to the depot.

Among the companies that went to the front from Clarke County were the Troup Artillery, Athens Guards, Clarke Rifles, Georgia Troopers, Ritch's Company, Mell Rifles, Johnson Guards, and Highland Guards. Lumpkin's Battery, White's Company, Cook's Company, the Oconee Rangers, Lipscomb Volunteers, and the Thunderbolts organized for local defense.

Among the major battles in which Clarke County troops fought were the Seven Day battles, Crampton's Gap, Sharpsburg, Fredericksburg, Chancellorsville, Brandy Station, Gettysburg, and the Crater. Many of the troops who left expecting a quick victory and a safe turn never came home.

Postal officials in the South were in a quandary at the outbreak of the Civil War. After the states had seceded and the Confederate government was formed, it was no longer acceptable to use the old United States postage, yet the Confederacy had not begun to issue stamps. The problem was solved by the issue of provisional stamps by each postmaster. These were replaced when the new Confederate stamps arrived. The extremely rare stamp shown here was issued in Athens by postmaster Thomas Crawford. It has a white design on a purple background. Stamp courtesy of Gary Doster

This photograph was taken of the Hodgson brothers in their Home Guard uniforms. They are, from left to right: Will Hodgson, age eighteen, artillery; Edward R. "Prince" Hodgson, age sixteen, artillery; Rob Hodgson, age fourteen, cavalry. Photograph courtesy of Mr. and Mrs. Edward R. Hodgson III

After graduating with first honors from the university, Benjamin Mell, seen here in his Confederate uniform, enlisted in the Mell Rifles. The company had been organized by his father, Patrick Mell, who was a Baptist minister and vice-chancellor of the university. The senior Mell was forced to remain at home because of "domestic afflictions," so the command of the unit passed to Captain Thomas U. Camak when they were mustered into service in August 1861.

Known also as Camak's Company, they were officially Company D, Infantry Battalion, Cobb's Legion, Georgia Volunteers. The unit fought until captured two days before the surrender at Appomattox. Benjamin Mell became third corporal in the outfit. He was killed on September 17, 1862 at Sharpsburg, Maryland. Photograph courtesy of University of Georgia Libraries Special Collections

A device designed by an imaginative inventor in an effort to help the South win the War Between the States has become one of Athen's most familiar landmarks. The famous double-barrel cannon was cast at the Athens Foundry and Machine Works in 1862 to the specifications of its designer, John Gilleland, a local housebuilder.

Each barrel was to be loaded with a cannonball connected to the other by an eight foot chain. When fired, the balls were supposed to separate, pull the chain taut and sweep across the field, mowing down Yankees. When tested out on the Newton Bridge Road near Athens, the weapon did not perform as expected.

A contemporary reported that when fired, the projectile "had a kind of circular motion, plowed up an acre of ground, tore up a cornfield, mowed down saplings, and the chain broke, the two balls going in opposite directions. One of the balls killed a cow in a distant field, while the other knocked down the chimney from a log cabin." The observers "scattered as though the entire Yankee army had been turned loose in that vicinity" (Brockman, Secret Weapon).

Gilleland sought to have the weapon adopted in spite of the poor showing it had made at its debut. It was taken to Augusta for tests, which were not conducted to the satisfaction of the inventor. He wrote angry protests to Richmond, all to no effect. Colonel G. W. Rains of the Augusta Arsenal explained to the War Department that the device could not be made to work because there was no way to assure that the two barrels would fire at precisely the same time.

Further efforts by Gilleland to gain the support of Governor Joseph Brown for his project failed, and the cannon was placed at the town hall to be used as a warning of approaching Federal troops. After the war the cannon was fired to celebrate Democratic political victories.

It disappeared in 1891, turning up four years later in the hands of a junk dealer. Rescued by the city fathers and mounted on a new carriage, the cannon was placed on College Avenue near the Confederate monument where it appears in the photograph. When the monument was moved to Broad Street, the cannon was given a place of honor on the lawn of City Hall. Several years ago, a small landscaped park was created on City Hall grounds with the cannon as centerpiece.

The house seen behind the cannon in the photograph was the Eustace Speer House, which occupied the southwest corner of Washington and College. Photograph courtesy of University of Georgia Libraries Special Collections

"If our cause has gone down in gloom, it is not their fault. They have done all that men can do." The same could be said for those who had supported them at home. Athens was no longer the same town the soldiers had left. Many friends and loved ones had been killed or injured, and the community looked forlorn. "The streets were unlighted, washed into gullies or overgrown with grass," remembered Augustus Hull. "No new houses had been built, no old ones repaired. Broken windows were covered with paper, broken fences propped with stakes." There was little business and only the factories showed signs of life.

Another, and even more dramatic change had occurred as a result of the war—the emancipation of slaves. When the federal troops occupied Athens in May 1865, the freedmen from the surrounding countryside flocked to town to join local blacks in celebrating their freedom. They soon built shanty towns on the edge of the city. Conditions were deplorable and a smallpox epidemic broke out. There was tension between blacks and whites, but surprisingly little violence. By 1867 the former slaves were adjusting to their freedom and were purchasing homes, securing jobs, organizing a volunteer fire company, and establishing churches. After the Reconstruction acts were passed by Congress, which disenfranchised former Confederate officials and enfranchised the freedmen, two Athens blacks, Alfred Richardson and Madison Davis, were elected to represent the area in the Georgia General Assembly. Richardson, considered a radical, survived two shootouts with the Ku Klux Klan. Davis, regarded as a moderate, served quietly and effectively until he withdrew his name from consideration during his third campaign. He remained an influential black leader in the community for many years thereafter.

As conditions became more settled, a surprising economic revival took place in Athens. Businesses

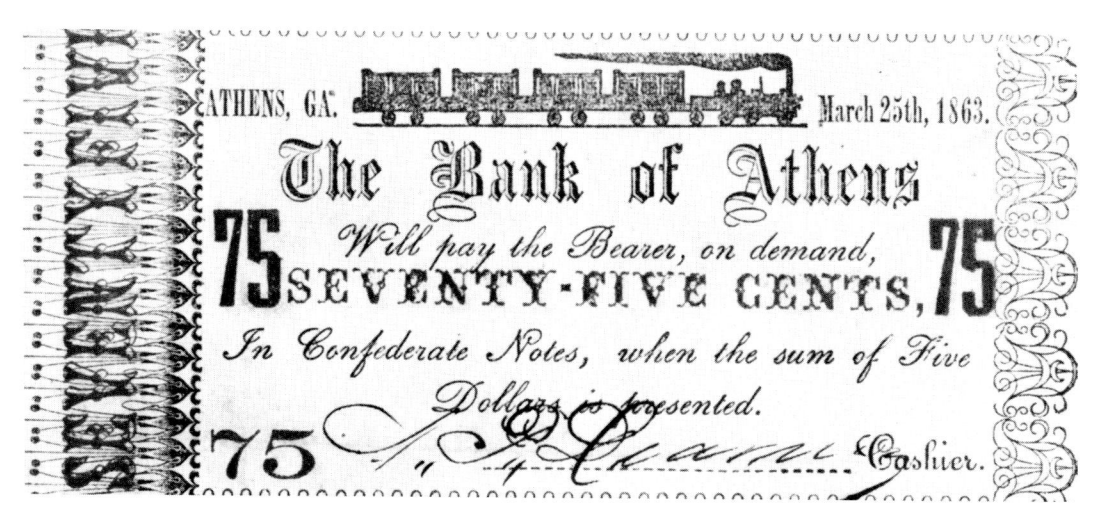

During the War Between the States, there was a great shortage of coins in the South. To remedy this situation, local banks issued paper money in denominations of less than one dollar. This note in the amount of seventy-five cents was issued in 1863 by the Bank of Athens. When a person had accumulated enough of these small bills to total five dollars, the bank would redeem them for a Confederate note. Banknote courtesy of Gary Doster

began to multiply, and new buildings were constructed in the downtown area replacing some of the older homes. New houses in the eclectic Victorian styles were erected on Prince and Milledge avenues and in Cobbham. The university opened again in January 1866, and enrollment was soon swelled by returned Confederate veterans who received free tuition, books, board, and clothing from the state. An equally important and farther reaching development for the university was the establishment of the State College of Agricultural and Mechanical Arts, a land grant college made possible by the federal Morrill Act. After long debate, the university was chosen as the location for this new school, and Moore College was erected in 1872.

The new growth and activity did not cause the city to lose it reputation for grace and beauty, however. John Muir, the famous naturalist who visited Athens on his thousand-mile walk from Kentucky to Florida in September 1867, wrote this description in his diary: "Reached Athens in the afternoon, a remarkably beautiful and aristocratic town, containing many classic and magnificent mansions of wealthy planters, who formerly owned large negro-stocked plantations in the best cotton and sugar regions farther south. Unmistakable marks of culture and refinement, as well as wealth, were everywhere apparent. This is the most beautiful town I have seen on the journey, so far, and the only one in the South that I would like to revisit."

The Postbellum era in Athens saw the growth of governmental services and the development, for the first time, of modern public utilities. After years of agitation by local citizens, Athens was finally designated county seat of Clarke County in 1871, and the county offices were consequently moved from Watkinsville. A new courthouse and jail were soon erected on Prince Avenue. The angry citizens of Watkinsville and the lower part of the county succeeded, however, in having a new county carved out of Clarke. In 1875 Oconee County was born, leaving Athens as county seat of the smallest county in the state. In 1872 the intendant and warden system of government for the city was replaced by the mayor and council form which is still in use today. The new governing body soon created a board of health, which was short lived but revived in the 1890s. By 1881 the city boasted a three-man police force consisting of a chief, a lieutenant, and a sergeant. A modest street paving program was begun in 1885 and expanded during the next fifteen years. Paving materials included vitrified brick, granite blocks, and even creosoted wood blocks. These last proved impractical on the College Avenue hill since the summer heat made them so slick that horses had difficulty keeping their footing. In 1891 a municipal fire department replaced the old volunteer companies, and the city had professional fire protection for the first time.

Modern utilities first appeared in 1882 when Bell Telephone installed lines to its first thirty-six subscribers. By 1900 it served 234 customers with local and long distance lines. In the 1890s the streets were lighted by electricity and by the middle of that decade, the Athens Railway and Electric Company was offering service to private subscribers made possible by the development of hydroelectric power on the Oconee River. The same company provided efficient streetcar service through the downtown and along Prince Avenue, the Boulevard, Barber, Milledge, and Lumpkin streets. The Oconee also provided water for the city waterworks plant, which was built in 1893, and sixteen miles of mains supplied water to local residents.

One of the most important developments of the period occurred in 1885 with the establishment of a public school system in Athens. The next year temporary buildings were provided on Oconee, Meigs, Foundry and Baxter streets. In 1887 two ten-room, two-story brick schools were erected, one on Washington Street for white students and one on Baxter for blacks. In 1893 the Baxter Street School was remodeled for white students, and two new black schools were constructed, East Athens and West Broad Street schools. Private schools also continued to play an important role in local education. The Lucy Cobb Institute developed into one of the South's finest girls' schools under the direction of Miss Mildred Rutherford; and the Home School for young ladies, operated by Sophie and Callie Sosnowski, earned a favorable reputation around the state. Other schools included Mrs. E. A. Crawford's school and the Grove School, taught by Misses Moss and Bacon. Knox Institute, which had been founded by the Freedmen's Bureau in 1868, and Jeruel Academy provided excellent instruction for black students.

In 1891 the legislature created a State Normal School as a branch of the university, and it was located at the old Rock College on Prince Avenue. For three years, only summer sessions were held, but in 1895 the General Assembly appropriated money for a more permanent program. After the turn of the century, the Normal School became an important institution in the community.

During the Postbellum period, the university saw relatively little progress and growth, with the exception of the college of agriculture. Constant assaults were made against the university by supporters of denominational colleges who thought that the school posed a threat to their programs. There was, in addition, constant bickering among faculty and trustees over the curriculum. In 1899, though, the university began a new direction under the guidance of a newly-elected chancellor, Walter Hill. The 1870s, 1880s, and 1890s were times that were recalled fondly by many graduates as an era when the school was small and intimate friendships developed among students and faculty. The last two decades also saw the development of an organized athletic program and the beginning of intercollegiate sports.

Other forms of entertainment were also popular. Deupree Hall was erected shortly after the war, and traveling shows and local productions were held here exclusively until the opening of the New Opera House in 1888 with the production *Erma, the Elf*. Dances were favorites of young and old alike, but only the quadrille and the reel were, at first, considered acceptable. The waltz was thought to be "off color" and was avoided by all proper ladies. Great parties, too, were given on special occasions: President Cleveland's inauguration in 1884, Winnie Davis's visit in 1887, and William Jennings Bryan's speech in 1898. Social and patriotic organizations flourished. The Knights of the Golden Eagle and the Royal Arcanum joined the Masons, the Y.M.C.A., the American Legion of Honor, and other groups in providing social outlets and community service.

The people may have put the war behind them, but those who gave their lives for their state and community were not forgotten. Confederate Memorial Day was first observed on April 26, 1866, and seven years later the cornerstone was laid for a monument to those killed in the conflict. The United Daughters of the Confederacy and Confederate veterans organizations kept alive the memory of those that had fallen.

The last decade of the century was a particularly exciting and prosperous time for Athens. Many new businesses were established, and the face of downtown was dramatically changed as it became a bustling commercial center. By the turn of the century, three new railroads, the Southern, the Central of Georgia, and the Seaboard provided rail service in every direction. Small towns grew up along the tracks and retail businesses opened to serve the communities. Athens merchants developed a thriving wholesale trade to supply the new towns. Most of Athens's citizens welcomed the new era, but progress had its price. Augustus L. Hull offered this ironic assessment of the Postbellum era: "Railroad facilities brought in new citizens with a demand for houses and lots. Then history repeated itself and the handsome old lots were cut up

Rufus K. Reaves left Athens on April 29, 1863, a private in the Athens Guards. The company was sent to Portsmouth, Virginia where it was attached to the Third Regiment, Georgia Volunteer Infantry, as Company K. It served until the surrender at Appomattox. According to A. L. Hull, Reaves returned from the war with less than fifty dollars. Within twenty-five years he was worth $150,000.

He was known for his public spirit, and he never failed to participate in any civic undertaking or charitable organization. Reeves was an organizer and director of the Northeastern Railroad when the first train pulled into Athens in 1876, and was appointed by the governor in 1893 as a receiver for the road until it was bought by the Southern Railroad for bonded indebtedness.

He was a partner in the wholesale grocery firm of Reaves, Nicholson & Company, which also dealt in cotton, fertilizers and rope. Reaves was also an agent for the checks, yarns, cottonades, and jeans made by the Athens Factory. He was elected mayor of Athens in 1886. Daguerreotype, courtesy of Rufus Reaves Paine, Sr.

and sold off or built up with cottages. Old homes have passed from the hands of the family. New neighbors with bay windows and little hoods and towers and ginger-bread work are crowding them; fine old trees have been cut down; the familiar mud is gone; the gentle cow no longer lies across the pedestrians' way; there are no secluded walks left for the amorous swain, no gates for him to lean upon as he lingers to say good-bye, and the glare of the arc light has robbed the evening stroll of all its sentiment. And what is all this due to except the rushing competition of soulless corporations? It is enough to make a socialist of a man of sentiment to think of it."

Although dramatic changes took place in Athens between 1861 and 1900, this was a period that many looked back on with fond memories. The era can still come alive today in the memoirs of Edward B. Mell, Sylvanus Morris, and Tom Reed.

After becoming a prosperous merchant, Rufus Reaves purchased this home on the corner of Washington and Thomas streets. It was built before the war by Dr. Richard D. Moore, one of Athens's most outstanding citizens. During the war Dr. Moore generously treated the families of soldiers free of charge. Later, he was instrumental in persuading the city to give the money for the construction of a building to house the college of agriculture. It was named Moore College in his honor. A gas station presently occupies the site of the Moore-Reaves House just north of Old Fire Hall Number One on Thomas Street. Photograph courtesy of Rufus Reaves Paine, Sr.

In Memory Of
Georgia's Gifted Statesman,
Noble Patriot, Eloquent Orator, And Brave Defender, Generous Friend, Sage Counsellor,
GEN'L. HOWELL COBB,
Born Sep. 7, 1815. Died Oct. 9, 1868.

"O Gracious God! not paintless is our loss;
A glorious sunbeam gilds thy sternest frown;
And while his Country staggers with the Cross,
He rises with the Crown."

DEDICATED To the People Of Georgia.
By P.P. Enston, Prof. of Penmanship.

Howell Cobb probably achieved a greater degree of national prominence than any other Athenian in the nineteenth century. Although born in Jefferson County, Georgia, he moved with his parents, John A. and Sarah Cobb, to Athens when a small boy. He graduated from the University of Georgia in 1834 at age nineteen and immediately married Mary Ann Lamar, one of Georgia's wealthiest and most prominent women.

Following his admission to the bar in 1836, he entered politics for the first time, remaining active politically until after the War Between the States. He was elected solicitor general in 1837 and became a member of Congress in 1842. Because of his strong support of the Union and his effort to keep Southerners in the national Democratic party, he was elected Speaker of the House in 1849.

His support of the Compromise of 1850 earned him the hatred of the die-hard Southern Rights Democrats. Nevertheless, he remained popular at home and was elected governor of Georgia in 1851 with the largest majority up to that time. After the election of his friend James Buchanan to the presidency in 1856, he was appointed secretary of the treasury.

When Lincoln was elected, he returned to Georgia and became a strong supporter of secession. He was sent as a delegate to the Montgomery Convention which organized the Confederacy and might have been elected president if it were not for the opposition of his old Southern Rights enemies.

During the war he served as a major general and was in command of the District of Georgia. After the war, he again practiced law. Following his death in New York in 1868, this memorial broadside was issued. Two of Howell and Mary Ann Cobb's houses still stand in Athens, one at the north end of Pope Street behind Emmanuel Episcopal Church and the other on the corner of Hill and Harris. *Photograph courtesy of University of Georgia Libraries Special Collections*

In 1862 Cook and Brother, an arms manufacturing firm that was forced to flee New Orleans because of the approach of Federal troops, purchased sixteen acres from the Athens Manufacturing Company at the junction of the North Oconee River and Trail Creek. Additional land was purchased, and buildings for the factory and workers' housing were constructed. The factory began operations on Christmas Day, 1862, and by the following June the plant was valued at almost $700,000.

The principal product of the factory was the Enfield-model rifle. Agents scoured the countryside for old brass, and the stocks were produced from local wood. An ordnance inspector declared that the guns were the finest he had seen of Southern manufacture, although there were minor problems with some of the firing mechanisms.

The operatives at the factory formed themselves into a home guard unit and established a breastwork, which still exists, on the hill overlooking the factory and river. One of the owners of the factory, Major Ferdinand Cook, was killed at the defense of Savannah. The operations were closed when hostilities ended. The Athens Manufacturing Company repurchased the land and factory at a sheriff's sale in 1870 and moved its weaving operation there from the factory downriver.

At the time this photograph was taken (circa 1895), the building was being used as a cotton factory. The bridge seen on the right of the photo crossed the Oconee at the foot of Broad Street. It was replaced by an iron bridge early in this century, which was in turn supplanted by a concrete bridge during the 1970s. The Check Factory, as the weaving operation was called, prospered during World War I and survived the Depression. After the death of A. G. Dudley, president of Athens Manufacturing Company, in 1947, the building was sold to Chicopee Mills, a division of Johnson and Johnson.

The old factory was enlarged and altered, losing its battlements and ornamental brickwork in the process. Johnson and Johnson recently gave the mill complex to the University of Georgia. It now houses the offices of the Small Business Development Center and the Physical Plant. Photograph by David Earnest; courtesy of University of Georgia Libraries Special Collections

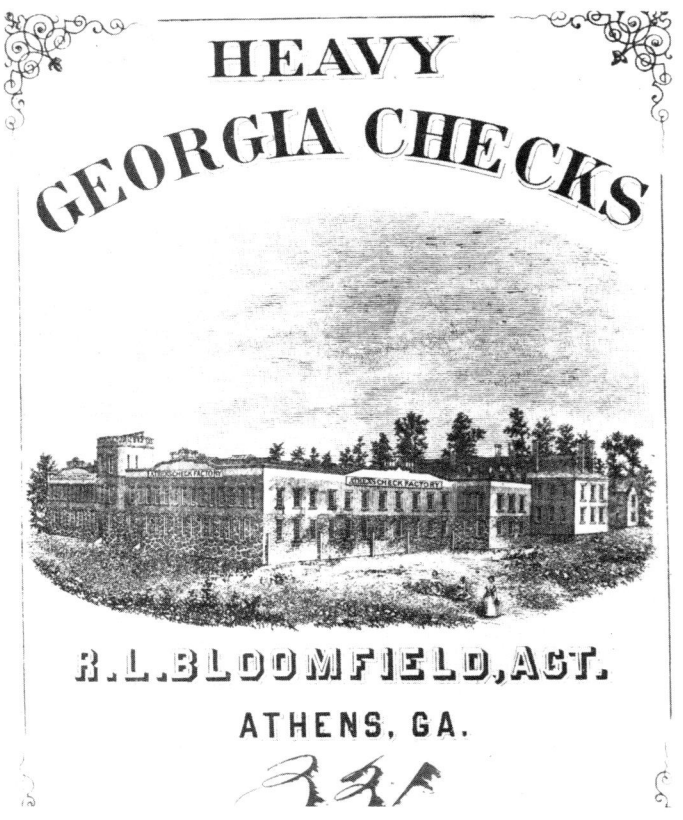

The bolts of cloth produced by the Athens Manufacturing Company at the Check Factory bore labels like the one shown here. The label has an engraving of the factory as it appeared before 1897 while R. L. Bloomfield was president and general agent of the company. Label courtesy of Gary Doster

The peaceful rural scene shown in this 1890s photograph has long since vanished, and it takes an imaginative observer to reconstruct it when visiting the location today. Located at what is now the intersection of Milledge Circle and Westlake Drive, the old Bobbin Mill produced the dogwood bobbins which were used by the local cotton factories in manufacturing cloth.

Power was supplied by water impounded by the dam (shown at the left) which passed through the wooden sluice to the overshot waterwheel at the factory on the right. The factory disappeared when the area began to develop in the second decade of this century, and the site is marked only by the rock shoals and a small park maintained by the Bobbin Mill Garden Club. Photograph by David Earnest; courtesy of University of Georgia Libraries Special Collections

Before the organization of a municipal fire department in 1891, Athenians depended on volunteer companies for fire protection. The first companies were organized before the Civil War and became a fixed part of the scene in Athens until the organization of a municipal fire department in 1891.

The tournaments held each year to determine which company could unwind its hose and set up its ladders the fastest were important social occasions in the community. The building in the photograph housed the oldest continuous volunteer company, the Hope Fire Company. A. L. Hull reported that the Confederate flag flew first over this structure.

The piece of equipment proudly displayed here with the members of the company is a hose reel, which was pulled to the scene of the fire by the men themselves. The hose was then attached to the steamer which pumped the water out of cisterns (and then later, water hydrants) to put out the fire. The building stood in the center of Washington Street between College and Lumpkin, facing west, in front of the present police department building. Photograph courtesy of University of Georgia Libraries Special Collections

This watercolor, which shows Athens as a peaceful, small town at the close of the Civil War, appeared on a Christmas card in 1866. The two tall steeples on the left belong to the Methodist (far left) and Presbyterian churches. The building in front of the Methodist church with the short tower is the old Town Hall.

The church on the far right of the picture is the old Emmanuel Episcopal Church, which stood where the C&S Bank Building is now located. In the middle ground are houses belonging to Mr. Hillyer and the Reverend Mr. Henderson. Photograph courtesy of University of Georgia Libraries Special Collections

After the end of the War Between the States, Federal troops occupied the buildings of the university. In December 1865, Chancellor Lipscomb went to Augusta and succeeded in freeing the college buildings from military occupation. Classes began again in January of 1866, with seventy-eight students in attendance. In that year, the sophomore class, which graduated in 1868, stood for this photograph.

Members of the faculty are in the front row, seated, from left to right: William L. Jones, James P. Waddell, Patrick H. Mell, Chancellor Andrew A. Lipscomb, Williams Rutherford, Louis Jones, and L. H. Charbonnier.

Standing behind the faculty are: Howell Jackson, Charles S. DuBose, William P. Mitchell, Julius L. Brown, N. V. McKibben, L. L. McClesky, Reese Crawford, A. L. Mitchell, J. P. Rucker, George Goetchius, R. A. Russell, and Peter W. Meldrim.

Second row, standing, left to right: A. H. Alfriend, S. W. Barnett, H. P. Myers, H. Whitman, Charlie Goodman, J. H. Casey, Hamilton Yancey, Bowdre Phinizy, E. B. Young, R. B. Hodgson, W. R. Mims, and E. H. McLaren.

Between the second row and last row in the left corner: W. Dennis, and Henry W. Grady (with hat on).

Last row: Davenport Jackson, S. F. Wilson, B. P. Hollis, W. Bailey Thomas, William Parks, W. C. Smith, Horace Beene, W. W. Thomas, George Bancroft, W. A. Carlton, Robert Toombs (nephew of the statesman), and J. H. Bethune. Photograph courtesy of University of Georgia Libraries Special Collections

Henry W. Grady, orator, journalist, and spokesman for the New South, was born on May 24, 1850 in this one-and-a-half story cottage which stood on the corner of Jackson and Hoyt streets. T. Remsen Crawford, writing in the New England Magazine in 1890 described it as a "four room, frame building with veranda in front, over which fragrant honeysuckle gracefully climbs, modest and lowly, yet comfortable and convenient."

This photograph was taken by Professor David Earnest shortly after that description was written. By the mid-1950s the house had been destroyed, and Frank Basham was running a welding and machine shop on the site. That, too, fell to the urban renewal wrecking ball in the 1960s.

William S. Grady, Henry Grady's father, came to Georgia about 1846 from the mountains of North Carolina. At the beginning of the War Between the States, William organized the Highland Guards and was elected captain. He was killed at Petersburg, Virginia. His wife, Anne Gartrell Grady, was still living in Athens (with her daughter Mattie Grady) at the time the above sketch was written. Photograph courtesy of University of Georgia Libraries Special Collections

At the close of the Civil War, Henry W. Grady and his mother moved into this imposing Greek Revival mansion on Prince Avenue which had been purchased by Grady's father in 1863.

General Robert Taylor, a planter and cotton merchant from Savannah, purchased the land on which the house stands in 1843 to build a summer home. He moved to Athens shortly thereafter so his sons could attend the university and constructed this elegant residence. It was sold by his estate to William Grady in 1863.

Henry Grady lived in the house only about three years before graduating from the university in 1868. It continued to be used as a residence until purchased by the city of Athens in 1966. The Athens Junior Assembly, now the Junior League of Athens, leased the house in 1968 and has restored and maintained it. It is used by the League as its headquarters and is rented for parties, receptions, weddings, and other social occasions.

The Taylor-Grady House was listed in the National Register in 1976 and has been declared a National Historic Landmark. It is the only known house associated with Henry Grady that survives. Grady often referred to it as "an old Southern home with its lofty pillars, and its white pigeons fluttering down through the golden air." Photograph courtesy of University of Georgia Libraries Special Collections

The gentleman on the arms of the two bathing beauties in this photograph is Henry W. Grady, a native Athenian who had become a national celebrity by the time of his death in 1889 at the age of thirty-nine. After graduating from the university in 1868, he briefly attended the University of Virginia but left in 1869 to become a reporter for the Atlanta Constitution.

He later became associate editor of the Rome (Georgia) Courier and soon purchased his own paper. In 1872 he bought an interest in the Atlanta Herald, which folded four years later because of financial difficulties. He returned to the Constitution and about 1880 bought a quarter interest in the paper. Grady assumed the post of managing editor and used this pulpit to preach the gospel of the New South.

He called on Southerners to throw off the shackles of the past and embrace a new prosperity founded on diversified farming, manufacturing, and the development of the region's natural resources. On December 22, 1886, he delivered his famous "New South Speech" in New York City. Assuring his audience that the days of slavery and secession were behind the South, he pictured the area as a place of harmony and progress that was striving for even greater achievements.

This approach, while it did little to increase Northern investment in the South at that time, struck a responsive chord in Northerners and Southerners alike and fostered the beginning of reconciliation between them. This speech made Grady a national figure, and he toured the country extensively, delivering orations on a similar theme. Exhausted by his travels, Grady contracted pneumonia and died after returning from a trip to Boston. Photograph courtesy of University of Georgia Libraries Special Collections

Musical entertainments have always been popular with Athenians. In the days before movies and television, virtually every child received some form of musical training and was often called on to perform for guests at home. Recitals and concerts were always well attended. This sextet of university students was photographed at a Washington's Birthday concert on February 22, 1867.

The performers are: seated, left to right, Samuel W. Barnett, William W. Thomas, and George Bancroft; standing, left to right, Alfred H. Alfriend, William L. Dennis, and Augustus Longstreet Hull. Photograph courtesy of Richard Patterson

55

This photograph, taken about 1868, shows the members of the Chi Phi fraternity at the University of Georgia. Henry Grady, standing second from the left, and several of his classmates founded the Eta Chapter in 1867. Interfraternity rivalry was particularly strong at that time, and these Chi Phi's were known for vigorously defending their honor against all comers.

In an impromptu speech to a group of Alpha Tau Omega alumni in his Atlanta Constitution office some years later, Grady seemed to have mellowed a bit from his college days. "The old rivalry between the Alpha Tau's and the Chi Phi's has died out," he said. "We used to fight each other, and your crowd once gave me an awful whipping. But it is all over; we are reconstructed, and we will shake hands across the bloody chasm."

The young man standing on the left next to Henry Grady is Walter B. Hill, a graduate of the class of 1870. He later served a brief term as chancellor from 1899 to 1905. It was his vision of what the university could be that led it from the traditional small liberal arts school of the nineteenth century toward the diversified institution of today. Although he served only six years, he is regarded as one of the greatest administrators in the history of the university. Photograph courtesy of University of Georgia Libraries Special Collections

The five ladies in this 1870 photograph were considered among the belles of Athens in the years after the war. Four of the group were sisters, daughters of Dr. James S. Hamilton and Rebecca Crawford. The Hamilton sisters were popular among the beaus of the era, and an invitation to a party at their Milledge Avenue home was highly prized.

The ladies are, from left to right: Sarah Hamilton, Louise Hazelhurst, Ethel Hamilton, Natalie Hamilton, and Emily Hamilton. Photograph courtesy of Mrs. David Robert Cumming

The Milledge Avenue home of the celebrated Hamilton sisters was completed after the beginning of hostilities in 1861. It exemplifies the architectural complexity of late Antebellum mansions in Athens and forms, with its combination of Federal, Greek Revival, and Italianate elements, a link with the elaborate, eclectic houses of the late nineteenth century.

Dr. James S. Hamilton, who bought the lot from the university and began his house in 1857, made a fortune from textile manufacturing at the Princeton Factory. The house was completed after four years by Ross Crane, the most celebrated contractor/architect of that day. The ornamental iron work, ordered from Wood-Perot Foundry in Philadelphia at a cost of $2,100, was shipped into the port of Savannah just before it was sealed off by the Union blockade.

In the years after the war, the house was often the site of lavish parties. As a result of a dispute over the estate of Dr. Hamilton, the house was sold on the courthouse steps in 1900. It was purchased about 1906 by E. R. Hodgson, president of the Empire State Chemical Company. It was acquired by Alpha Delta Pi sorority in 1939 and is still maintained and used by the sorority as a dormitory and chapter house. *Photograph (1930s) courtesy of University of Georgia Libraries Special Collections*

At the time this photograph was taken about 1875, the Confederate monument stood in the center of the intersection of College Avenue and Washington Street. Although fund raising efforts had begun in 1866, it took six and a half years for the Ladies' Memorial Association to raise the $4,444.44 construction cost by holding concerts, auctions, and a memorial fair. To help, the students of Lucy Cobb Institute and the Home School presented a May Queen pageant.

The cornerstone was finally laid on May 5, 1871, and the monument was dedicated on June 3 of the following year. University Chancellor Andrew Lipscomb composed the inscriptions, and a sculptor, Markwater of Augusta, was chosen to execute the work.

Because it posed a hazard to traffic, it was moved about the turn of the century to a median in front of City Hall. It was later moved to its present location on Broad Street. Some in the community sought to move it again because its location was deemed inconvenient, but the Banner-Herald reported that the fight to keep the monument where it was was won by "those who believed some good had come out of the past and that it was worth a minute in the whirl of going somewhere to contemplate where they had once been." *Photograph from Davis's Souvenir Album; courtesy of University of Georgia Libraries Special Collections*

This photograph shows Moore College as it appeared in 1875, a year after its completion. The building was given to the university by the city of Athens to house the college of agricultural and mechanical arts which was located at the university in 1873. Dr. Richard Moore, a popular and respected physician, organized the drive to secure the building, and it was named for him.

Professor L. H. Charbonnier was the architect, and M. B. McGinty was brought to Athens as the contractor. Athens had no good contractor at the time, and McGinty soon established himself as the successor to Antebellum builder Ross Crane. According to A. L. Hull, McGinty built every house of any pretensions in Athens from 1874 to 1890.

When the agricultural school moved to Connor Hall in 1909, Moore College was used by the engineering, physics, and astronomy departments until 1959, when it was remodeled to house the Department of Modern Foreign Languages. It is the only building in the French Second Empire style on the college campus. Photograph from Davis's Souvenir Album; courtesy of University of Georgia Libraries Special Collections

Lewis Green was one of the most familiar figures on campus from the 1870s through the 1890s. Born about 1811, he had been the slave of John Christy, publisher of the Southern Watchman. He was blind and so was given the task of turning the crank which operated the press. After emancipation, he sold apples on the college campus, sang, and passed the hat.

He was a great friend of the students who called him "Old Tub." He was often called on to lead them in hymns and spirituals when they gathered under the trees in front of Old College. One of his favorites was "Angels Bid Me Come":

> Look over yonder, what I see
> Angels bid me come;
> Two tall angels coming after me,
> Angels bid me come.
>
> Chorus:
> Rise and shine mourners,
> for angels bid me come.
>   (Mell, Reminiscences)

Green is shown here seated on the steps of the Chapel with his grandson Charley during the early 1890s. He lived in a small cottage west of the campus. Photograph by Telamon Cuyler; courtesy of University of Georgia Libraries Special Collections

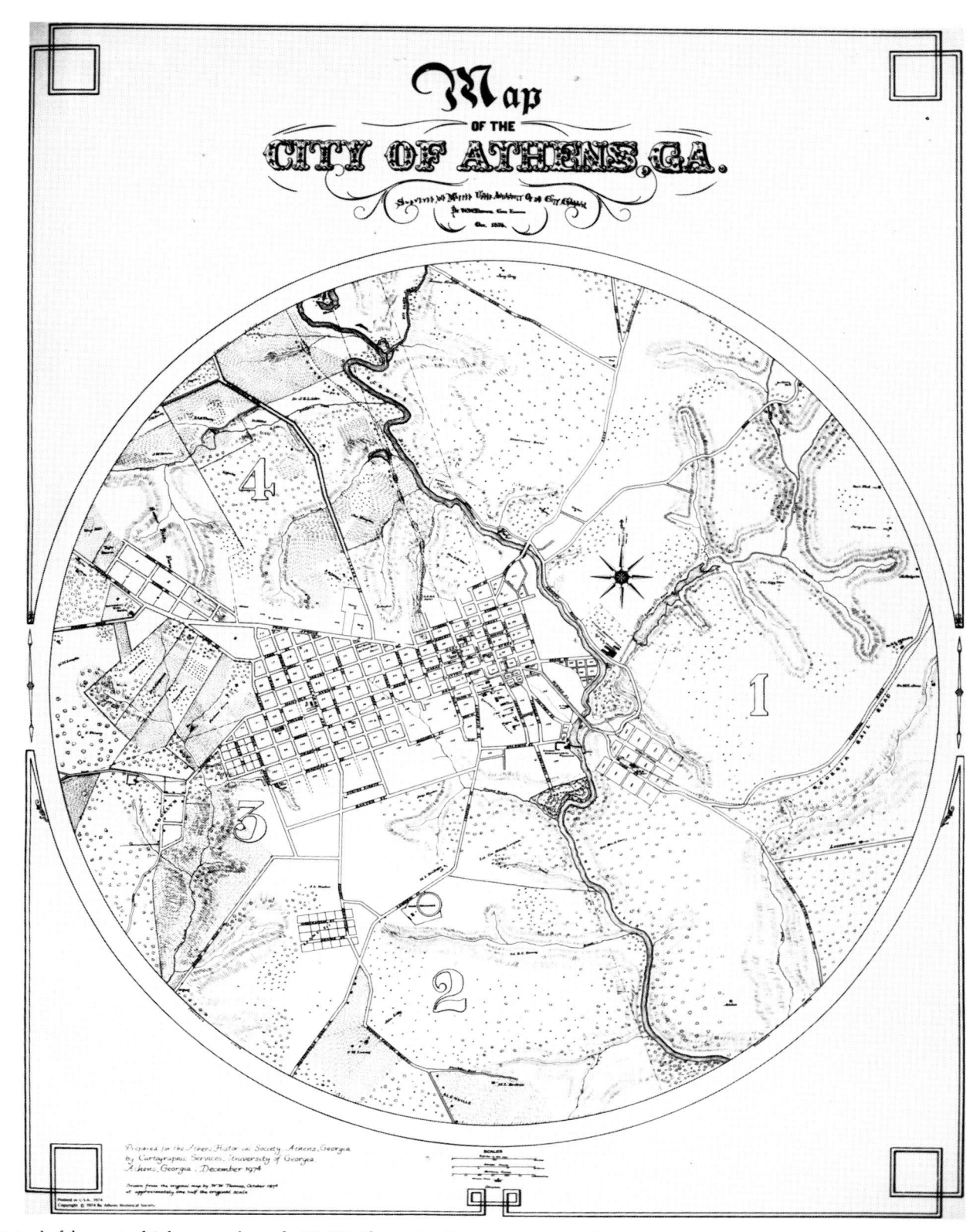

The original of this map of Athens was drawn by W. W. Thomas in 1874 and shows the extent of the town at that time. The grid pattern of streets extended from Foundry Street on the east in the downtown area west through Cobbham, across Milledge Avenue to about Rock Spring Street. It was bounded on the north by Prince Avenue and by Baxter Street on the south.

The only development in East Athens was that near the Athens Manufacturing Company Check Factory and on Carr's Hill at the terminus of the Georgia Railroad. The fair grounds were located along South Lumpkin near the present university track.

The area shown on the map is now almost completely developed, with only a few wooded enclaves as reminders of the rural character of much of the community in the 1870s. This map was reproduced for the Athens Historical Society on the centennial of its first issue by the Cartographic Services of the University of Georgia. Map courtesy of the Athens Historical Society

Although established before the war, Lucy Cobb Institute did not develop its reputation as one of the finest girls' schools in the South until the Postbellum period. This photograph was taken in 1875 during the administration of Mrs. A. E. Wright as principal. When she departed in 1880 to open a school of her own, she took most of the pupils with her, and Lucy Cobb was found to be in debt and badly in need of repairs.

Under her successor, Miss Mildred Rutherford, the school began to grow and prosper. She remained as principal, except for a few brief periods, throughout the remainder of the school's existence. Miss Millie was a strong believer in the Bible, the Lost Cause, and female virtue. She would not let the girls go out to the fence to talk with the boys. They were allowed only closely supervised visits in the parlors on the main floor and were forbidden to wave from the windows of their rooms on the second and third floor.

In the early years, classes were held in the main building, but about the turn of the century, Alumni Hall and Margaret Hall were built to the rear of the building, and later a gymnasium was added. On the left end of the porch in the photograph is one of the two goat statues that became symbols of the school. Unfortunately, they were frequently the objects of pranks of university boys and finally wound up, it is said, at the bottom of the Oconee River.

The school lasted until the Depression of the 1930s when it was transferred by the trustees of the school to the university. It has been used at various times as a girls' dormitory, office space, sorority housing, and storage space. During the 1960s, the upper story had deteriorated so badly that it was removed.

The Friends of Lucy Cobb, a non-profit group of Lucy Cobb alumnae and friends of the school, were organized during the 1970s to seek a way to preserve this important landmark. The Lucy Cobb complex will be restored to house the University's Carl Vinson Institute of Government. Photograph from Davis's Souvenir Album; courtesy of University of Georgia Libraries Special Collections

This is the way one of the parlors of Lucy Cobb appeared about the turn of the century. The painting over the mantel is one of eighteen given to the school by George I. Seney, its principal benefactor, from his personal collection. It was here that the girls were allowed to entertain their gentlemen callers under the watchful eye of Miss Millie. Photograph by Hajos; courtesy of University of Georgia Libraries Special Collections

This photograph of the interior of the Seney-Stovall Chapel shows the stage arranged for a musical performance. The Hook and Hastings organ in the center of the stage was given by George I. Seney after the completion of the chapel to the school he always called his "Little Daughter."

After the turn of the century, the Windsor chairs were replaced by wooden auditorium seating. Otherwise, the arrangement of interior looks today much as it does in this picture. Photograph courtesy of University of Georgia Libraries Special Collections

After becoming principal of Lucy Cobb, Miss Millie Rutherford felt that there was a need for a proper place to hold chapel and assemblies. She conceived of the idea of having each of the girls draw the names of prominent philanthropists and write individual letters to them asking for help. Miss Nellie Stovall wrote to George I. Seney of New York who responded with a promise of $10,000 if $4,000 could be raised locally. The matching money was quickly raised, and the cornerstone was laid in 1882.

The unusual octagonal brick building, designed by Athenian W. W. Thomas, was dedicated in 1885. After the school was acquired by the university in 1931, the chapel was used as a theater until the Fine Arts Building on campus was built. A leaking roof caused considerable damage to the interior of the buliding, and it might have been destroyed if it had not been for Dean of Men William Tate, who helped secure a new roof for the building.

The entire Lucy Cobb campus was placed in the National Register of Historic Places in 1970, and as a result a $50,000 matching grant from the United States Department of the Interior was made available in 1979 to begin exterior renovation. The work was completed in early 1981. The chapel now awaits interior restoration. The chapel is shown in the center of the photograph, with Alumni Hall to the left and the main building to the right. Since this photograph was taken, Alumni Hall has been demolished and the chapel has lost its tower. The tower has not been reconstructed in the first phase of restoration. Photograph courtesy of University of Georgia Libraries Special Collections

Mildred Lewis Rutherford, one of the most notable women of her era in Georgia, was known as an educator, writer, historian, and moving force behind many of the civic and patriotic organizations in Athens. She was the daughter of University Professor Williams Rutherford and Laura Cobb, the lady whose anonymous letter led to the founding of Lucy Cobb Institute.

Mildred entered Lucy Cobb in 1860 and graduated eight years later. She taught briefly in Atlanta before returning to her alma mater where she spent the remainder of her life as a teacher, serving three terms as principal. She and her sister, Mary Ann Lipscomb, guided the school through most of its history.

Miss Millie's interest in the history and traditions of the Old South led her to write a number of books and pamphlets on the subject including The South Must Have Her Rightful Place in History and The South in History and Literature. She served as historian general of the United Daughters of the Confederacy and was widely known for her speeches, which she often delivered in Antebellum costume.

She was a leader in most of the women's organizations of the day, including the Y.W.C.A., Bessie Mell Industrial Home, Athens Mission Board, and the Athens Memorial Association. There were few civic and cultural activities in which she did not participate.

Believing that the young ladies committed to her charge should be exposed to the life and culture of the old world, Miss Millie conducted a number of guided tours of Europe. This photograph was taken in Paris during one of these trips. Photograph courtesy of University of Georgia Libraries Special Collections

This house stood directly across the street from Lucy Cobb Institute and was the home of the school's long-time principal, Millie Rutherford. Originally built as a cottage by Ferdinand Phinizy in the late 1870s, it was extensively remodeled and enlarged.

Miss Millie lived in the house until it burned about 1926. She then moved to Dearing Street where she lived until her death shortly thereafter. The building stood on the corner, and the yard extended beyond where the two-story brick building housing a chiropractic clinic is now located. Photograph courtesy of University of Georgia Libraries Special Collections

Parades gave the Lucy Cobb girls a welcome opportunity to go beyond the front fence and to show that their reputation for beauty was well deserved, as long as they did not show too much.

These demure ladies are shown riding in a flower-festooned carriage in one of the many parades that were enjoyed by Athenians about the turn of the century. Photograph from the Lipscomb family papers; courtesy of University of Georgia Libraries Special Collections

One of the private schools remembered fondly in Athens was conducted in this modest frame structure which was located in the side yard of the Moss Home on the corner of Cobb and Franklin streets. Known to the students of the 1880s as the Grove School; it was organized by Miss Julia P. Moss for members of the Moss family and their friends. Miss Moss was assisted in her teaching duties in the two-room school by Miss Mary Bacon.

Each year the school held closing exercises so that the students could show proud parents and friends what they had learned. At the June 12, 1885 ceremony, Minor Nicholson declaimed "Life, a Mighty River," Albin Dearing discussed "The True Glory of a Nation," James Barrow recited "Composition on the Camel," and Barrett Phinizy delivered an oration on "Oh! Why Should the Spirit of Mortal Be Proud?"

In 1934 the alumni held a reunion at the Georgian Hotel. Miss Moss had died, but Miss Bacon was honored by her former students. In February 1979 the school was destroyed by the collapse of one of the large oak trees. Photograph courtesy of John Bondurant

Madame Sophie Sosnowski and her daughter Callie were widely recognized for their contributions to female education in Athens in the last half of the nineteenth century. Born in 1809 in Baden, Germany, Madame Sosnowski married a wounded Polish nobleman in 1835 and shortly afterward, migrated to the United States.

Living first in St. Louis and then in Erie, New York, Madame Sosnowski moved south in 1850 where she taught at Charleston, South Carolina; Montpelier, Georgia; and Columbia, South Carolina. After the destruction of Columbia by Sherman, she moved to Athens and became principal of Lucy Cobb Institute in 1862.

In 1869 Madame Sophie and Callie opened the Home School for young ladies which they operated first in a house on Hill Street and then in the Joseph Henry Lumpkin House on Prince Avenue. The school was particularly known for its instruction in French, German, and music. Madame Sosnowski died in 1889. Her papers are at the University of South Carolina. *Photograph courtesy of the South Caroliniana Library*

Another of Athens's well known private schools for young ladies was run by Mrs. E. A. Crawford in the 1880s and 1890s. The school was first conducted on the corner of College and Dougherty streets downtown. It later moved to Prince Avenue, and finally was located at Mrs. Crawford's home on Hill Street.

This White Victorian house still stands on the north side of the street in the middle of the block between Milledge Avenue and Franklin Street. It was later the home of Mrs. Crawford's daughter Annie. The curriculum of the school consisted of instruction primarily in French, music, and the social graces, but also offered the basic components of reading, writing, and arithmetic.

These young ladies are shown dressed in their minuet costumes for a school performance during the 1890s. *Photograph courtesy of Marguerite Thomas Hodgson*

The effort to establish a public school system in Athens began about 1879, but it was not until 1885 that the people voted by a majority of 603 to establish a school system under an act of the legislature and to issue bonds for the erection of school buildings.

The first school to be opened was the Meigs Street School which was housed in the old buildings of the Athens Academy. The board of education soon erected the Market Street School (later the Washington Street School), seen in this photograph. It housed both grammar and high schools, the latter of which was originally the seventh through ninth grades. The first tenth grade was added about 1906.

Regulations in those days were quite strict. One rule provided that "any pupil found in that portion of the ground assigned to the opposite sex will be subject to immediate suspension" (Athens Advertiser). After only twenty years of use, the building was demolished about 1909, and construction of the Georgian Hotel, which still stands on the northwest corner of Washington and Jackson streets, was started. Photograph courtesy of University of Georgia Libraries Special Collections

Edward B. Mell, a student at Washington Street School, recalled some years later an entertaining diversion for the students. "There was a parrot which was in a cage on the back porch of a residence next to the school," he related, "and some of us stopped in the afternoon each day to tease it. We would say, 'Hello, Polly' several times, then Polly would reply, 'Good bye.' We kept this up until Polly, in seeming anger, would tell us to 'Go to hell!' We were satisfied then and left Polly in peace" (Mell, Reminiscences).

The family that lived in the house took in borders and provided meals to a number of university professors. Polly, her family, and some of those who dined with them are shown here. Photograph courtesy of Mr. and Mrs. Paul Hodgson

Jeruel Academy was established in 1881 by the Jeruel Baptist Association, a group of mostly rural black churches. In 1886 a new building was completed on the corner of Pope and Baxter streets, where it remained until 1956.

This photograph shows the building as it appeared in the 1890s. During its history, the school experienced three name changes. Sometime between 1910 and 1914 the name was changed to Jeruel Baptist Institute, and in 1924 it became Union Baptist Institute. During the 1930s the trustees voted to eliminate the word Baptist from the name, to indicate that it was open to all denominations.

By 1914 Jeruel offered a curriculum which included college preparatory courses, elementary English, kindergarten, theology, and music, as well as such industrial courses as sewing and cooking. The campus facilities included a chapel, classrooms, library, laboratories, and dormitory rooms for boys and girls. The school was directed in its early years by the Reverend John H. Brown, who fostered interracial cooperation and encouraged whites to assist the school's programs. He held a farmer's conference at the school each year to train local black farmers in modern agricultural methods and stimulate their interest in his school.

Another principal that had a major impact on education in Clarke County was Professor C. H. Lyons, Sr. He graduated from Jeruel in 1901, returning there in 1908 to teach after receiving his degree from Atlanta Baptist College. Fourteen years later he became principal, a position he would hold until the school was incorporated into the public school system. Following his death in 1955, the Clarke County School District named Lyons Junior High School in his honor.

Harry "Squab" Jones, long-time trainer for the University of Georgia football team, coached the Union Institute football squad for a number of years. The school was closed in 1956 after the merger of city and county school systems. Photograph from An Era of Progress and Promise; courtesy of Michael Thurmond

The Reverend John Brown is shown seated in a carriage in front of the Jeruel Academy Principal's Home. The house was located on land acquired by the University of Georgia about 1910 for the development of South Campus. Photograph from An Era of Progress and Promise; courtesy of Michael Thurmond

This is a photograph of the faculty of Jeruel Academy about the turn of the century. The school's principal, the Reverend John H. Brown, stands on the far left. Photograph from An Era of Progress and Promise; courtesy of Michael Thurmond

The Bessie Mell Industrial Home was established in January 1889 by Bessie Rutherford Mell. First called the Athens Industrial Home, the name was changed after Mrs. Mell's death to recognize her important work. Before the days of welfare, this charitable institution provided help to needy women, particularly from mill worker families. With a motto of "do good as we have the opportunity," the ladies provided food, medicine, and medical attention to the sick and assisted the needy in any way they could, including providing rent money for aged and feeble women.

Their main activity was teaching women skills that they could use to supplement their income. They cut out garments and paid workers to make them, selling the completed clothes to reinvest in cloth to begin the cycle again.

Their facilities were located in the former home of Dr. James Carlton on the north side of Washington between Jackson and Thomas streets. In 1910 the Y.W.C.A. moved into the house, and the following year it was sold by the Industrial Home and the proceeds given to help the Y.W.C.A. purchase the Stevens Thomas House on Pulaski Street. The Clarke County Courthouse and a parking lot are now located on this site. Photograph courtesy of Richard Patterson

This stock certificate was issued by the short-lived Athens Street Railway Company organized by William P. Dearing in 1870. The object of the railroad was not to carry passengers, but to facilitate the transportation of freight from the Georgia Railroad depot on the east side of the Oconee River to the merchants in town.

The drayage charges were a burden to the merchants, and the organizers hoped to undercut the dray lines' business. However, just the opposite happened. They dray lines reduced their charges, and the street railway went out of business. While they were in operation, they used flat bed cars which were pulled by mules and delivered freight as far as College Avenue. Certificate courtesy of Rufus Reaves Paine, Sr.

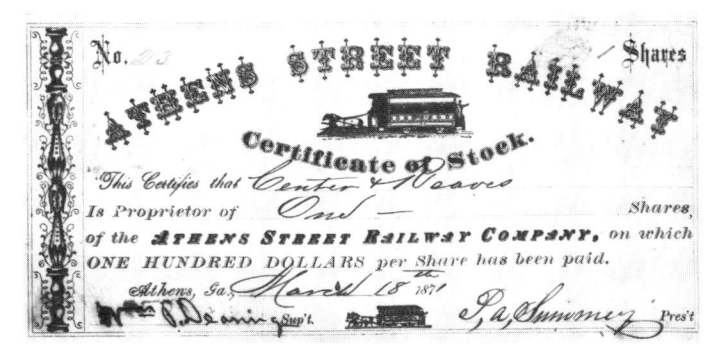

This photograph of Broad Street looking east from the university arch was taken about 1885. Only two familiar landmarks can be found in the photograph: the cast iron fence which enclosed the university campus, and the old National Bank of Athens (with the pointed gable and battlements) in the left foreground. The street level storefront of the bank has been changed, but the upper story remains the same.

All of the other buildings visible in the photograph have undergone substantial changes or have been replaced in the intervening years. The mule-drawn streetcar was one of those operated by the street railway company organized by Mr. Snodgrass in 1885. Photograph courtesy of University of Georgia Libraries Special Collections

There was no immediate move to erect a new courthouse after the county seat was transferred from Watkinsville to Athens in 1871. For a time, the old Town Hall in Market Street was used for a courtroom while an extensive debate over a location for the new structure ensued. Finally, in 1875 the Athens Georgian reported that "the contract for building the Court House was awarded to Messrs. Eaves, McGinty & Co., for $27,597.50. It is to be erected on the old Stevens lot on Prince Avenue." Three buildings, designed by University Professor L. H. Charbonnier, were rapidly erected: a courthouse, a jail, and a jailer's house.

This post card view shows the building as it appeared about the turn of the century. When the present courthouse was built downtown in 1913, the structure was remodeled and became Athens High School. After the high school's present facility was built in the early 1950s, the courthouse was demolished and property divided.

The eastern part of the lot was sold to the Coca-Cola Company, and Finley Street was extended through the site of the old building to join Prince Avenue. The jailer's house was demolished in 1980, leaving only the jail, now used as a warehouse, as a reminder of the old Courthouse Square. Two fast food restaurants, Wendy's and Captain D's, were erected on the front of the lot in recent years. Post card courtesy of Gary Doster

The tree seen in this photograph is the subject of one of Athens's most enduring legends. The story goes that Dr. W. H. Jackson, a university professor, loved the old white oak under which he had spent many hours as a boy and as a man. Hoping to preserve the tree, he drafted the following deed: "I, W. H. Jackson, of the County of Clarke, State of Georgia, of the one part, and the oak tree...of the County of Clarke of the other part, witness, that the said W. H. Jackson, for in consideration of the great affection which he bears said tree, and his desire to see it protected, has conveyed, and by these presents does convey unto the said oak tree entire possession of itself, and of the land within eight feet of it on all sides."

No record of this transaction can be found in the courthouse, and its value, if found, would be somewhat dubious. Professor Jackson did, however, accomplish his goals and gave rise to a delightful story. The tree was enclosed by chains and granite posts, and a marker was placed on the site. About the turn of the century a sleet storm damaged the tree (shown here) and it finally died many years later. In 1946 the Junior Ladies' Garden Club planted a replacement, reputedly a seedling of the original tree. It still stands on the corner of Dearing and Finley streets. Photograph by David Earnest; courtesy of University of Georgia Libraries Special Collections

The high daylight basement and wide verandas of this house seem appropriate for the home of a retired businessman from Savannah. John W. Nevitt lived in this house for a number of years after moving to Athens from the coast. The unusual porch posts, which form Gothic arches, and the rustic "stick" furniture make this an interesting scene.

Sylvanus Morris recalled happy times he spent at the house in his youth and characterized the owner as dignified and reserved (Morris, Strolls).

When the daughters of Jefferson Davis came to Athens during the fair in November 1877, they were entertained at a luncheon given for them by Mr. Nevitt.

The house stood across from the old courthouse on the north side of Prince Avenue at its intersection with Barber Street. It was demolished about 1900. Bells Supermarket now occupies the site. Photograph (circa 1880-1888) courtesy of Georgia Department of Archives and History

The house shown in this photograph was built in 1857 by J. H. Rucker on the northwest corner of Broad Street and Milledge Avenue. It was the scene of a brilliant reception given by the owner and his mother for Miss Winnie Davis, daughter of Confederate President Jefferson Davis, in November 1887. Mr. Rucker had the house substantially remodeled inside and out in 1889-90 in anticipation of a wedding that never took place.

Joseph M. Hodgson bought the house in 1896. Hodgson was a partner in Hodgson Brothers' Wholesale Grocery, later King and Hodgson, and served as a county commissioner. After his death in 1935, the house was rented to Alpha Omicron Pi sorority and later to Delta Tau Delta fraternity. It was sold in 1962 to the Varsity Restaurant and was demolished. Photograph courtesy of Marguerite Thomas Hodgson

Ice cream suppers were popular social events during the 1890s in Athens. The lively scene above, captured by a photographer at one such event, is uncharacteristically animated for a Victorian era photograph. The two ladies in the dark hats are Helen and Olivia Carlton, identical twin daughters of Henry H. Carlton, builder of Cloverhurst, the house illustrated on the facing page. Photography courtesy of Mrs. Lanier Orr

Henry Hull Carlton, physician, lawyer, legislator, congressman, and owner of the Athens Banner, built Cloverhurst, this elaborate Victorian era mansion about 1890. In 1901, the house was sold to Judge Hamilton McWhorter who moved to Athens in that year from Lexington where he had developed a lucrative law practice and had served on the bench of the Northern Judicial Circuit from 1890 to 1895. McWhorter remodeled the house, replacing the delicate Victorian porch with the more classical one shown in the photograph. Before retiring to Cloverhurst in 1918, he had become general counsel for the Southern Railroad in Georgia, Alabama, Florida, and Mississippi. The house stood on a hill to the west of Milledge Avenue.

The present Cloverhurst Avenue was once the private driveway to McWhorter's home. When the house was demolished after his death, Cloverhurst Avenue was extended through the former site and the area was developed. Photograph courtesy of University of Georgia Libraries Special Collections

The Victorian era brought about not only a change in architectural styles, but also a taste for more elaborate interior furnishings. The Ware-Lyndon House is an example of an Antebellum house which was redecorated during that era, shown here at the time of the wedding of Moselle Lyndon to Thomas Alexander Burke in 1897. While it is furnished in typical Victorian fashion, the structure remains much as it was in the days before the war, with its elegant marble mantels and simple woodwork. Stenciling does, however, elaborate the wall surfaces.

The house was built circa 1850 by Edward R. Ware, a prominent Athens physician and was sold to Edward S. Lyndon in 1880. Dr. Lyndon was a successful druggist and owner of a millwork company. It was his daughter Moselle that was married here in 1897. In 1939 the city of Athens purchased the property with playground bond money. It was used as offices and as a recreation center until 1973 when it became a cultural center.

The Lyndon House today serves as a gallery, an instruction center, and an arts organization meeting place. Additional renovations were made in the summer of 1981. Photograph courtesy of Mrs. Edward B. Hodgson, III

Both houses in this photograph were designed by Athens architect W. W. Thomas in the 1890s. The house on the right was built for William Pinckney Welch and his wife, Margaretta White, about 1890. It was in this house that a reception was held for President-elect William Howard Taft when he visited Athens as a guest of the university just prior to his inauguration in January 1908.

According to tradition, officials at the university felt that there was not a suitable place on campus to receive the president-elect, so they asked Mrs. Welch to have the party at her home.

When she died in 1921, the house went to her niece, Mrs. George Dudley Thomas, who lived there until her death in 1955. The Clarke County School System purchased it in that year. It was used for classes for Athens High School and finally as an office building for the board of education. It was damaged by fire and demolished. The Southern Bell building is now located on this South Milledge Avenue site.

The house next door to the Welch House was owned by J. H. Fleming and his wife, Alice Thomas, a sister of the architect. It is said that Mrs. Fleming saw a picture of a similar house in a magazine and had her brother draw up plans for it in 1895. It is now the location of Phi Kappa Psi fraternity. Photograph courtesy of Margurite Thomas Hodgson

Billups Phinizy, a wealthy cotton factor, had this house built for his family in 1890. A long-time president of the Southern Mutual Insurance Company, Phinizy also had business interests in the Georgia Railroad and Banking Company, Athens Railway & Electric Company, Southern Manufacturing Company, and Bank of the University.

He was a partner in the building of the Georgian Hotel, a trustee of Lucy Cobb Institute, and chairman of the committee that oversaw the building of the new Clarke County Courthouse in 1912-13.

His Milledge Avenue home was a classic of the Queen Anne style with its irregular massing, turrets, decorative shingles, iron cresting, classical details, and moldings of every description. It was probably the most elaborate example of its type in Athens.

After the death of Mrs. Phinizy in 1949, the Thomas Tillmans lived briefly in the house. It was rented to the Kappa Sigmas for a number of years until sold to the Chi Omega sorority in 1960. The house was demolished and replaced by a new chapter house. Photograph (1930s) courtesy of University of Georgia Libraries Special Collections

The Thomas-Carithers House, a veritable "wedding cake" of classical detail and decoration, was built in 1896 by W. W. Thomas, Athens's most accomplished nineteenth century architect, for his own home. Its design is said to have been influenced by a visit to the 1893 Columbian Exposition in Chicago, where the Neo-Classical Revival dominated the design of the exposition buildings.

Although trained in civil engineering, Thomas pursued a career in business, rising to the presidency of the Southern Mutual Insurance Company in 1894. He also served as first chairman of the Clarke County Commission and was appointed to the commission for building the new Georgia State Capitol in Atlanta in 1883. After Thomas's death in 1904, the house was leased and finally sold in 1909 to the George Henry Hulme family. James Y. Carithers, organizer of the Athens Electric Railway, city council member, and state senator, purchased the house in 1913.

Carithers died after living only four years in the house, but his widow remained until 1939 when she sold it to the Alpha Gamma Delta sorority, Gamma Alpha House Corporation. They adapted part of the house for living quarters and added a dormitory wing to the rear. The sorority undertook a major refurbishing of the exterior and the principal downstairs rooms in the summer of 1981. The house, which is located on the corner of Milledge and Baxter, is listed in the National Register of Historic Places. *Photograph courtesy of Richard and Georgia Hightower Patterson*

This photograph of the entrance hall and one of the flanking sitting rooms was taken in 1897 while the Thomases were living in their Neo-Classical house on Milledge Avenue. These principal rooms have fourteen foot ceilings, ten foot high doors, and parquet floors.

Below the cornice is a frieze of rose garlands with goat heads. The woodwork is dark oak. The Alpha Gamma Delta sorority has tried to preserve the character of these rooms, which the members use for social functions and chapter activities. *Photograph courtesy of Richard Patterson*

White Hall, one of Georgia's most magnificent Victorian mansions, was built in 1891 by John R. White, a prominent banker and industrialist. The style is eclectic, combining Queen Anne and Richardsonian Romanesque elements. Quality materials, fine craftsmanship, and attention to details are evident throughout. After his mother's death, White constructed his new house (shown here) on the site of the original White Hall, built by his father. In 1906 the older house was moved to Dillard, Georgia, where it still stands.

Although no documentation exists for the assertion, the design of the house has been attributed to W. W. Thomas. Family members recall Mrs. White chastizing Thomas for the design of the staircase. When Mrs. White died, Mr. White married Lena H. Towns, his children's governess, in 1917. She redid the house, painting over its exquisite paneling and woodwork and covering the floors with grey carpet.

The house remained in the White family until 1936 when the property was acquired by the Georgia Rural Rehabilitation Corporation. The land was deeded to the university for an experimental forest, and the house was later converted into offices and laboratories for the School of Forest Resources. When a new building was completed for the school on campus, the house was carefully restored with funds from the sale of timber in the experimental forest. The restoration has received several awards from preservation organizations. Photograph by Jim Lockhart; courtesy of Georgia Department of Natural Resources, Historic Preservation Section Section

This photograph is of the wedding party gathered on August 10, 1892 for the marriage of Asbury H. Hodgson, a wealthy widower, to Miss Sally Paine, a sister of Mrs. John R. White. This was the first major social event held in the White's new mansion, White Hall. The wedding guests traveled the short distance from Athens to Whitehall Community on a private railroad car owned by the groom. Photograph courtesy of Marguerite Thomas Hodgson

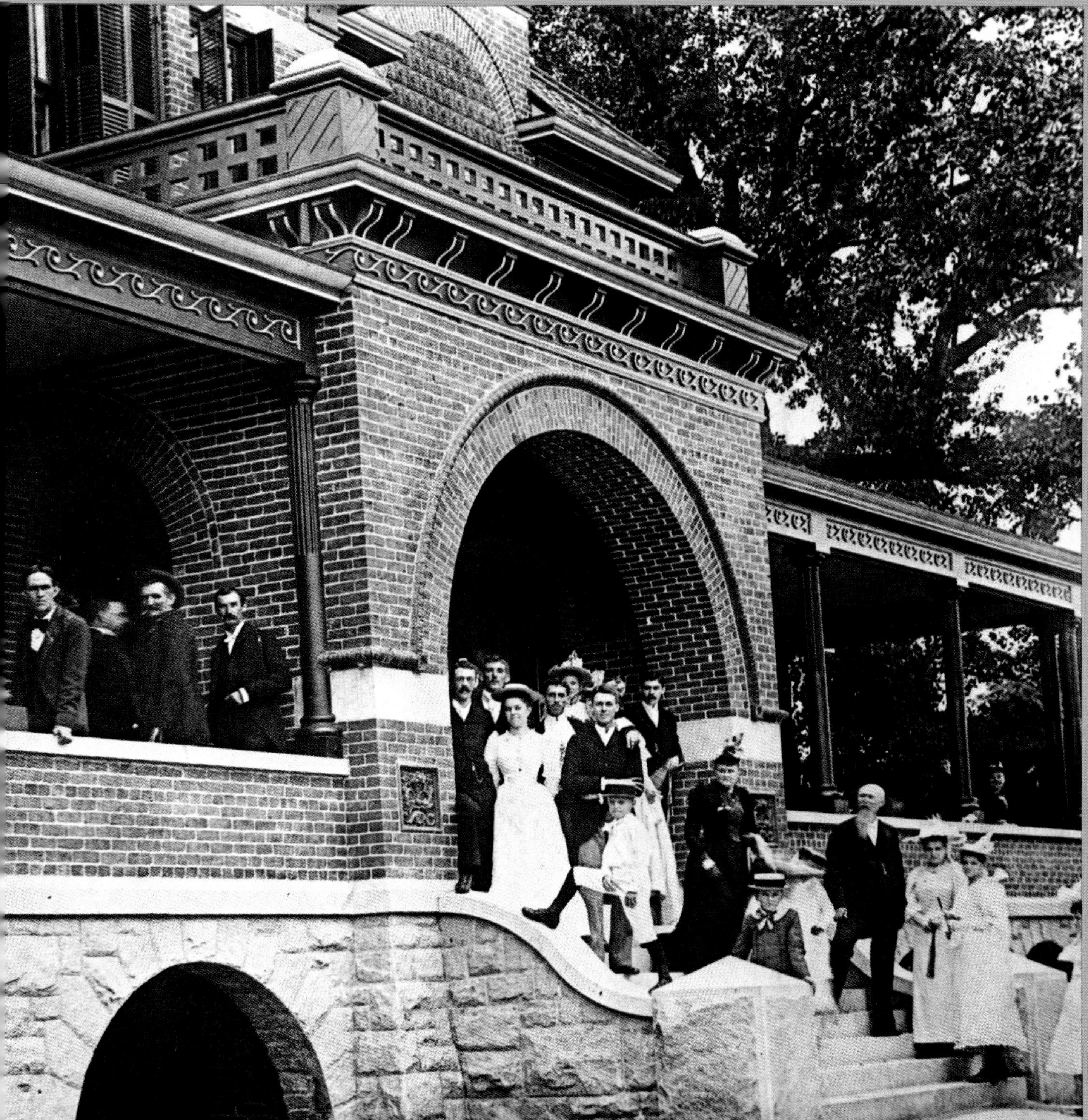

Monroe Bowers "Pink" Morton was one of Athens's most noted and affluent black citizens at the turn of the century. Although he was born a slave and had little formal education, Morton became a successful businessman. He was active in Republican politics and was a delegate to the convention that chose William McKinley as the party's candidate for president in 1896. The following year he was appointed postmaster of Athens.

By 1914 he had become editor and publisher of the Progressive Era and owned between twenty-five and thirty buildings in the city. He was also a contractor, and he participated in the construction of the Wilkes County (Georgia) Courthouse and the government building in Anniston, Alabama.

His most enduring monument is the Morton Theatre, a black vaudeville house, which he built on the corner of Washington and Hull streets in 1910. It became the center of black cultural activities in Athens and also housed the offices of many prominent black professionals. Pink Morton died in 1919, but his legacy lives on in buildings like the Morton. Photograph courtesy of Athens Newspapers, Incorporated

M. B. Morton lived in this Victorian era house on the corner of Prince and Milledge avenues from the 1880s until his death in 1919. Prince Avenue was once one of the most fashionable streets in the city, and Morton's house occupied a prominent corner location in that neighborhood.

On the left of the photograph through the trees may be seen a part of the Central Presbyterian Church which stood on the opposite corner. Both of these buildings are now gone, the church replaced by Dunkin Donuts and the Morton House by Flowerland. Photograph courtesy of University of Georgia Libraries Special Collections

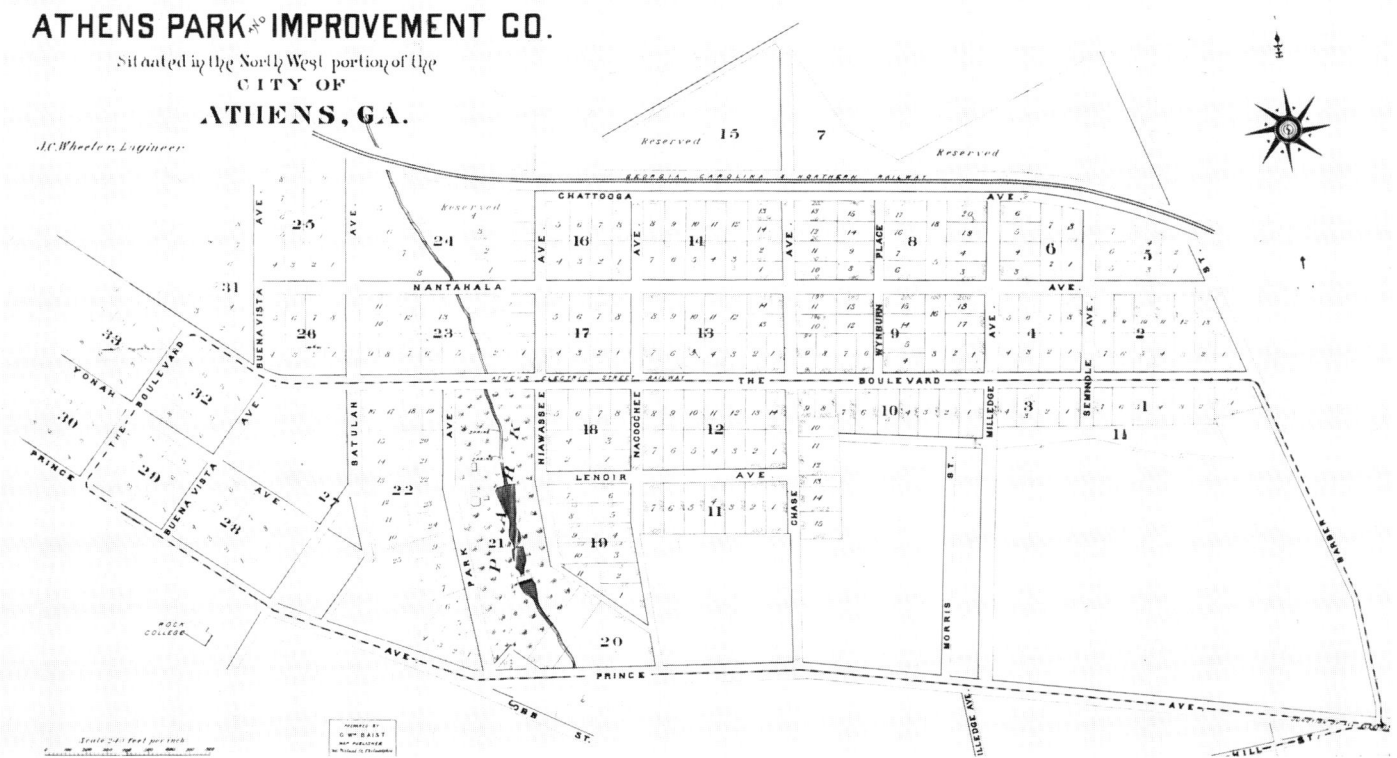

In 1890 the Athens Park and Improvement Company was organized and purchased 300 acres of land north of Prince Avenue and west of Barber Street. They cleared the land, laid out a mile-and-a-half long avenue through the heart of it, and began subdividing it for sale. The development of this area was made possible by an agreement reached with the street railroad to switch from mules to electricity and thus open the area to easy access from the heart of the city.

The "streetcar suburb" was a phenomenon sweeping the country in the days before the advent of the automobile; and the Boulevard, as the area became known because of its wide central street, was Athens's own version. It was a well planned development with a twenty-one acre park and land reserved along the railroad for industrial development. Those living east of the park were within the city limits and enjoyed the benefits of city schools, lights, and water. For those purchasing lots to the west of the park in Buena Vista Heights, there was the advantage of no city taxes. There was a little something for everyone in the Boulevard.

A number of larger homes in a variety of Victorian styles were soon constructed along the Boulevard itself and many less elaborate but substantial homes rose on the adjacent streets. When the Southern Manufacturing Company bought part of the land north of railroad tracks for its factory, the workers' houses were built along Nantahala and Hiwassee avenues. There was a mixture of incomes and lifestyles in the development area. The development was not a financial success for its backers, but it became in the long run an asset to the city.

With the coming of the automobile, suburbs opened further out of town, but, by and large, the area developed by the Park and Improvement Company remained a viable in-town area. It remains so today in a time when an in-town location is again becoming desirable, and efforts have begun in recent years to restore many of the substantial older homes. This map shows the original layout of the development in 1890. Photograph courtesy of University of Georgia Libraries Special Collections

This delightful rural scene was photographed during the 1890s in what is now the heart of the Midtown neighborhood. The meadow along the east side of Bloomfield where Hall Street now intersects was a favorite spot for picnicing and picking wildflowers during this period. Two of those in the photograph, Minnie Power and John Wilbanks, married in 1899.

The area, which was laid out by industrialist Robert L. Bloomfield, began to develop in the late 1880s. The new street railway on nearby Milledge Avenue helped to foster further growth around the turn of the century. Now many of the older homes are being restored, and the neighborhood, which was at one time beginning to deteriorate into a student rental area, is now on the upswing. Photograph by Claude Maddox; courtesy of Lucile Wilbanks Johnson

This photograph was taken at the old streetcar barn which was located off the Boulevard on land given to the railway by the Athens Park and Improvement Company as an inducement to extend their lines through the new development. In 1885 a Mr. Snodgrass from Texas organized the first street railway in Athens designed to carry passengers. He went from town to town organizing the railroads, garnering his profit from the money left from the sale of bonds after the expenses had been met.

His streetcars were powered by small mules which he sent in from Texas, and his three cars were called "Lucy Cobb," "Pocahontas," and "No. 2." The mules had a hard time of it in wet weather, having to walk on the rails on Milledge Avenue near Lucy Cobb to keep from getting bogged down in the mud.

When the line went into receivership, it was bought by E. G. Harris, who electrified the line and went into business with the Athens Park and Improvement Company. When the venture again failed, the line was bought by J. Y. Carithers, W. S. Holman, and others. They built dams and power plants at Mitchell Bridge and Tallassee Shoals to provide the electricity, replacing the small steam plant on Boulevard.

By 1910 they supplied power to the Athens Water Works, Southern Manufacturing Company, Empire State Chemical Company, Athens Foundry and Machine Works, and Athens Coca-Cola Bottling Company, among others, and provided electric street lights for the city. Photograph (1890s) courtesy of Athens Newspapers, Incorporated

Military companies were popular on campus throughout the nineteenth century, and all the young boys in town looked forward to the time when they, too, could join the university boys who stepped around, held their heads high, and dressed in a uniform. The uniform was an essential ingredient and only two Athens merchants furnished them, F. W. Lucas and M. G. & J. Cohen. They had to be tailor-made to assure a proper fit and were usually quite expensive. This photograph shows the properly uniformed companies drilling on Herty Field.

From 1867 until his retirement in 1898, Colonel L. H. Charbonnier was in charge of military training. He was a Frenchman and graduate of the French military school of St. Cyr. He taught engineering and mathematics at the university in addition to drilling the student companies.

The buildings behind the cadets are, from left to right, the Old Library, the Ivy Building, Demosthenian Hall, and the Chapel. The Ivy Building was built in 1831 as a classroom building and was used at the time this photograph was made (near the turn of the century) by several departments. The law school and English department had the first floor, while modern languages and engineering occupied the second. Photograph courtesy of University of Georgia Libraries Special Collections

This photograph is a self-portrait of Claude Maddox, one of Athens's most prominent photographers during the 1890s. He took a number of photographs that appeared in the university's annual, the Pandora, during this decade. He favored more casual or informal poses for his subjects, and his photographs all have a certain flair about them.

Maddox moved away from Athens about 1900 but returned some years later. He died at his 258 Springdale Street home during the 1930s. Photograph courtesy of Lucile Wilbanks Johnson

Field Day was an event that university students always looked forward to in the spring. There were athletic contests in which the young men could demonstrate their athletic ability before the assembled crowds, and all attending enjoyed the picnic that followed. During the 1880s and 1890s Field Day was held at the old fair grounds race track, which was located about where the university track is today. The main contests were in track and field, but other events such as wrestling and chasing a greased pig were also included.

This photograph was taken on Field Day 1893. The Pandora of that year reported that it was the most successful ever held on campus. Records were broken in the running high jump, the hammer throw, the half mile run, and the three legged race, while the winner of the fifty yard dash tied the best time on record. Photograph courtesy of University of Georgia Libraries Special Collections

There were no intercollegiate sports at the university until the 1880s, and for some time thereafter they were looked on with disfavor by a number of university trustees. There was a long and bitter struggle among trustees that began in 1892 when Dr. W. H. Felton, an opponent of dancing and all frivolity as well as intercollegiate sports, introduced a resolution to discourage baseball.

A substitute motion was passed which provided: "In the opinion of the Board the indulgence of students of the University in interstate and intercollegiate football or baseball contests during the college term may be harmful in its influence, and further that students shall not be permitted to leave the University to give Glee Club or other exhibitions during the term."

The following year, trustee Augustus L. Hull offered a resolution declaring that the previous one was only advisory and that decisions as to athletics should be left to the faculty. The motion passed and college athletics at Georgia were on firm ground, enjoying the strong support of Chancellor Boggs.

Georgia's first intercollegiate football game was played against Auburn on Washington's Birthday in 1892. It was not a propitious beginning. Georgia lost. In the years since that game, the university has established a strong football program which achieved its first national championship almost eighty-nine years afters the first loss to Auburn in Atlanta. The scruffy team of rowdies shown in this photograph was the team of 1895. Each member purchased his own uniform from the McGregor Company, which supplied athletic equipment as well as college textbooks.

The team had a winning season, losing only their opening game in Athens to Sewanee, 8-12. In the remaining games, they beat Wofford, 10-0; Auburn, 10-8; South Carolina College, 40-0; Augusta Athletic Association, 66-0; and the Savannah Athletic Association, 22-0. Photograph by Maddox Brothers; courtesy of University of Georgia Libraries Special Collections

Baseball was first introduced to Athens in 1868 by Bill Hodgson. It soon became the town's most popular game, and two teams, the Dixies and Pop and Go's established statewide reputations. By the mid-1880s, the college was fielding intercollegiate teams. The 1885 team played a celebrated game at Union Point against Emory College. The score was tied in the ninth inning and Georgia had two outs. Jim Mell, a freshman, came to bat and immediately got two strikes against him. On the next pitch he hit a home run, winning the game for Georgia. Chancellor Barrow, then a young professor, was so excited he ran the bases behind the student.

The baseball game in progress in this photograph was being played on Herty Field, an open area west of the Chapel and New College below Moore College. It was named after Charles Holmes Herty, who was the university's first athletic director. The field was used for baseball and other sports until after the turn of the century. When the land was acquired for South Campus, Sanford Field was constructed, and baseball games were played there. *Photograph courtesy of University of Georgia Libraries Special Collections*

The 1896 Pandora identified the group shown in this photograph as the Varsity Boat Crew, although they appear more like a track team with shotput and cleated shoes. They were photographed in the McDannell studio on a set replete with artificial grass and a painted pastoral backdrop. *Photograph courtesy of University of Georgia Libraries Special Collections*

Looking like fugitives from a Georgia chain gang, the university lacrosse team posed for this 1890s photograph. The sport was apparently popular for only a few years before disappearing. It has been resurrected once again in recent times. *Photograph courtesy of University of Georgia Libraries Special Collections*

The Old North Campus of the University is shown here as it appeared about the turn of the century. The building on the left with the turret is now occupied by Athens Refrigeration. The first floor store front has been altered and the turret removed, but otherwise its exterior remains much as it was. Terra cotta cherubs still gaze down upon pedestrians walking along the Jackson Street side of the building.

Above the roof of this building, the gable roof of Phi Kappa Hall can be seen. The building with the cupola in the upper left of the photo is Science Hall. It was constructed in 1898 and stood only until 1903 when it was gutted by a fire which destroyed the chemistry department and chancellor's office. It was replaced in 1905 by Terrell Hall, designed by Professor Charles Morton Strahan.

To the right of Science Hall are Old College, New College, the Toombs Oak, the Chapel, Demosthenian Hall, Moore College, the Ivy Building, and the old Library. In the center of the photograph, behind the iron fence, are four tennis courts. The building at the lower right is the old National Bank of Athens building with its crenelated parapet. Photograph by Hajos; courtesy of University of Georgia Libraries Special Collections

Students of the 1870s and 1880s complained that good theatrical performances were few and far between, but they seldom organized plays or programs of their own. About 1888 the students finally staged a performance of Ingomar at Deupree Hall, the city's principal theater or opera house. Thomas Reed, later university registrar, recalled that he was costumed in a pair of old shoes cut down to look like sandals, trousers rolled up to his knees, and a pink satin cape which he had borrowed from Mrs. Howell Cobb.

Although greeted with acclaim, this was the only student performance until the Thalian Dramatic Club was organized in the 1890s. The Thalians are shown here in costume for one of their plays in the mid-90s. The group continued to stage plays after the turn of the century, becoming part of the Thalian-Blackfriars organization.

After the university acquired Lucy Cobb Institute in the 1930s, the Seney-Stovall Chapel was used as a theater until the completion of Fine Arts in 1941. Today, several plays are performed each year by students in the university's drama department. Photograph courtesy of University of Georgia Libraries Special Collections

83

Card playing was always a popular diversion among students but one which, in the early days, could bring about the expulsion of any who were caught. By the end of the century, the practice, while not encouraged, was dealt with less harshly. When Dr. Mell was chancellor (1879-1888) he knocked on the door of a student's room to deliver a message and was told to "scratch under." On entering, he found the young man and three companions playing cards. He simply delivered his message and left.

When the boy later came to him to find out what was to be done, the chancellor told him that his room was his "castle" and took no further action. "This made a profound impression on the boy," it was reported, "and he made an entire change in his manner of life. Later on he became one of the famous lawyers of the state" (Mell, Reminiscences).

The photograph of this card game in the 1890s was taken by Telamon Cuyler, a student, and undoubtedly, a participant himself. Photograph courtesy of University of Georgia Libraries Special Collections

This engraving from the 1890s shows the building originally known as Lester Hall. It was built by Thomas N. Lester on the northwest corner of Clayton Street and College Avenue sometime after 1875. Pope Barrow, who had the second floor corner office, was a prominent attorney, United States senator, and judge of the superior court. Future Chancellor David Barrow, Law School Dean Sylvanus Morris, and Judge E. K. Lumpkin studied law with him there, and many years later Judge Lumpkin moved his office to the same location.

The lower floor was used by Hodgson Brothers for their wholesale grocery business, which later became King and Hodgson and was moved to the building in the triangular intersection of Broad and Oconee streets, now Farmer's Hardware.

The building illustrated here was then known as the Shackelford Building and was the location at one time of Orr Drugs and the chamber of commerce. The cotton warehouse, which appears at the left, is gone; but the main building remains. Engraving courtesy of Marguerite Thomas Hodgson

The first Y.M.C.A. was organized in Athens in May 1857 by Young L. G. Harris, Williams Rutherford, Dr. R. D. Moore, Thomas R. R. Cobb, and a number of other prominent men from the university and town. The War Between the States disrupted the new organization, which was not reconstituted until the 1880s. In April 1889 the cornerstone for a new building was laid on the former site of Junius Hillyer's law office on the corner of Clayton and Lumpkin streets.

When the three story building was completed it offered a gymnasium, swimming pool, bowling alley, and a reading room, as well as rooms for young men to rent. Bible classes, personal workers' classes, and Sunday meetings were held here regularly. The ground floor storefronts were rented to merchants to help provide income for the association. Edward E. Jones was credited with organizing and directing the effort that resulted in the construction of the new building.

The building was demolished after the second Y.M.C.A. was built two blocks south on the corner of Lumpkin and Broad in the second decade of this century. The site was then occupied by the Elite Theatre building which survives today as the Georgia Theatre. Photograph (circa 1900) courtesy of University of Georgia Libraries Special Collections

In the summer of 1891, Athens finally got the direct connection with Atlanta and the Eastern Seaboard it had long sought when the Georgia, Carolina, and Northern Railroad, later part of the Seaboard system, came through Athens. A fine new passenger depot was constructed on North College Avenue.

This photograph shows the depot as it appeared shortly after its completion, with buggies lined up in front and a train at the station. The depot is still standing, but passenger service disappeared a decade ago. It is now used by the Seaboard Coast Line Railroad for offices. Photograph from the author's collection

The old covered bridge across the Oconee River and the railroad trestle constructed in 1891 appear in this 1890s photograph by Professor David Earnest. The new trestle made a dramatic crossing above the old bridge which had for years provided a link between downtown Athens and Barberville, an outlying community located along what is now North Avenue between the river and the bypass.

The bridge continued to provide one of the principal river crossings in Athens until well into the twentieth century. A four-lane concrete bridge now spans the river here. Athens's last covered bridge, crossing the Oconee at Elm Street not far above this site, stood until 1965 when it was moved to Stone Mountain Park. Photo courtesy of University of Georgia Libraries Special Collections

Athens was the scene of an interesting experiment that began in the 1890s and lasted through 1907—the operation of a city-owned dispensary. In 1885 the "dry" forces had succeeded in getting a local prohibition ordinance passed in Athens, but "blind tigers," selling illegal liquor were set up everywhere. "Our city has been full of barrooms since prohibition went into effect and they [are] constantly increasing," wrote the editor of the Banner. "They are making prohibition a farce."

The liquor being sold was not only illegal but also often adulterated so that many people became ill. By 1891 it was apparent that prohibition would be defeated at the polls. The prohibitionists came up with the idea of establishing a city-owned-and- run dispensary that would sell pure liquor and thus put the illegal bars out of business. The proposition passed by a narrow margin. Local attorneys Andrew J. Cobb, Henry Tuck, and George Thomas drew up the state enabling legislation, and aided by the lobbying efforts of local ministers, professors, and even Chancellor Boggs, succeeded in getting the bill through the General Assembly on August 3, 1891.

The Athens Dispensary was thus the first created in the country. It was governed by a board of three commissioners who set the rules in accordance with the governing statute. Some of the regulations provided that sales were to be cash only; liquor could be sold only between sunrise and sunset Monday through Saturday, election days and holidays excluded; all liquor had to be analyzed by a chemist; no university students could buy liquor without written permission of the chancellor; and the minimum purchase was one pint and the maximum amount allowable was two gallons.

Macon C. Johnson, a clerk at Hodgson Brothers, was made manager and sold $900 worth of liquor in the first three days the dispensary was open. The idea was greeted with interest all over the country and the city received many letters of inquiry. "Pitchfork" Ben Tillman, the governor of South Carolina, was so impressed that he forced a statewide dispensary system through the legislature in his state.

Soon the very prohibition forces that brought the dispensary into existence began to attack it. The manager, Macon Johnson, was expelled from the Baptist church for selling liquor, even though his minister and congregation had urged him to take the job in the first place. He said in his defense that "it seems monstrous to me that the members of the church should want to exclude me for selling liquor in the dispensary when nearly everyone buys it from me."

A move was begun in 1906 to close down the dispensary, but the action of the General Assembly the next year made that unnecessary. Statewide prohibition went into effect on January 1, 1908. The last bottle of wine was sold at the Athens Dispensary at 1:30 p.m. the previous day. The photograph shows men lined up in front of the dispensary to buy some of a new shipment of liquor being unloaded in barrels from the wagon in the street. The store was on East Broad Street near the present location of Christian Hardware. Photograph courtesy of University of Georgia Libraries Special Collections

This one pint gin bottle was sold by the Athens Dispensary during its sixteen years of operation. Bottle courtesy of Charles Brockman; photograph by William B. Winburn; courtesy of Athens Newspapers, Incorporated

This photograph of one of Athens's volunteer fire companies was taken in the 1880s at the corner of Jackson and Broad streets, probably during one of their drills or tournaments. The fire engine or "steamer" is pumping water from an underground cistern. These cisterns provided the source of water for fighting fires from the 1850s until a water system was constructed in the 1890s.

The buildings on the right housing the businesses of George W. Calvin and Lowe and Company have been replaced, but the structure seen dimly through the smoke and mist, the old National Bank of Athens, is still standing. Photograph courtesy of Athens Newspapers, Incorporated

In 1882 Moses and Simon Michael opened a small dry goods firm with the shelves half full of goods. Within a few years it had become the largest and finest department store in the area. Michael Brothers was first located on the southeast corner of Broad and Jackson streets where the Athens Refrigeration building presently stands.

By the early 1890s, the growth of the business required a move to larger quarters and the building in the photograph was constructed on the southeast corner of Clayton and Jackson streets, replacing a Chinese laundry. Within a few years, the Michaels had to rent additional space, and in 1906 they built a new retail store to the left of this building, retaining the old five-story structure for their wholesale trade.

Both buildings were destroyed by a disastrous fire in 1921. The present Michael Brothers building was built on the former site following the fire. It still stands today as the restaurant, retail, and office development known as Park Plaza. Photograph courtesy of University of Georgia Libraries Special Collections

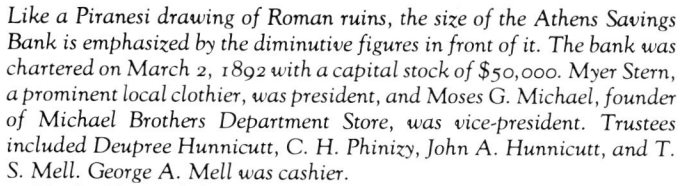

Like a Piranesi drawing of Roman ruins, the size of the Athens Savings Bank is emphasized by the diminutive figures in front of it. The bank was chartered on March 2, 1892 with a capital stock of $50,000. Myer Stern, a prominent local clothier, was president, and Moses G. Michael, founder of Michael Brothers Department Store, was vice-president. Trustees included Deupree Hunnicutt, C. H. Phinizy, John A. Hunnicutt, and T. S. Mell. George A. Mell was cashier.

The building is believed to incorporate an earlier two-story brick store building which was raised to three stories when the present facade was added about 1886. It is one of the few commercial examples of the Richardsonian Romanesque style in the city.

About the turn of the century, the Athens Savings Bank was flanked by the National Bank of Athens on the right and the American State Bank on the left. It is said that in times of financial panic, the banks passed money from one to another through the back windows to meet depositor's runs on one of the banks and thus restore customer confidence. In 1928 the Athens Savings Bank sold the building to the National Bank which, in 1950, sold it to Charles Parrott, Sr.

For a number of years the structure housed the insurance office of Charles Parrott and Associates. It is still in use as a commercial building. Engraving courtesy of James E. Kibler

By 1889 J. H. Huggins had located his store in this building on East Broad Street. The business, which had been organized many years earlier, had located at various times in buildings all up and down Broad. Huggins was one of the best known dry goods stores of the period and maintained a large stock of merchandise.

H. T. Huggins, son of the proprietor, J. H. Huggins, and later himself owner of the store, stands in the doorway. The building stood on the south side of the street between Spring and Jackson streets.

Huggins later moved to Washington Street next to the Courthouse. The building was razed during urban renewal in the 1960s. The last location of the business, which had become an auto parts supplier, was on Hancock near Wilfongs. The business was sold by the family in 1979 and closed not long thereafter. *Photograph courtesy of T. K. Huggins*

T. Fleming & Sons was, according to Charles Morton Strahan, the leading hardware and agricultural implements company in Athens during the 1890s. They carried a wide variety of items which ranged from nails to a popular buggy known as the Classic City Buggy. Other items included sashes, doors and blinds, fire arms, ginning machinery, and farming implements of all kinds. They were the sole agent for Princeton Factory's cotton rope.

The business was located in the elegant Richardsonian Romanesque building shown in their advertisement in the Southern Banner. The three-story, granite-trimmed brick building is located on Clayton Street between Thomas and Jackson streets. A number of commercial establishments, including the successor firm of Fleming and Dearing, have occupied the premises over the years.

The street level storefront has been altered by the removal of the granite arches, but the upper stories remain essentially as they appear in the photograph. *Photograph courtesy of University of Georgia Libraries Special Collections*

This view of College Avenue looking north from the university arch was photographed in the 1890s by a college student, Telamon Cuyler. The ox-drawn wagon in the foreground was a common sight on Broad Street in the days before automobiles and trucks.

The building on the right was the McGregor Company, a book and stationery store founded in the 1870s and which is still in business at another location today. The other buildings in that block along College Avenue look much like they do today. In the second block is the mansard-roofed Southern Mutual Insurance Building which was replaced by the present structure in 1908.

Beyond Southern Mutual is the tower of the Baptist church on the corner of Washington and College, and in the far distance is the old water tower. *Photograph courtesy of University of Georgia Libraries Special Collections*

This view, also by Telamon Cuyler, was taken just inside the university arch. Across Broad Street on the corner of College Avenue is the Commercial Hotel. This building was built before the war as the Newton House and was remodeled and renamed the Colonial Hotel in the late 1920s.

The iron work on the balcony is typical of the ornamental cast iron which graced many of Athens's buildings in the nineteenth century. Photograph courtesy of University of Georgia Libraries Special Collections

The Southern Banner was founded in 1832 by Albon Chase and John Nesbit and was operated by them for many years. After the financial panic of 1837, they made a great deal of money by becoming the official organ of many counties in Northeast Georgia whose own local newspapers had failed. The newspaper passed through many hands during the remainder of the nineteenth century, becoming finally the Athens Banner.

Among the prominent editors of the period were James Sledge and Anderson Reese, both strong advocates of secession on the eve of the Civil War and men who carried on a lively debate with John Christy, editor of the Whig Southern Watchman. In the 1850s the Banner was located in a wooden building on the northeast corner of the Broad and College intersection. By the 1870s it had moved to the corner of Broad and Spring streets.

One day a young lady, who had been offended by something printed in the paper, came into the second floor office and asked a printer if he were the publisher. He unwarily said that he was, and she shot him with a pistol. All of the printers left in a great hurry, many by the windows. The identity of the lady and the fate of the printer remained undisclosed. (Hull, Annals) At the time this photograph was taken, the Banner had moved to the west side of Jackson Street between Broad and Clayton. The building is still standing, occupied on the ground floor by two retail firms.

When the staff members were photographed outside their offices in 1898, H. J. Rowe was the lessee and business manager and James O'Farrell was editor. Rowe is the hatless man fourth from the right, and O'Farrell is standing sixth from the right with his hands clasped in front of him. Photograph by Claude Maddox; courtesy of Lucile Wilbanks Johnson

The house on the right in this photograph was owned in the Antebellum period by Charles Dougherty, a noted lawyer and judge of the Western Circuit. The house faced College Avenue between Washington and Hancock at the crest of the highest hill in the downtown area.

Sometime after Dougherty's death in the mid-1850s, the house was purchased by Colonel John I. Huggins, a well-known local merchant. His son-in-law, S. M. Herrington lived in the house and had his law office in the small building at the left. When the old Town Hall and Market was abandoned in 1893, the city purchased the Herrington House for city offices. It was demolished when the present City Hall was built on the site in 1903-04.

The law office on the corner was used by the city engineer until it, too, was demolished to make way for City Hall. The famous double-barrel cannon may be seen in the median in front of the house. The photograph was taken during the time city offices were located here in the 1890s. Photograph by David Earnest; courtesy of University of Georgia Libraries Special Collections

This photograph of a funeral procession on College Avenue was taken before 1898 when the old Baptist church at the corner of College and Washington was demolished and a new brick structure erected. The tower of the old church is seen in the upper left. The hearse, drawn by two white horses seen in the lower right, is turning the corner onto Broad Street, heading toward Oconee Hill Cemetery.

The funeral may have been that of Williams Rutherford, a university professor and prominent Baptist, who died in August 1896. The photograph is from one of the scrapbooks kept by his daughter, Mildred Lewis Rutherford. Photograph courtesy of University of Georgia Libraries Special Collections

This montage from Hajos's Photo-Gravures shows the most prominent churches in Athens as they appeared at the end of the last century. The First Methodist Church erected the church shown in the photograph in 1852 on the site of the congregation's first church, built on a lot given to them by Thomas Stanley in 1824. Though considerably altered, the building shown here still stands.

The Christian Church building illustrated here stood on the corner of Pulaski and Dougherty streets, across Dougherty from the present structure. It was erected in 1884, some eight years after the congregation had been organized. In 1915 the present edifice replaced the one shown in this photograph.

St. Joseph's Catholic Church was organized toward the end of the nineteenth century. Prior to this time Athens's Catholics had been served by priests who came from Washington or Sharon to celebrate Mass. The Right Reverend Bishop Gross, Bishop of Savannah, acquired the property shown in the photograph, which was originally the University of Georgia Law School, on the property of T. R. R. Cobb at the corner of Pulaski and Prince. This building was used until the present church was constructed in 1913.

From the time the Athens Baptist Church was organized in 1830 until its church on the corner of College and Washington streets was dedicated in 1860, the congregation met in a small frame building on the college campus near the Broad and Lumpkin intersection. In 1898 the building shown in the photograph replaced the 1860 structure. It, in turn, was demolished after the present First Baptist Church building was opened on the corner of Pulaski and Hancock in 1921. Fulton Federal Savings now has a drive-in window on the corner where the church in the photograph stood.

First Presbyterian Church was established on the college campus in 1820 by Dr. Moses Waddel, president of the university and the church's first pastor. A church was constructed on the present site of Academic Building. It stood until the present building, shown in the photograph, was finished in 1856. The steeple was once surmounted by a gigantic hand, carved of wood and guilded, with a finger pointing heavenward. It was removed before this photograph was taken. Since the turn of the century, the steeple has been removed completely, and a new portico with columns extending across the front has been built.

Emmanuel Episcopal Church was organized in 1842, and the following year Bishop Stephen Elliot appointed the first wardens and vestrymen. The first rector of Emmanuel was William Bacon Stevens, a professor at the University and author of A History of Georgia in two volumes. He was later Bishop of Pennsylvania. Their first church was built where the C&S Bank now stands on the corner of Clayton and Lumpkin. It was demolished in 1892 and the congregation met in a small frame building until the present church, shown in the photograph, was completed in 1899. A tower was added about 1925.

The Congregation Children of Israel was organized in Athens in the early 1870s. For the first twenty-five years Moses Myers was president of the congregation, and his building on College Avenue was used for services before the synagogue in the photograph was built in 1884. It stood on Hancock Avenue across from the rear of the Courthouse until demolished by urban renewal in the late 1960s. The congregation is now located on Dudley Drive. Photograph courtesy of University of Georgia Libraries Special Collections

Tallulah Falls, in the North Georgia Mountains, has always been a popular place for Athenians to escape the summer heat. In 1854 the General Assembly passed an act authorizing the construction of a railroad from Athens to near Clayton, Georgia. The Northeastern Railroad was not chartered, however, until 1871. It extended from Athens only as far as Lula, where it joined the Southern Railroad.

By 1882 the line which was to become the Tallulah Falls Railway had been extended from Cornelia, on the Southern System, to Tallulah Falls. This permitted Athenians to travel with ease to the cool mountains in the summer. Passenger service on the Tallulah Falls Railway ended in 1946, but by that time automobiles had replaced trains as the means of reaching the falls.

This photograph from the 1890s shows a group of passengers ready to board the train to Lula, the first leg of the trip to Tallulah Falls. Photograph courtesy of Georgia Department of Archives and History

This group of young people from Athens are shown posing for their photograph during an outing to Tallulah Falls around the turn of the century. Photograph courtesy of Mr. and Mrs. Paul Hodgson

On March 17, 1898, William Jennings Bryan, Democratic nominee for president in 1896, in 1900, and in 1908, visited Athens. A group of university students, upon learning that Bryan was to speak in Atlanta and Augusta, invited him to come to Athens. On the morning of the seventeenth, he was met by a large crowd at the Seaboard depot and escorted by the mayor and a delegation of prominent citizens to the Commercial Hotel where he dined before going to the campus.

A crowd of 3,000 gathered for his speech on Herty Field behind New College. After his introduction by H. H. Carlton, Bryan spoke at length in favor of an income tax. He decried the decision of the Supreme Court which had declared it unconstitutional and advocated an amendment to the Constitution to permit it. He attended a reception following the speech at the Library and was entertained by John W. Welch at his home on Milledge Avenue.

That evening he lectured on free silver at the Opera House. The following day Bryan attended church services and left for Atlanta on the train. This photograph shows Bryan speaking to the gathering on Herty Field. Photograph courtesy of Richard Patterson

Professor David Earnest photographed the crowd gathered for a balloon ascent in downtown Athens during the 1890s. The launching took place on the corner of Washington and Lumpkin streets behind the Methodist parsonage. The Methodist church can be seen at the left, and the water tower near the Herrington House at right. Photograph courtesy of University of Georgia Libraries Special Collections

Fairs, carnivals, and circuses were always popular with Athenians. In the days before the Civil War when circuses would pitch their tents on the corner of Broad and Thomas streets where Athens Bank is now located, the whole town turned out, incuding the university boys who were forbidden to participate in such frivolity. The faculty minutes contain numerous references to disciplinary actions against the students who tried to sneak in to see the circus.

In the 1870s the fairgrounds were located on South Lumpkin Street near the present university track. When that area began to develop, fairs and carnivals were held all over town, wherever a space was available. In 1900 the downtown merchants organized a carnival which was held on Broad Street and College Avenue. They printed up an elaborate brochure touting the benefits of locating in Athens and brought in a number of traveling shows.

This photograph shows Broad Street looking east from the corner of College during the fair. All of the buildings were decorated, and the attractions were set up in the streets. The attraction just to the left of the large tent was billed as The Galveston Horrors. The carnival must have been a success because the merchants sponsored another large fair the following year. Photograph courtesy of University of Georgia Libraries Special Collections

The first bicycle to appear in Athens was made by Richard Schevenell, a French carriage maker, and ridden by his son Len on Broad Street in 1869. For a rider with "plenty of strength, plenty of time and lots of patience, it did pretty well," according to A. L. Hull.

The boy with the bicycle in this photograph was Frederick Grady Hodgson, son of E. R. Hodgson. The young rider eventually became an orthopedic surgeon and taught at Emory University in Atlanta. Photograph courtesy of Mr. and Mrs. Paul Hodgson

A photographer captured this scene of a daring aerial feat being performed in the middle of Broad Street during the carnival of 1900. A large crowd had gathered in the street between the arch and the Commercial Hotel, while others enjoyed a better vantage point on the hotel's balcony.

Other attractions such as The Snake Eater may be seen in the background in College Avenue. Photograph courtesy of Georgia Department of Archives and History

This strange photograph was taken at the entrance of an attraction called The Snake Eater at the 1900 carnival. The tent was located in the middle of College Avenue where the curious onlookers had gathered to get a preview of some of the acts which could be seen inside. Photograph courtesy of Georgia Department of Archives and History

It's not the mysterious East, but Clayton Street in Athens during the 1901 Wheat and Oat Fair. The camel was one of the many attractions brought to town for the gala event. Photograph courtesy of Richard Patterson

Chapter Three
1901-1940

Athens entered her second century on a note of optimism. The town had grown from a tiny settlement on the edge of Indian territory to a bustling community of more than 10,000. A strong commercial and industrial base had developed, serving the entire Northeast Georgia region. The city's two major state institutions, the university and the state normal school, made important economic, social, and cultural contributions to the community. This firm foundation permitted the city to sustain a continued steady growth over the next four decades in spite of the twin blows of the boll weevil and the Great Depression. By 1940 the city's population had more than doubled to 20,650.

In 1904 the City Fathers erected an elegant new city hall which stands today as a monument to their civic pride and confidence in the city's prosperous future. A new federal building, a county courthouse, a large new hotel, and a multi-story office building quickly followed in a four-block area of downtown along Washington Street and College Avenue, a section that had been, only a few years before, a quiet residential district. Other public facilities were soon constructed to serve the growing population. Two new fire stations, one on Prince Avenue (1901) and the other on Thomas at Washington (1912), replaced the old volunteer company buildings; and soon modern fire trucks supplanted the horse-drawn vehicles of an earlier era. Space in the old Oconee Hill Cemetery even proved to be inadequate, so additional land was acquired across the river, and an iron-truss bridge was erected to join the new section with the old.

The memory of army wagons mired in the mud during the late Spanish American War prompted a major street paving program, and miles of cement sidewalks were laid. Water lines were extended to serve new customers who built homes in the older residential areas—Milledge Avenue, Boulevard, Bloomfield Street, Cobbham, East Athens—and new areas were opened for development in Five Points and the area west of Milledge Avenue. This growth was at first spurred by convenient streetcar service and later encouraged by the easy access the automobile made possible.

New public schools were built to serve the growing population—Barrow, Chase Street, Oconee Street, and College Avenue—and improvements were made to existing facilities. A new high school on Childs Street proved inadequate only six years after completion, and the upper classes removed to the renovated old courthouse in 1915. Blacks, too, benefited from the local interest in public education. By 1914 the only black four-year public high school in Georgia was located in Athens. Private schools continued to flourish during the early years of the new century—Lucy Cobb, Knox Institute, Jeruel Academy—but most ceased to function during the hard times of the Depression. Before their demise, though, they trained many of the community leaders that charted the city's course through succeeding decades.

In 1901 the university celebrated the centennial of its opening with great fanfare. Chancellor Hill used the occasion to rally the Alumni Society to support the institution and his view of its future as a modern, progressive school. Although Hill did not live to see his dream become a reality, by the end of the Barrow Administration in 1926 much had been accomplished with the help of the alumni and the generosity of George Foster Peabody. The campus was greatly extended, and new buildings were erected. Others were enlarged or renovated, including Old College, which in 1901 was abandoned, derelict, and threatened with demolition. New schools and colleges—Forestry, Pharmacy, Education, Commerce, Journalism, and the Graduate School—were established. An act of the General Assembly created a new college of agriculture out of the agricultural programs of the old A&M College; and the Agricultural Extension Service (made possible by the Smith-Lever Act, passed by Congress in 1914 under the sponsorship of Georgia's Senator Hoke Smith) helped university programs reach Georgia's farmers and homemakers through a system of county agents and home demonstration workers.

The streets of downtown Athens were still lined with trees when this photograph of College Avenue, looking north from Clayton Street, was made just after the turn of the century. The Confederate monument is located in the center of the Washington Street intersection in the middle ground. A drinking trough for horses can be seen in the foreground. On the right of the photo is the old Baptist church. Beyond the church, the street was still residential. Photograph courtesy of Isabel Wier McWilliams

One of the most dramatic changes wrought during this period was the admission of women to the university. Barriers were lowered in 1911 when women were permitted to earn a master's degree for summer school work; and in 1918, the trustees narrowly adopted a resolution admitting women on a vote of twelve to eleven. An editorial in the student newspaper, the *Red and Black*, welcomed the change, but a flurry of letters from diehard traditionalists predicted the demise of the university. While change did come, their dire predictions proved to be unfounded, and women students became fully integrated into the life of the campus under the guidance of the first two deans of women, Mary Lyndon and Ann Wallis Brumby.

During these same years, the young state normal school continued to grow and develop a comprehensive program of teacher education and training. The school and its students became an integral part of the Athens community, and the growth of the state normal campus stimulated develoment of an area known as Normaltown adjacent to the school along Prince and Oglethorpe avenues.

In 1932 the statewide system of colleges and universities was reorganized under a board of regents. In Athens, this change merged the state normal and the college of agriculture with the university proper. This consolidation set the stage for the unprecedented growth which transformed the university campus during the 1930s. The federal New Deal programs, which grew out of the economic crisis of the Great Depression, made possible, really for the first time, the development of an adequately equipped, modern, physical plant. Seventeen new buildings were erected between 1935 and 1940, including six dormitories, a science building (LeConte Hall), a practice school (Baldwin Hall), the Forestry Building, the Agricultural Extension Building, the Dairy Building and Dairy Barn, a classroom building for English and modern foreign languages (Park Hall), the Fine Arts Building, the home economics group, and Snelling Hall cafeteria.

The four decades between 1900 and 1940 saw not only the expansion of the physical plant and the diversification of academic programs, but also the tremendous growth of collegiate athletics. Shortly after the turn of the century, Sanford Field on the newly-acquired South Campus replaced the old Herty Field as a facility for football, baseball, and track. By 1920, however, Herman Stegeman still coached baseball, basketball, and football almost single-handedly. A new era for intercollegiate sports at Georgia was ushered in with the dedication of Sanford Stadium in 1929. Alumni and fans, who were now more mobile and could come to Athens to see the Bulldogs play, demanded and got a professionally staffed athletic program. By 1940 the days of Herty Field were only a faint memory.

Campus life, too, changed during this period. While the strictures of those days might appear rigid by today's standards, they were a far cry from the inflexible rules of Alonzo Church's time. Fraternities and sororities became increasingly important as social outlets, assuming a role once filled by the literary societies. The admission of women students, greeted less than enthusiastically by Athens girls who had heretofore commanded the entire attention of the college swains during the academic year, also brought a change in the campus social life. Dances and parties became more frequent occurrences, social clubs and organizations flourished, and new extra-curricular activities made the campus a more exciting place than ever.

One important factor that contributed to the growth and development of both town and university during this forty year period was the extensive transportation network that connected Athens with the rest of the state and the nation. During the early years of the century, the railroads continued to carry the bulk of passenger and freight service. In 1906 the Gainesville Midland, Athens's fifth railroad line, opened new warehouses and a freight depot along Foundary Street between Broad and Hancock. In the same year, the Central of Georgia spent $150,000 on a new depot (which burned in 1981) on Mitchell Street near the campus. By 1926 Athens was served by twenty-four passenger trains a day. The days of the ascendency of rail transportation were numbered, however, with the appearance of automobiles on the streets of Athens at the turn of the century. Highways became the arteries of commerce, and Athens was on the route of the early major connectors. The Bankhead Highway (the nation's longest, stretching from Washington, D. C. to San Diego) gave the town connections with Atlanta and Greenville, South Carolina and points beyond. Engineering Professor Charles Morton Strahan and a delegation of leading citizens helped to assure that the Atlanta-Augusta Highway (now U. S. 78) was routed through Athens. The Calhoun Highway, the Stone Mountain Highway, and the Macon Highway, provided access to the east, west, and south. Sales and service facilities and gasoline stations became important components of the local economy, and the automobile and new highways helped expand the territories of the more than 200 traveling salesmen that operated out of Athens. The 1930s marked the beginning of mass bus travel. During that decade, several bus stations served

The summer of 1901 was an exciting time in Athens. That year marked the beginning of not only the twentieth century but also the city's second century. The Athens Banner issued a special centennial issue in June which chronicled the progress of the city during its first hundred years, highlighting the important people that had made local history during that period.

In July the city celebrated by sponsoring the Athens Wheat and Oat Fair. The fair originated as an effort to encourage crop diversification. Local farmers were urged to plant wheat as a badly needed midsummer cash crop, and oats as a superior food for livestock. Prizes were offered for the largest yield of wheat or oats grown on three-acre and one-acre plots. A. L. Malcom of Statham in Oconee County won the grand prize of $100 in gold for the best three acres of wheat, totaling 121¾ bushels.

A large gathering was held at the Opera House presided over by John R. White of Whitehall. The keynote speaker was T. B. Terry, a prominent wheat grower from Ohio, who spoke on the benefits of wheat production. There was a reception at the Athenaeum Club and a big barbecue. A parade was held downtown on Clayton Street where there were booths and attractions set up for the entertainment of the fairgoers. At the same time the fair was going on, there were also conventions of newspaper editors and wholesale grocers that swelled the population of the town, creating a festive atmosphere.

This photograph shows some of the activities during the fair on Clayton Street. The view is looking east from the College Avenue intersection. A large triumphal arch was erected across Clayton Street for the parade to pass through, and the buildings were decorated with bunting and banners. The building on the far left of the photograph is the old Southern Mutual Building. The building to its right, then a drugstore, was replaced not many years later by the Stern Building, now occupied by George Dean's.

The next building was for many years Tony's Restaurant, a familiar local landmark. The McLellan Building still stands, although its tower has been altered, and the building at the end of the block was remodeled and now houses Foster's Jewelers. The building at the far right of the photograph is the old Scudder Jewelry Building. This interesting structure with pressed metal details is now occupied by Beussee's Florist, The Chocolate Shop, Cookies and Company, Serendipity, and the law office of Gene Mac Winburn. Photograph courtesy of Georgia Department of Archives and History

The young ladies of Lucy Cobb Institute also joined in the festivities at the Wheat and Oat Fair. Their elaborate float, one of the units in the parade, was photographed on Prince Avenue in front of the Taylor-Grady House. Photograph courtesy of Georgia Department of Archives and History

the Old South, Queen City Coach, and Wilkes bus lines. When the Union Bus Terminal opened in 1940, bus travel had begun to rival rail transportation. Finally, the early years of the twentieth century saw the beginning of the Air Age. Georgia's pioneer aviator, Ben Epps, built and flew planes in Athens as early as 1907, and air service soon joined rail and highway transport as part of the network connecting the city with the outside world.

Industries which depended on the transportation network thrived, along with firms that provided products for local consumption. Among the industries listed in a 1926 chamber of commerce brochure were eight cotton mills; the largest wooden handle manufacturing plant in the South; eight wholesale groceries; two wholesale hardware companies; one wholesale drygoods company; two wholesale seed houses; two wholesale drug companies; four ginning machinery distributors; three foundries and machine works; four sash, door and lumber plants; three bakeries; three fertilizer plants; three candy factories; two marble and granite works; two cotton oil mills; two shirt factories; a cotton compress and warehouse; a mattress and spring bed factory; a flour mill; a brick and tile manufacturer; a coke and gas plant; an ice and cold storage plant; a creamery; an ice cream plant; an oil refining company; a mill and machinery supply company; a bookbinding and stationery manufacturing company; and a broom factory. Retail firms also prospered, and the downtown business district expanded into adjacent residential areas. A black business district grew up around the intersection of Washington and Hull streets, known as "Hot Corner." The Morton Theatre, the Samaritan Building, and Union Hall housed black-owned businesses of every description and offices of professionals such as doctors, dentists, and insurance companies.

The one-two punches of the boll weevil and the Great Depression at the beginning and end of the 1920s dealt severe blows to previously thriving businesses and industries. Many did not survive, but others rose to take their places. The Depression brought economic hardship to many, yet contemporary commentators acknowledged that Athens fared much better than the large cities of the North or the devastated countryside of the Cotton South.

World War I disrupted the pattern of life in the community during the seventeen months of active United States involvement, but there was no great or lasting impact on Athens or the university. The textile factories thrived on the increased wartime production, and cotton prices soared, bringing prosperity to the hard-pressed cotton farmer for the last time before the boll weevil arrived in great numbers. Local boys went off for training to Camp Gordon (then in Atlanta) and Camp Wheeler in Macon. As they had done during the War Between the States, the townspeople saw them off at the railroad depots. They also went to the depot to cheer and wave little American flags for the soldiers who passed through town on the train. A student army training corps was established at the university, but programs had barely gotten under way when the war ended. There were shortages in many staples. The scarcity of sugar forced the Athens Coca-Cola Company to cease operations for a time, and the lack of coal for heating had to be met by cutting wood. As meat, too, became scarce and expensive, rabbit became a regular item on many tables in town. To make matters worse, Athens felt the effects of the great flu epidemic, and

The wide-eyed ostrich may not have enjoyed standing for this photograph with three children on its back, but the young man sitting between his two sisters seems to be enjoying the unique experience. The circuses and fairs that came to Athens gave people their first look at exotic animals that they had only read about in books. The obliging photographer preserved the event for many years of enjoyment. Photograph courtesy of Georgia Department of Archives and History

many died. The winter of 1917-18 was a particularly severe one, with heavy snow and ice in January. In spite of all the hardships, Athenians continued to have fun. On January 18, a dance described as "one of the most important events of the season for the younger set," was held at Costa's. Throughout it all, patriotic feeling continued to run high in Athens. War Bonds sold well and the kaiser was thoroughly hissed and booed at the picture show. After the war, those that had died on Flanders fields were not forgotten. The university erected War Memorial Hall in their honor, and an Athenian, Moina Michael, originated the idea of the memorial poppy.

Throughout the war and Depression, good times and bad, Athenians led active social lives. Movies provided a new popular form of entertainment. For ten cents you could see the *Perils of Pauline* at the Strand and enjoy a serving of ice cream for only a nickel at Ye Garden. Drugstores and ice cream parlors were, in fact, the most popular gathering places of the day. Many still recall Costa's, Patricks, and the Old P. A. Young people danced at Woodruff Hall on campus and at the Georgian Hotel (where they could take lessons at the Arthur Murray Studio) and listened to records at Bernsteins Furniture, Dorsey's, or Durden's Music Store. In 1928 Athens's first radio station, WTFI, went on the air, and many local residents soon acquired radio sets. After the station moved to Atlanta in 1937, a group of Athenians organized WGAU, still an Athens institution.

Four country clubs thrived during the era: Westlake Country Club, Cloverhurst, a Jewish club on Pinecrest, and the present Athens Country Club. They provided facilities for golf, swimming, dances, and parties. Card parties became a popular form of entertainment, and Augustus L. Hull lamented that "at the present time gentlemen are practically barred from society and all the ladies do is play cards." They rarely, he said, played the piano or sang anymore. Women did, however, become more active in public life after winning the right to vote in 1919, and their social, charitable, and patriotic organizations continued to thrive. Some of the more important were the Hebrew Benevolent Association, the Ladies' Garden Club, the W.C.T.U., the United Daughters of the Confederacy, the Y.W.C.A., the Civic League, the D.A.R., the Bessie Mell Industrial Home, and the Athens Woman's Club. Men's organizations were similarly active.

By 1940 the small college community had been replaced by a modern prosperous town. Many still remembered, however, where they had come from. Sylvanus Morris, writing in the middle of the period, said, "We rightfully congratulate ourselves upon these evidences of prosperity. But let us not forget that they were made possible by the men and women of former days. Our priceless heritage is the unconquerable spirit which laid firm and sound foundations of material, intellectual and moral excellence." His admonition appears to have been forgotten by many during the following forty years in the heady days of post-World War II prosperity.

In 1903 the city government demolished the old Herrington House which it had been using for city offices since abandoning the old City Hall and Market House in 1893. Plans for a new building were drawn by L. F. Goodrich of Augusta who narrowly beat Atlanta architect J. W. Golucke in the design competition sponsored by the city. Bonds were issued in the amount of $50,000 and the building was erected by the city engineer, Captain J. W. Barnett.

When completed, the building stood ninety-nine feet high from granite basement to eagle weathervane. It was 103 feet across the front and 85 feet deep and housed city offices, an armory for the local militia company, and an office for the Athens Chamber of Commerce. This post card view shows the building as it appeared about the time of World War I. A particularly interesting feature in the photograph is the American flag. The caption on the back of the card notes that it was an illuminated "electric flag," installed on April 11, 1916 in observance of Flag Day. No one today seems to recall what happened to this unusual city landmark.

The City Hall, however, is still in use, having narrowly escaped becoming a parking lot during the heady days of urban renewal in the late 1960s. Photograph courtesy of University of Georgia Libraries Special Collections

The original plans for City Hall called for a spacious auditorium that could accomodate 300 people for public meetings. Over the years it has been used for public hearings, for city council meetings, and for court hearings.

This photograph shows the interior as it appeared before the ceiling was lowered to provide additional space for second floor offices and a small meeting room. In 1960 the balcony was partially removed, and in 1972 the ceiling was completely lowered, creating a one-story auditorium. The remaining smaller room is still used for its original purposes. Photograph courtesy of Athens Newspapers, Incorporated

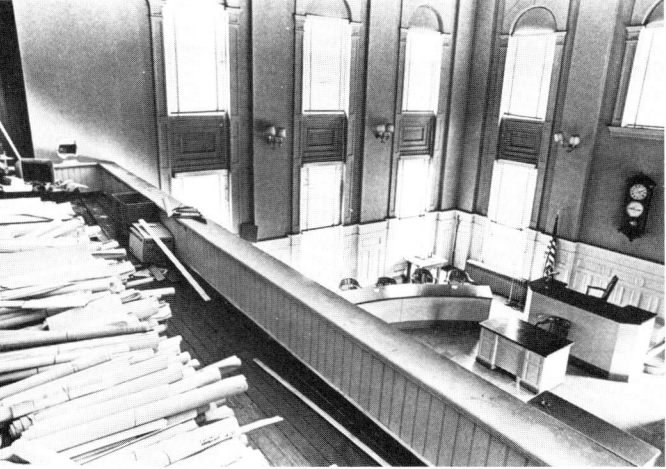

The Athens Police Department is shown assembled for inspection during an official function held on the north lawn and portico of City Hall about 1910. Dressed in Keystone Cops uniforms, the officers are formidably armed with shotguns.

The building in the background is the old Federal Building, now First American Bank, which was completed in 1905, one year after City Hall had been finished. The governmental complex was complete when the Clarke County Courthouse was built one block to the east in 1913. Photograph courtesy of Georgia Department of Archives and History

The Cobb-Deloney Camp of the United Confederate Veterans was organized in Athens in 1894 and named for two of Athens's most illustrious soldiers who had died in the late war: Thomas R. R. Cobb and William G. Deloney. Cobb was killed at Fredericksburg, and Deloney was wounded at Jack's Shop, was captured, and died of his wounds at the Old Capitol Prison in Washington.

The surviving veterans lined up on the steps of the new City Hall during their reunion in 1906 to have this group photograph made. About 1920 the camp hosted a state convention of the United Confederate Veterans, but many in this photograph did not live to participate in that event. Photograph courtesy of Charlie Williams, Chase Street Liquors

This view, taken about 1905, shows College Avenue as it appeared at the turn of the century. The horses in the foreground are drinking from troughs that were located in several intersections downtown and provided with running water. Behind the buggy is the Commercial Hotel as it looked before its remodeling in the 1920s.

The two-story building to the right of the hotel is still standing, as is the adjacent Myers Building, site of a then popular department store, Moses Myers and Company. Schlotsky's Sandwich Shop occupies the lower floor of the building today. The similar three-story building on the corner has been demolished and replaced by the one-story Marilyn Shoe Store.

Across Clayton Street on the left is the Hodgson/Shackelford Building and beyond it the cupola of City Hall. At the right of the photograph is the old Southern Mutual Building which was moved to allow construction of the present building in 1908. Beyond that is the tower of the First Baptist Church, demolished in the 1920s. The Confederate monument appears in the median in the middle of College Avenue. Photograph courtesy of Gary Doster

In 1899 the first automobile appeared on the streets of Athens, driven by John R. White of Whitehall. It was said to have created more of a stir than when the first buggy, owned by Elizur Newton, made its appearance many years before. Writing in 1923, Sylvanus Morris said that he had interviewed four or five people who had owned the first car in Athens, so he settled the issue by declaring that they must have come at the same time. Morris noted that at the time he was writing there were about 2,000 registered automobiles in the county, but added, "Whether or not the drivers thereof own them is not a matter of inquiry here."

The car in the photograph, certainly among the earliest in town, is shown being driven by Mrs. Harry Hodgson in 1904. Photograph courtesy of Mr. and Mrs. Edward R. Hodgson, III

Athens entered the Air Age in 1907, just four years after the Wright Brothers' historic flight at Kitty Hawk. Ben Epps, Georgia's first aviator, is shown here in front of this shop on Washington Street with the plane he built and flew briefly that year.

After dropping out of Georgia Tech in the fall of 1904, Epps returned home to Athens and opened an electrical shop. He was soon tinkering with motorcycles and early automobiles. By 1909 he was appointed official inspector of the autos entered in an Augusta-Athens-Atlanta race. Shortly after the Wrights' flight in 1904, he began experimenting with airplanes.

The one shown here resembled the first Wright plane, except Epps's was a monoplane, not a biplane like the one flown at Kitty Hawk. According to published reports, this plane became airborn on its maiden flight but crashed. The following year, Epps built a biplane, which also was demolished in a crash. A similar fate awaited his 1909-10 monoplane which was powered by an engine mounted in front, had four landing wheels, and was controlled by a steering wheel.

Epps had been flying during this time in planes which he had purchased, and in 1919 he and L. M. Rolfe established the Rolfe-Epps Flying Service to offer flight instruction, passenger flights, and aerial photography. He continued to fly until his death in a crash in 1937. Photograph courtesy of Evelyn Epps Galt

Although the beginning of the twentieth century marked the dawn of the Auto Age, there was still a demand for buggies and wagons in Athens for many years. In 1902 William and Frank Griffeth moved to Athens from nearby Bogart to open the Griffeth Implement Company. In 1908 they were advertising that "in buggies, carriages, surreys, runabouts and stanhopes, this company acknowledges no superior."

This photograph from that period shows half of their "vehicle department." In addition to passenger vehicles, the company stocked or manufactured a complete line of farm equipment including their own "Griffeth Hand Pea Planter," an invention of Frank Griffeth's. Their three-story building was located at 448-465 East Broad Street adjacent to Athens Hardware Company (the old Franklin House). The University of Georgia Business Services Building occupies the site today. Photograph courtesy of University of Georgia Libraries Special Collections

In the years between the Civil War and 1920, cotton was the principal crop in the countryside surrounding Athens. Virtually every available acre was put into its production, and as the land lost its fertility, larger and larger amounts of commercial fertilizer were needed to produce a crop. While many of the small farmers did not prosper under this one-crop agricultural system, the cotton factors, fertilizer manufacturers, and farm implement suppliers in Athens reaped a substantial profit.

In 1910 the Banner declared that Athens was one of the largest cotton markets in the world, leading all of Georgia's cities in wagon cotton receipts. More than 150,000 bales passed through the warehouses here in some of the better years. World War I brought additional prosperity as prices soared to a high of thirty-five cents per pound. The end of the war caused prices to plummet to seventeen cents a pound by 1920, and the ravages of the boll weevil brought a virtual end to the thriving cotton business in the city within a few years. Dean William Tate, who remembered 1920 as the last bumper year for cotton in Athens, recalled the following scene downtown:

> Cotton weathers well, and hundreds of bales were on the sidewalk—one on the edge of the street, one on the sidewalk, a third atop these two. We students were asked in our chapel meetings not to smoke on the street, to avoid setting fire to this "white gold"—a contemporary phrase. It was all down one side of Broad, one side of Lumpkin, in fact, on every street corner where space permitted.

This photograph, taken shortly before World War I, shows cotton being hauled and stacked on Thomas Street. The building on the left, which was then a cotton warehouse, is still standing today, used by Thornton Brothers paper company. The building behind it is the Franklin House, which faces Broad Street. The rear wing, seen here nearest to the warehouse, was removed by a recent owner of the Franklin House. Photograph courtesy of Georgia Department of Archives and History

This photograph, taken about the time of World War I, shows one of several cotton gins that operated in Athens during that period. This one was located on the north side of Oconee Street on the Armstrong and Dobbs property. The wagons of loose cotton were brought to the area on the right where the cotton was taken up. After the seeds were removed, it was compressed and baled and emerged on the left, ready for shipping.

It is said that the first cotton raised west of the Oconee River was planted by Daniel Easley (near the site of the later Athens Factory) from a bushel of cotton seed he had brought back from the low country. Not knowing how to plant the seed, he broadcast it like wheat or oats so that it could not be cultivated. The fertile ground and favorable weather combined to produce a good crop in spite of its manner of planting. The close-growing plants produced the whitest cotton patch many old timers had ever seen. From this modest beginning came one of the pillars of Athens's economy which lasted over 100 years. Photograph courtesy of Georgia Department of Archives and History

These twin Neo-Classical houses, connected by an Ionic colonnade, were constructed in 1902 by two of Athens's leading merchants, brothers Moses and Simon Michael. Moses and his wife Emma lived in the house on the right, 596 Prince Avenue, while Simon and Annie Michael occupied the adjoining 598 Prince. Built between two of Athens's most impressive Greek Revival mansions (the Taylor-Grady House and the University President's House), the Michael houses reflected the classical detailing and monumental scale that made Prince Avenue legendary.

Moses Michael, one of Athens's most prominent civic leaders, died in his house in 1944 at the age of eighty-two. Some time after the houses were built, the connecting colonnade was removed, supposedly because of a family feud. The houses were demolished in the 1960s to make way for two out-of-scale insurance buildings, incompatible with their surroundings. The fate of these landmarks has befallen a number of majestic Prince Avenue structures, yet some remain to remind the visitor what the avenue was once like. Photograph courtesy of T. H. Milner, Jr.

This bird's eye view map published by Fowler and Downs of Morrisville, Pennsylvania, shows Athens as it appeared in 1909. The view is looking northwest across the Oconee River from Carr's Hill. Photograph courtesy of University of Georgia Libraries Special Collections.

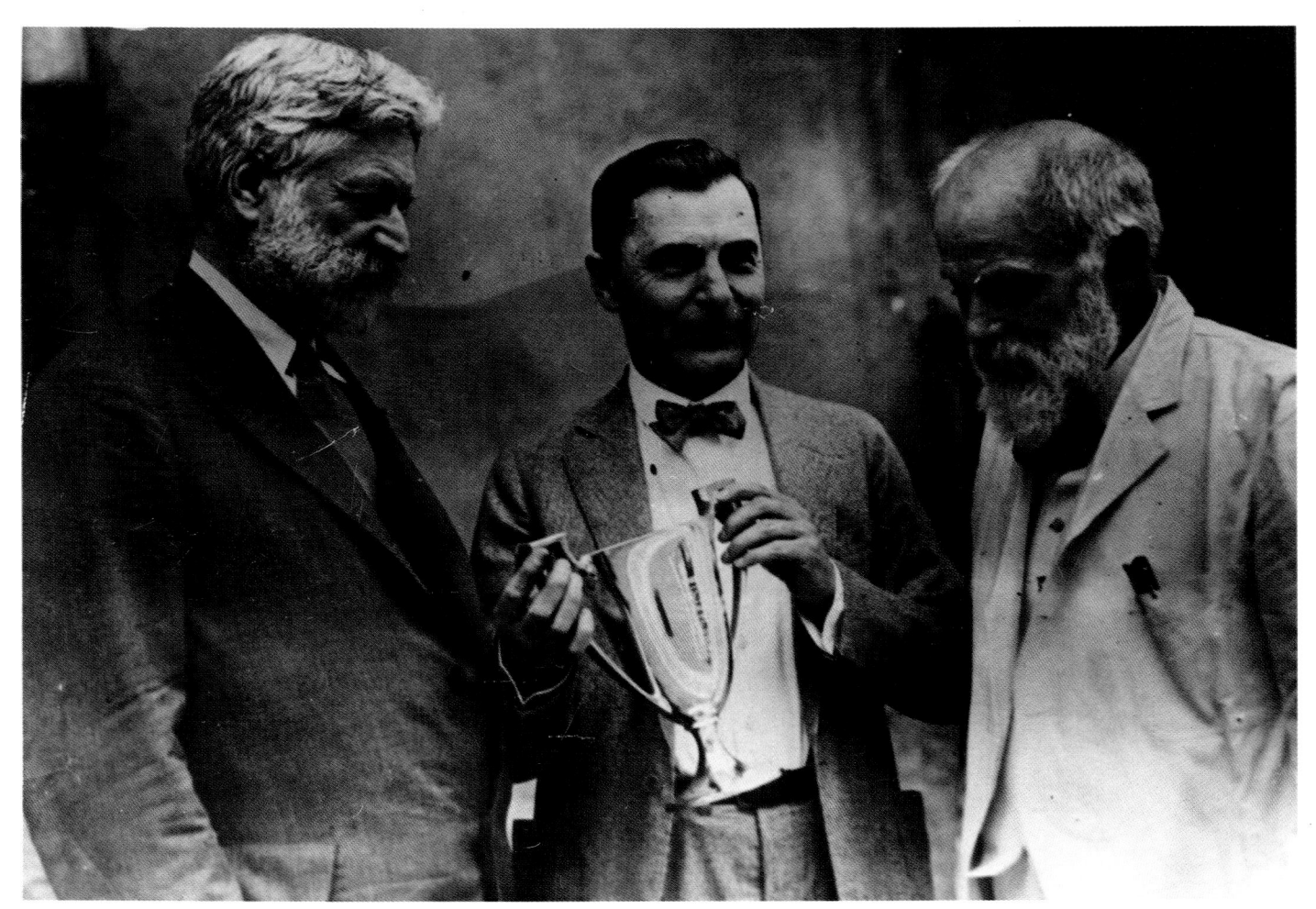

The three men in this photograph—George Foster Peabody, Harry Hodgson, and Chancellor David Barrow—were largely responsible for translating the goal first articulated by Chancellor Hill into a reality: the transformation of a small liberal arts college into a modern university.

George Foster Peabody, a native of Columbus, Georgia, who had grown up in New York and made a fortune in investment banking, first came to Athens during the university's centennial celebration in 1901. He soon became a close friend of Chancellor Hill and a generous supporter of the university. During a meeting of the Southern Educational Conference in Athens the following year, Peabody gave the university $50,000 for a new library. Other gifts, including $60,000 for the War Memorial Fund in 1920, raised his total contribution to more than $250,000. When the creation of a college of agriculture as part of the university was proposed in 1904, Peabody paid the expenses of the leaders of the General Assembly on a trip to Madison, Wisconsin, to see the college of agriculture there. This trip galvanized support for the new college in Georgia.

Harry Hodgson, a graduate of the class of 1893 and a prominent Athens businessman, was one of the moving forces of the Alumni Society for many years and a staunch supporter of efforts to expand and diversify the university. In 1920 he organized the War Memorial Fund, which resulted in raising over one million dollars. The proceeds of the campaign were used to create an endowment for the university and for the construction of Memorial Hall, John Milledge Dormitory, and the Commerce-Journalism Building.

While Chancellor Barrow always gave Harry Hodgson credit for the success of the War Memorial Fund drive, Hodgson ascribed its success to Barrow. The chancellor's leadership was crucial to the success of the new initiatives, and his administration was one of the most important in the history of the university. New schools and colleges were created, the campus was extended and new buildings were erected, the faculty was expanded and salaries were increased, women were admitted, financial support was increased from private sources and from the state, and enrollment exceeded 1,000 for the first time. In gratitude for his efforts, the General Assembly named Barrow County for this popular educator. *Photograph courtesy of University of Georgia Libraries Special Collections*

This library building, the second to be constructed on the university campus, is one of the lasting visible results of George Foster Peabody's generosity. Construction on the $50,000 building designed by architect Haralson Bleckley began in 1903 and was completed the following year. It was used as the main library of the university until the completion of the Ilah Dunlap Little Library in 1953.

The street in front of the building was closed after the photograph was taken, and the area is now part of the landscaped quadrangle. Photograph courtesy of University of Georgia Libraries Special Collections

Five thousand dollars was appropriated by the General Assembly in 1905 to provide furnishings for the library interior seen in this photograph. This scene was familiar to thousands of college students who read and studied here between 1905 and 1953. Then the interior was substantially remodeled to serve as gallery, office, storage, and work space for the Georgia Museum of Art. Photograph courtesy of University of Georgia Libraries Special Collections

At the beginning of this century, the university campus consisted of only thirty-seven acres remaining from the original Milledge purchase. Chancellor Hill recognized the need for additional land on which the university could expand and turned his attention to the area which lay across Baldwin Street to the south of the old campus. A committee of the Alumni Society known as the Land Trust was formed to acquire additional acreage.

Among the first properties purchased was the house and remaining acreage of Governor Wilson Lumpkin's farm, then owned by his daughter, Martha Lumpkin Compton (for whom Atlanta was originally named Marthasville). In 1907 she transferred the property to the university with the provision that the land would revert to her heirs if the house were ever moved or destroyed. Dean of Men William Tate often reminded the administration of this agreement, saying that as his wife, the former Susan Barrow, was one of those heirs, they would move into the chemistry building if the Lumpkin House ever came down.

Governor Lumpkin had designed the house for his residence in 1842 and supervised its construction of native stone dressed on the site. On its completion in 1844 he wrote, "I have endeavored to put a piece of my character in its stone walls...and until this building falls down, or is destroyed, there I stand to be praised, or lampooned, as the work may be thought, to be good or bad, by the beholder."

Connor Hall, which houses the college of agriculture, was built beside the Lumpkin House on its high hill in 1909. The house has been used as a dormitory, a classroom building, a branch library, the Institute of Ecology, and a computer center. The building is known today as the Rock House. The photograph was taken after the construction of Connor Hall, which appears on the right. Photograph courtesy of University of Georgia Libraries Special Collections

This photograph shows Connor Hall as it appeared shortly after its completion in 1909. Its construction had grown out of the efforts of Chancellor Hill to create a real college of agriculture as a division of the A & M College which had been established under the Morrill Act. The building was designed by Edward A. Dougherty and erected by the firm of E. B. Fitts & Company of Atlanta for $94,000. It was named Conner Hall for J. J. Conner, first chairman of the board of the agriculture college, and was formally dedicated on January 18, 1909. Although gutted and substantially remodeled in the 1970s, Connor remains the main building of the College of Agriculture.

The railroad tracks in the photograph provided access to the city for the Macon and Northern Railroad (later part of the Central of Georgia) in the late nineteenth century. The laying of the tracks stirred some controversy at the time, as they came close to Oconee Hill Cemetery. In recent years they provided a place for students to watch University of Georgia football games in Sanford Stadium, which was constructed in the depression in front of Connor Hall in 1929. In 1981 this tradition was ended by the enclosure of the east end of the stadium. Photograph courtesy of Anne and Branch Howe

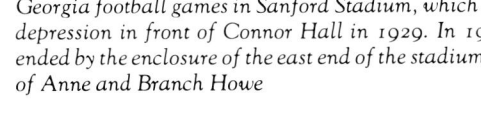

After the acquisition of the South Campus in the first decade of the century, a new athletic field was constructed to replace the inadequate facilities of Herty Field on the Old North Campus. It was erected on the low ground along Tanyard Branch east of the Lumpkin-Baxter Street intersection and was named for Steadman V. Sanford, who had become a professor in 1903 and was later to be elected president. The field was used for all major college sports until a new football stadium, also bearing Sanford's name, was built to the east of this site in 1929.

In 1943 Stegeman Hall was constructed on the old Sanford Field site. This view of the field, looking toward the northwest, was taken near the site of the present Gillis Bridge. The stands were built against the hill where the bookstore parking lot is located. They seated about 7,000 for baseball with another 3,000 accomodated on temporary bleachers for football. Dean Tate remembered that any student that tried to sit in the covered stands with a date was immediately ordered to the open bleachers with the boys.

The photograph shows a group of cadets marching on the field, and the large puff of smoke is coming from a cannon which had just been fired. Photograph courtesy of University of Georgia Libraries Special Collections

The game of push ball took the campus by storm for a few years near the beginning of the century. The object of the game was for one team to push the huge ball through the opposing team's goal. The mad scramble that ensued often became rather rough.

Chancellor Barrow, dressed in his topcoat and derby hat, acted as referee in this game, photographed about 1910. The game was played on Sanford Field. The push ball craze lasted only a few years, finally disappearing by the 1920s. Photograph courtesy of University of Georgia Libraries Special Collections

The early years of the twentieth century saw the rapid growth of the State Normal School, which had been founded in the 1890s and located in the old building of the University High School at the intersection of Prince and Oglethorpe avenues. Before the turn of the century, funds were raised to construct a second dormitory (Bradwell Hall), a president's cottage, and the old Auditorium. President Samuel D. Bradwell almost single-handedly developed the curriculum and conducted the courses to train new teachers and provide continued education for those already teaching. The school was so popular that some students had to be housed in tents on the campus.

In 1901 Eugene C. Branson succeeded Bradwell as president and immediately launched a drive to secure additional funds for building and program development. He was supported by gifts from the Carnegie Foundation, George Foster Peabody, James M. Smith, the United Daughters of the Confederacy, and private citizens from around the state. This outpouring of support helped persuade the General Assembly to provide regular appropriations for the school.

The success of Branson's efforts was apparent in the appearance of the campus by the time of his resignation in 1912. The buildings shown in the engraving drawn about this time are, from left to right: the president's cottage (1897); Gilmer Hall (the old University High School, 1859); the dining hall, to the rear of the quadrangle (1906); Bradwell Hall (1896); the old Auditorium, nearest the street (1898); Smith Building (1906); Winnie Davis Hall (1902); the Carnegie Library (1910); and the Muscogee Practice School (1902). The small gazebo-like structure beside the street was the "Buzzard's Roost," a streetcar stop.

Jere M. Pound was elected in 1912 to replace President Branson. He enjoyed the longest presidential tenure, guiding the school until its merger with the university in the 1930s. Two additional major buildings were erected during his administration, Miller Hall (1917) and Pound Auditorium (1917). In 1933 the Normal School became the Coordinate Campus of the University of Georgia, and housed female students. It was acquired by the United States Navy in the 1950s for its Supply Corps School.

The curriculum of the Normal School included the theory and practice of teaching, English, mathematics, geography, primary methods, kindergarten teaching, vocal music, psychology, drawing, and domestic science. Classes began at eight-thirty in the morning and lasted until six-thirty in the evening with a two-hour break for dinner at midday. Recitations were supplemented with guest lectures by university professors and other prominent local citizens. The scholastic year was divided into four terms of ten weeks each, with a vacation from mid-December to mid-March. The school offered a diploma for a complete course, a teaching certificate, and an elective course for continuing teachers. The State Normal School became an important component of Georgia's educational system and an integral part of the Athens community. Engraving courtesy of University of Georgia Libraries Special Collections

Canning clubs, which gave young women practice in cooking and preserving food, were very popular in the early years of the century. These clubs, along with the corn clubs and cotton clubs for boys, were forerunners of the 4-H. In this photograph the instructors are judging the canning efforts of the girls in the club. Photograph courtesy of Mrs. J. B. Adams

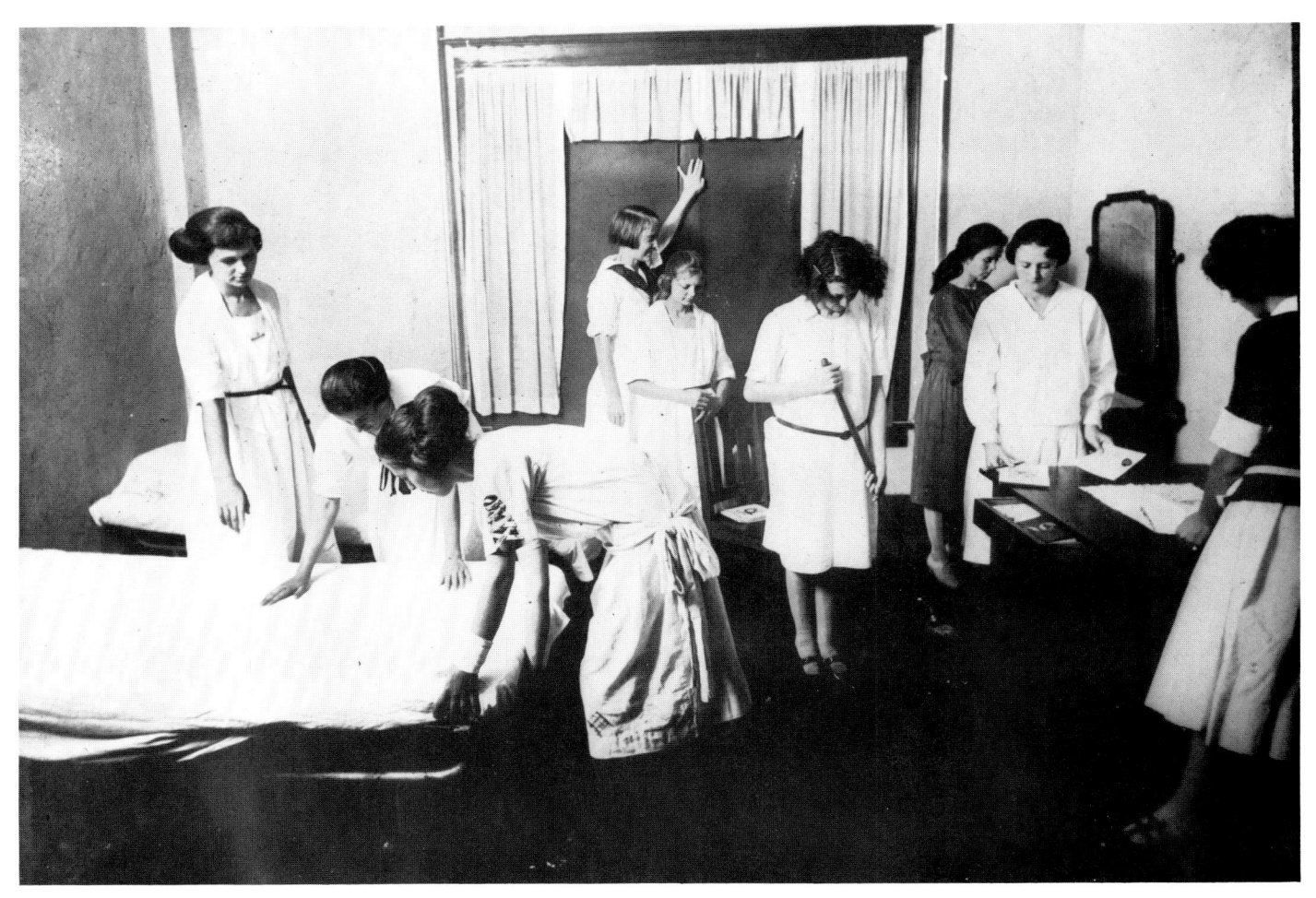

A domestic science department was established at State Normal in 1901 and first located in a renovated servant's house. A kitchen was equipped for cooking instruction, and a dining room was set up. Two teachers were paid by George Foster Peabody, who soon gave additional money for the expansion of the domestic science program. The students shown here are making up beds, sweeping, and working at other housekeeping chores in one of the school's practice rooms. Photograph courtesy of Mrs. J. B. Adams

The Young Women's Christian Association at the State Normal School grew out of the religious work of Miss Ida Young, who joined the faculty in 1897. In 1906 the Normal School Chapter became a charter member of the National Y.W.C.A. Miss Moina Michael, seated in the center of the photograph wearing a lace collar, became the secretary in 1913 and was the guiding force of the organization until the school merged with the university in the 1930s. A great deal of emphasis was placed on Bible study by the association, and courses were arranged for each class. The chapter won several honors in Bible study, mission study, and social welfare at the Panama Exposition in 1915.

Other organizations at State Normal included the following: the Altoria Literary Society; the Mildred Rutherford Literary Society; the Georgia Club, which promoted study of the state; the Round Table, which presented programs of readings, current events, and music as an opportunity for social interaction; L'Alliance Francaise; the Athletic Association; the Glee Club; and the Alumni-ae Association. Photograph courtesy of Annie Virginia Massey

Not to be outdone by the Lucy Cobb girls who always participated in local parades, the State Normal students seen here outfitted a flatbed truck as a float and joined the festivities. Photograph courtesy of Mrs. J. B. Adams

The continued strong development of downtown Athens after the turn of the century and the construction of the new City Hall and Federal Building in that area were factors which helped influence county officials to erect a new Clarke County Courthouse in 1913 on the corner of Washington and Jackson streets where C. A. Tucker's blacksmith shop had stood.

A bronze plaque in the lobby of the building credits prominent Atlanta architect A. Ten Eyck Brown with the design of the building, but contemporary newspaper reports recognize Professor Charles Morton Strahan for both the preparation of plans and supervision of construction. Strahan also served as a member of the building committee and held the title of Consulting Engineer.

The photograph shows the Clarke County Courthouse under construction in 1913. The general contractor was the Little-Cleckler Construction Company of Anniston, Alabama. Subcontractors and suppliers from all over the country were used on the project, but some local firms were represented.

L. M. Leathers was contractor for all cornice, sheet metal, and roofing work. The Dorsey Company supplied the furnishings, while Michael Brothers provided the linoleum and window shades. Bernstein Brothers sold the county the vault doors and the opera chairs which were used in the courtrooms. Photograph courtesy of University of Georgia Libraries Special Collections

This photograph shows the building as it appeared about 1918. The exterior remains virtually unchanged today. When the courthouse opened, the ordinary, clerk of the superior court, and offices of the tax assessor and tax collector occupied the first floor. On the second floor were the courtrooms of Judges Charles H. Brand and Henry S. West. County offices were located on the third floor. Sheriff Walter E. Jackson lived on the fourth floor with the prisoners.

The jail included a kitchen, a hospital room, a laundry room, and two padded cells for the insane, in addition to the other cells. There was also an open court on the roof for the prisoners to get fresh air. Photograph courtesy of University of Georgia Libraries Special Collections

This view of Hancock Avenue looking east from College Avenue was taken from the City Hall cupola in January 1914. On the right is the old Federal Building. Just visible behind it is the top floor of the Clarke County Courthouse, completed only the year before. The building on the left with the sign that urges the viewer to "Use Electric Light Power," was the headquarters of the Athens Railway & Electric Company. Originally constructed in 1876 on the corner of Clayton and College, it was taken down in 1906 and reconstructed on this site. It became the local office of Georgia Power after that company took over Athens Railway & Electric in 1926

Dean William Tate remembered it as a favorite place to study at night when he was a student in the early 1920s because it had a big room with well lighted tables. Other students were employed to watch the dials on the equipment at night. The building and the entire neighborhood behind and to the side of it fell to urban renewal in the 1960s. The Merrill Lynch office now stands on that corner. The fourth building to the right of the Athens Railway Building is the Synagogue of the Congregation Children of Israel, also demolished. Photograph by Scarlett and Noyes; courtesy of William John Russell

The E. D. Harris Drug Store was Athens's first black owned and operated drugstore. It was organized by Dr. W. H. Harris, a noted local black physician, who remained the largest stockholder. Dr. Blanche Thompson, the first black woman to practice medicine in Athens, was also a stockholder in the business. The proprietor was Dr. E. D. Harris. The store opened its doors in 1910 in the new Morton Building, but soon moved to the neighboring Samaritan Building. It operated in that location for many years. The Samaritan Building was located just east of the Morton Building on Washington Street, but was demolished in the early 1970s to make room for a parking lot.

This photograph shows the Harris Drug Store as it appeared while in the Samaritan Building. The Athens Banner praised the operation as a most complete drugstore and compared it favorably to many of the white drugstores of the city. Photograph courtesy of University of Georgia Libraries Special Collections

By 1916 the Athens Coca-Cola Bottling Company had moved its offices and plant to a building, shown here, on the corner of Washington and Lumpkin streets. It shared the building with the offices of Edwards Mills and the Mallison Braided Cord Company. This photograph shows the building as it appeared at that time. It was demolished. The C & S Bank drive-in window and parking lot now occupy this site. In 1926 the Coke Company moved to its present location on Prince Avenue. Photograph courtesy of Albert Sams, Sr.

The photograph above shows the interior of the McGregor Company, familiar to Athenians of several generations, as it appeared in 1912. In 1888 D. W. McGregor, a Scot from Dundee, purchased the Burk Bookstore which had been established during the 1870s on the corner of Broad Street and College Avenue. He soon developed the small business into a thriving concern which was popular with students and townspeople alike. The merchandise included books, athletic equipment, stationery, film, and other supplies for students and businessmen.

In 1904 a printing plant was established by McGregor in cooperation with the University Press, and in 1906 the company was incorporated. After the turn of the century, the store moved to Clayton Street into the building now occupied by the Logos Bookstore. It moved again in 1908, this time to its present location at 321 Clayton Street, shown here in the photograph.

The interior arrangement of the store remained the same until the 1980s when it was completely modernized. The company acquired additional property on Jackson Street in the 1920s and moved the printing plant into its Washington Street location in 1952. In 1981 the company opened a new warehouse and display room near Georgia Square Mall, but the old McGregor's continues to operate on Clayton Street. Photograph courtesy of Georgia Department of Archives and History

The Athens Coca-Cola Bottling Company, founded by L. C. Brown around the turn of the century, was originally operated out of a building on the corner of Hancock and Hull. By the time this advertisement appeared in 1906, S. B. Wilkins had become president of the firm and L. C. Brown was serving as secretary and treasurer. The building was later used by the Chero-Cola Company for its bottling plant.

In addition to Coke and Chero-Cola, there were a number of soft drink companies operating in Athens in the early part of the twentieth century. Deep Rock Ginger Ale, a company founded by the Abney brothers, had a plant on Clayton Street. Also on Clayton was the Red Rock Ginger Ale Company. The Viva Beverage Company and the Athens Bottling Works competed for the business of thirsty Athenians, along with the Bludwine Company, an Athens original. The building illustrated here is no longer standing. Photography courtesy of University of Georgia Libraries Special Collections

The saga of Bludwine, Athens's original soft drink, began in Watkinsville, Georgia, in 1894 when Henry C. Anderson began working on the formula for a cherry drink that could lure people away from alcohol. Anderson got together with a German chemist from Elberton, and they came up with a blend of fruit and grain extracts that Anderson wanted to call "G. D.," for good digestion. The cherry-flavored drink was finally placed on the market under the name "Bludwine," supposedly derived from the German Blut, or blood.

By World War I, the company claimed that it sold a million bottles a day in twenty-eight states. Although their advertising was careful to say that Bludwine was not being promoted as a medicine, it was claimed to have a tonic effect and to be an aid to digestion. Physicians were even prescribing it as a tonic for the blood. The company soon came under attack from the Food and Drug Administration. The government charged that the slogans "For Your Health's Sake" and "The Food Drink" were misleading. The company withdrew its health claims and removed the "l" from its name, becoming "Budwine."

In 1918 the company suffered a further setback, attributed to sabotage by the Anderson family, when a defective batch of soda water was delivered to over half of the distributors. By the time the company was purchased by Joseph Costa in 1929, only the Athens and Augusta plants remained. Budwine was really a sideline for the new owner, who was a partner in Costa's, the popular ice cream manufacturing firm with an ice cream parlor in the Southern Mutual Building. Eventually, both remaining plants were closed, but Budwine continued to be produced under an agreement with the local Pepsi bottler.

After Pepsi was sold to General Cinema in 1969, Budwine was available only at local Dairy Queens for nine months. The company received a reprieve when two bottlers, first in Macon and then in Thomasville, agreed to produce the soft drink. After Joe Costa's death, his son Butch and a partner, Shawn Cornell, took over the management of the business. By 1980 they had increased sales to 200,000 cases which were distributed in Georgia, North Carolina, Kentucky, Tennessee, and California.

Prospects now appear good for the survival and growth of an Athens tradition that goes back almost ninety years. This advertisement for Bludwine, touting the health benefits of the cherry-flavored drink, appeared in newspapers and magazines just after the turn of the century. Photograph courtesy of University of Georgia Libraries Special Collections

This group of children, enjoying bottles of Bludwine, were photographed in front of the company's old factory on Thomas Street below the Oconee Street intersection just before World War I. Photograph courtesy of Joseph Costa, Jr., II

When Joseph Costa took over the Budwine Company in 1929, he discovered this original Norman Rockwell painting stuffed in a trash can. The painting, which pictures a young boy drinking the old-fashioned cherry soda, is entitled Budwine Boy and Dog. *It was salvaged from the trash and restored, and remains in the possession of the Budwine Company. Photograph by Hal Brooks, Athens Newspapers, Incorporated, from the original; courtesy of Joseph Costa, Jr. II*

Before the days of motorized delivery trucks, Bludwine was distributed from horse-drawn wagons like the one shown in this turn of the century photograph. Photograph courtesy of Joseph Costa, Jr., II

C. A. Trussell, one of Athens's earliest automobile dealers, opened his Ford agency about 1918. Mr. Trussell is shown here seated with two ladies in one of the early Fords in his showroom. The dealership was located for many years downtown on Clayton Street at its intersection with Thomas. Trussell Ford's new facilities are now on the Atlanta Highway near the Oconee River Bridge. Photograph courtesy of University of Georgia Libraries Special Collections

The Athens Fruit Company, shown here about 1917, did a large business for many years in wholesale and retail fruits and vegetables in this Clayton Street location. Mr. and Mrs. Anthony Costa were the proprietors and at one time lived above their store. At the time this photograph was taken, an office above the store was rented to Dr. Charles L. Walton. Later a tailor, J. W. McQueen, occupied that space. The Costas were particularly known for their parched peanuts, which they sold for five cents a bag from the stand at the entrance. One hundred pound croker sacks of raw peanuts were stacked up to the ceiling.

The building now houses a retail establishment. The building to the right in the photograph, now Aurum Studios, was Martin Brothers Shoe Store at the time of this photograph. J. T. Anderson Real Estate, Dr. W. T. Hamilton, and Cobb Lampkin had offices on the upper floor. Photograph from the author's collection

When the Athens Fire Department was organized in 1891, much of the glamor and excitement associated with the volunteer fire companies was lost, but in return Athens got its first professional fire protection. The first two stations were those of the downtown volunteer companies—the Pioneer company's building on the corner of Washington and Jackson streets and the Hope company's hall in the middle of Washington Street. The horse-drawn equipment was very modern for its day, and the harnesses were arranged so that they could be dropped quickly over the horses.

There were fifteen paid firemen in those first years. In 1901 Fire Hall No. 2 was opened on Prince Avenue to replace the Hope company's hall, and the Southern Mutual Insurance Company presented Chief McDorman with a new buggy. In 1912 Fire Hall No. 1 was constructed at the eastern end of Washington Street, and the old Pioneer hall was abandoned.

The photograph here shows Fire Hall No. 1 with one of its early motorized trucks. The building was remodeled in 1980 to serve as the headquarters of the Athens Area Chamber of Commerce, after the department moved to the new fire station on North Jackson Street. Photograph courtesy of Athens Newspapers, Incorporated

These proud employees of Southern Bell Telephone Company were photographed in front of their new building on the southeast corner of Hull and Clayton streets in 1918. The structure, which cost $36,000 to build, was the fourth location of the telephone exchange in Athens. The first exchange on the second floor of the Scudder Jewelry Building at the corner of College and Clayton served thirty-six customers when it opened in August 1882.

Seven years later, the company moved its switchboards to the south side of Clayton Street over Ficketts Jewelry, replacing the old Law System with the newer Blake Transmitter. The following year the first toll line was run seven miles through Barberville to Winterville, and in 1892 a second long distance line was extended to Watkinsville, Bishop, Farmington, and Madison where it connected with the Augusta-Atlanta line. New improved services increased subscribers to a total of 234 by 1900. In 1906 the exchange moved again, this time to the third floor of the Talmadge Building on the southwest corner of College and Clayton. It was in this location that operations were disrupted by a serious fire about Christmas, 1908.

Service was begun in the new building seen in the photograph when Mayor A. C. Erwin pulled the string to "cut over" to the new exchange on June 21, 1918. H. J. Rowe made the first call to the Banner with the news. The yellow brick building is now the home of Padgett Business Services. Southern Bell headquarters is located in their new building on the Milledge Avenue site of the Welch House, demolished in the late 1960s. Photograph courtesy of Athens Newspapers, Incorporated

Fifty years ago, the children of Athens got to enjoy Christmas twice a year. In late August or September, children would gather on the lawn at Mrs. Alexander H. Davison's house on Prince Avenue to decorate a Christmas tree and bring presents. The decorations and presents were not for the participants, however, but for children in the Orient. The First Methodist Church supported Ella Leverett, a missionary in China, who would distribute the gifts to the children there at Christmas time.

The photograph here is of one of the "Christmas" parties about 1916. Several of the people are dressed in Oriental costumes which had been sent back by Ella Leverett. Photograph courtesy of Lucy Pound Huggins

These students, photographed in 1906, were members of the first tenth grade class in the Athens public schools. The tenth grade met at the Washington Street School until the completion of the new school on Childs Street in 1909. Photograph courtesy of Charles Brockman

Shortly after the turn of the century it became obvious that the facilities of the Washington Street School could not meet the needs of a growing school population. After becoming principal of the High School Department in 1907, Edward Baker Mell sought to remedy the situation by persuading the city to build a new high school building.

The Athens High School was opened in 1909 on Childs Street just off Prince Avenue behind the A. K. Childs House (J. H. Lumpkin House), and the Washington Street School was demolished to make way for the new Georgian Hotel. This photograph was taken soon after the opening of the new school, about 1910. The increased space made possible the addition of an eleventh grade in 1909, so the high school consisted of grades eight through eleven. Mr. E. B. Mell was principal and chemistry teacher. Mr. Cummings taught algebra; Miss Patti Hilsman, Latin; Miss Elizabeth Caldwell, English; and Mrs. Wyche, German.

The first high school baseball team was organized at Childs Street, but high school athletics were not what they are today—the boys had to hire their own coach. The school developed a good academic reputation, too, and by 1913 it was on the Southern accreditation list. The high school remained in this location only a few years, moving to the nearby old courthouse in 1915.

Renamed the Childs Street School, the building continued to be used until two youths set it on fire in February 1966. The insurance proceeds of a little over $100,000 did not nearly cover the loss. The building remained standing, a burned-out shell, for several years. It was finally razed and the property sold to St. Joseph's Catholic Church for use by its parochial school. Photograph courtesy of Gary Doster

The students photographed here about 1913 were enrolled in the cooking school at Athens High and Industrial School. The cooking school was the brainchild of Professor Samuel F. Harris, one of Athens's outstanding black educators, who saw the need for vocational education for working blacks.

Early courses were offered two afternoons a week. Discussions focused on food preparation, nutritional value of foodstuffs, and their relation to health. Later a night school was added to provide a more complete cooking program and to offer instruction in carpentry, brick-laying, and plastering as well. Professor Harris was appointed principal of Athens High and Industrial and supervisor of all black city schools in 1913.

When he was forced to resign in 1934, due to illness, Mrs. A. H. Burney, an instructor and assistant principal, served as principal until Aaron Brown was appointed the following year. In 1964 Athens High and Industrial School (which had moved into a new building on Dearing Street in 1956) became Burney-Harris High School in honor of these two educators. It is now a middle school.

This photograph was taken at the old Athens High and Industrial building which was on the corner of Reese and Church streets. The two-story wooden building is still standing, although no longer used as a school. Photograph courtesy of University of Georgia Libraries Special Collections

Knox School, the first for blacks in Athens, was established in 1868 and named for John J. Knox, a white official of the Freedmen's Bureau. It was reorganized as Knox Institute under the direction of the Reverend Louis S. Clark and became one of the schools of the American Missionary Association. Clark became principal of the school about 1886 and remained in that position until the school closed in 1928. The two-story white frame building in the photograph was located on the southeast corner of Reese and Pope streets across from Hill First Baptist Church. Classes were conducted on the ground floor, and boarding students lived upstairs.

In addition to academic subjects, the school offered, among others, industrial classes in carpentry, typesetting, printing, and sewing. Tuition in 1912 ranged from fifty cents per month for primary grades to $1.50 for special music courses. There were at that time eleven teachers and about 330 students. In this David Earnest photograph students and faculty are seen in front of the old building about the turn of the century. Reverend Clark can be seen standing at the front left, holding his derby hat in his hand. The lot on which this building was located is now a small park. Photograph courtesy of University of Georgia Libraries Special Collections

This view of the carpentry shop at Knox Institute was taken about 1910. Photograph courtesy of Michael Thurmond

Money for the construction of Knox Institute's handsome new building, photographed here in 1924, was contributed by Andrew Carnegie in 1912. Named Carnegie Hall in his honor, the twenty-one room structure was completed in the following year on the corner across Pope Street from the old building. The school's industrial department was housed on the lower floor, while the two upper floors were used for classroom instruction.

The curriculum included a standard college preparatory course, an elementary division, teacher training, domestic science, industrial courses, and music. Financial troubles finally forced Athens's oldest and largest private black school to close its doors in 1928. Beginning in 1933, the city leased Carnegie Hall for several years to house the Athens High and Industrial School. The building was later demolished, and the site is today a vacant lot. Photograph courtesy of University of Georgia Libraries Special Collections

When the United States entered World War I in 1917, the facilities of the university were offered to the government for special courses. The Students Army Training Corps (S.A.T.C.) was organized to train students for service in the armed forces. Four units were established: the collegiate army section, the collegiate navy section, the vocational army unit, and the Reserve Army Training Corps for students who were under age.

S.A.T.C. courses included Infantry, Artillery, Signal Corps, Aviation, and Pre-Medical, with emphasis on causes of the war, topography, hygiene, military law, radio, and mechanics. In 1918-1919, 617 students were enrolled in the collegiate sections and 533 were listed in the vocational sections. This photograph shows one of the units drilling on the quadrangle in front of Philosophical Hall.

Work had barely begun when the war ended in November 1918. The following June, a memorial service was held for the university alumni who had lost their lives in the war. Of the 1,663 alumni who had entered military service, forty-one were listed as casualties, ranging from one member of the class of 1880 to one of the class of 1919 (Brooks, The University of Georgia). Photograph courtesy of Anne and Branch Howe

All of the town's citizens were called upon to support the war effort in 1917 and 1918. The girls at Athens High School organized a chapter of the Red Cross and met after school to knit, roll bandages, and sew for the soldiers under the supervision of their teacher, Mrs. Ora Hart Avery.

The group shown in this photograph is gathered in one of the classrooms in the old high school on Prince Avenue to do their part by knitting socks and other garments. Photograph courtesy of Bertha Coffee Thurmon

This photograph shows the Georgia "tank" on Herty Field before the beginning of the senior parade. Photograph by Clifford Cagle; courtesy of Anne and Branch Howe

The controversial "Tech in 'Lanta" float is shown here on Herty Field with Moore College and the Chapel in the background. Photograph by Clifford Cagle; courtesy of Anne and Branch Howe

The emotions which were running high among the students during World War I gave rise to an incident that caused a serious rift between the University of Georgia and Georgia Tech that lasted for several years. During senior parade 1918, two floats reflected on the patriotism of Georgia Tech students and alumni. One float, in the shape of a tank, manned by uniformed "soldiers," was labeled "Georgia in France, 1917-1918." It was accompanied by a car driven by two students with a banner reading "Tech in 'Lanta, 1917-1918."

The four class presidents at Georgia were asked to apologize to their counterparts, but they refused. Charges and countercharges flowed back and forth. Some said that Chancellor Barrow got up from the meeting between the two schools and said, "Boys, let's go home." Another blamed an article in the Red and Black for inciting the disagreement. Several alumni blamed a sports column by Morgan Blake. One Tech alumnus claimed that uniforms had been stolen from Tech; others from Georgia countered that sweatshirts dyed yellow were used with Georgia uniforms.

Whatever the story, the upshot was the suspension of athletic contests between the two schools. Finally, according to Dean William Tate, Governor Clifford Walker asked the presidents of the two schools to get together in 1925 and quietly settle the matter. Tech and Georgia finally played again in 1926.

One of the lasting symbols to come out of World War I was the red poppy. Its adoption as the official memorial flower was the result of the efforts of an Athenian, Moina Belle Michael. At the outbreak of the war, Miss Michael left her position as social and religious director at the state normal school for an appointment to the Y.M.C.A. Overseas Headquarters at Columbia University. It was there that she first read a copy of Colonel John McCrae's famous poem, "In Flander's Fields," and was inspired to wear a red poppy in memory of the fallen soldiers. She penned her pledge in the following words:

> *Oh! You who sleep in "Flanders Fields,"*
> *Sleep sweet—to rise anew!*
> *We caught the Torch you threw*
> *And, holding high, we keep the Faith*
> *With all who died.*
>
> *****
>
> *And now the Torch and Poppy red*
> *We wear in honor of our dead.*
> *Fear not that ye have died for naught;*
> *We've learned the lesson that ye taught*
> *In Flanders Fields.*

When asked to select flowers for the Y.M.C.A. and Y.W.C.A. Overseas Conference in 1918, she went to Wannamakers and bought red silk poppies. Her idea caught on and spread. In 1920 the Georgia State American Legion Convention adopted the red poppy as its official memorial flower and succeeded in obtaining the endorsement of the National Convention of the American Legion in the fall of that year. Since that time, the red poppy has been sold to raise money for disabled veterans of all wars. This photograph of Moina Michael was taken in her memorial poppy garden in Athens, where she returned after the war. The flowers were grown from seed brought from Flanders fields. Photograph courtesy of University Archives

Moina Michael, The Poppy Lady, was one of only two Athenians to be honored by the issuance of a United States postage stamp. (The other was Crawford W. Long). The three cent stamp, which recognized her role in originating the idea of the World War I memorial poppy, was first issued in Athens on November 9, 1948. This photograph shows a first day cover of the Moina Michael stamp. Courtesy of University of Georgia Libraries Special Collections

About the turn of the century, the Y.M.C.A. and the University Alumni Society began efforts to raise money for a new building on campus. The two groups, however, could not agree on a site. The Alumni Society favored a location near the Lucas House, south of Baldwin Street, while the Y.M.C.A. preferred a Broad Street site.

The Y.M.C.A. finally withdrew from the project and the university began work in 1910 on the new building on Lucas Hill. More than $59,000 had been spent on the project when work was stopped for lack of funds. The building remained incomplete until the 1920s when money from the million dollar War Memorial Fund was made available to finish the structure.

The building was renamed War Memorial Hall, and a bronze plaque was placed in the rotunda to record the names of the university alumni who lost their lives in the war. Chancellor Barrow composed the inscription which appears around the rotunda: "In loyal love we set apart this house, a memorial to those lovers of peace who took arms, left home and dear ones and gave life that all men might be free."

In 1926 the university treasurer reported that nearly $217,000 had been spent to complete the building. During World War II, Memorial Hall was considerably enlarged by the United States Navy and later served as a student activities center. The photograph shows the building as it appeared during construction. Courtesy of University of Georgia Libraries Special Collections

This photograph of the Memorial Hall portico was taken during the 1960s before the construction of the Psychology-Journalism complex across Hooper Street to the north. Memorial Hall ceased to function as a student center upon completion of the new Dean William Tate Student Center. The building is now used for administrative offices and registration. Photograph from the author's collection

When the facilities of the old Y.M.C.A., which was built on the corner of Clayton and Lumpkin streets in 1889, no longer met the needs of a growing community after the turn of the century, an effort was launched to raise money for a new building. In 1912 a campaign raised pledges in excess of $100,000, but the project was slow in getting off the ground.

The Athens Banner published drawings of the proposed new building in February 1915. Work finally got under way, and by the time this photograph was taken in 1919 the building had been completed and was in use. The building stood on the southwest corner of Broad and Lumpkin streets facing the university campus.

After the present Y.M.C.A. complex on Hawthorne Avenue was completed in 1966-67 at a cost of more than $800,000 the old building was used for several years by the University of Georgia. It was demolished in the early 1970s. The rear of the property became a parking lot for the Holiday Inn, which constructed a small vest-pocket park along Lumpkin Street. Photograph courtesy of University of Georgia Libraries Special Collections

This photograph of the interior of the Y.M.C.A. was taken shortly after the building's completion. The main entrance is shown in the background, and in the foreground are a ping-pong table, pool table, and another game table. The building also had a swimming pool and other gymnastic equipment. Photograph courtesy of Mrs. J. B. Adams

In 1901 the Athens Y.M.C.A. established a summer camp in the mountains of North Georgia near Tallulah Falls. W. T. Forbes, the camp's founder, directed it for forty-two years. The 326-acre camp with cabins, sports-fields, a lake, and many other recreational facilities has served thousands of Athens's youngsters over the years. In some families, three generations of campers have attended "Big Y" in the summer.

The camp was begun, Forbes said, to be "a place where boys can spend vacations in the activities designed to develop them mentally, physically, and spiritually, and at the same time give them a happy camp experience." The camp has been doing just that for eighty years. In 1943 Forbes was succeeded by H. C. "Pop" Pearson, Jr., who directed the camp for three decades. John Simpson became director after Pop Pearson's death in 1972.

The camp is still in operation and as popular as ever. This photograph, taken in the 1920s, provides a view of the lake with a diving tower in the middle and several groups canoeing. Photograph courtesy of University of Georgia Libraries Special Collections

Each year before the boys went to "Y" camp at Tallulah Falls, the girls from the Y.W.C.A. got an opportunity to enjoy a two-week camping experience in the mountains. This photograph shows the girls all assembled at "Big Y" one summer about 1920. W. T. Forbes, the camp director, is standing on the left with the megaphone. Photograph courtesy of Lucy Pound Huggins

The Cloverhurst Country Club, located at the west end of Springdale Street, where Cloverhurst and Springdale now converge to form Bobbin Mill Road, was a favorite spot of many Athenians in the 1920s and 1930s. The private club was organized about 1918. A nine hole golf course and the clubhouse shown in this photograph were soon constructed.

The golf course was later expanded to eighteen holes, and a swimming pool was built. Dances held at the clubhouse were very popular among young Athenians of the period. The club was disbanded in the late 1930s, and the area was developed as a residential suburb. Photograph courtesy of University of Georgia Libraries Special Collections

This is the way that the south side of Clayton Street, from Jackson to Thomas, looked before the disastrous fire of 1921. The fire began in the basement of the Max Joseph Building (the four-story structure with the pyramid-roofed tower) on the evening of January 24, 1921. The building had been built in the 1890s as a department store, but by 1921 the basement and the first floors were occupied by the Denny Motor Company. The building also housed a restaurant, meeting rooms for several fraternal organizations, and the Athens Typographical Union.

After the firemen arrived they soon seemed to have the fire under control, but the gasoline in the tanks of the cars stored in the basement of Denny Motor Company sent flames licking across the street (to the right in the photograph) toward the 1906 Michael Brothers retail store. In spite of the firemen's efforts, the wooden window sashes caught fire and the flames quickly spread through that store and the adjoining four-story Michael's wholesale department.

The fire began to spread south toward Broad Street, and by 3 a.m., when it was near its peak, it could be seen in Monroe, twenty-five miles away. Mayor Andrew C. Erwin was forced to call the Atlanta Fire Department for help. In the next hour, the fire lept across Jackson Street and consumed the upper story of Citizens' Pharmacy (in the lower right of the photo), and only quick action by the fire fighters and a thick brick fire wall stopped the fire, driven by cold northeast winds, from spreading through Joseph Jewelry and the entire block toward College Avenue.

The Deupree Block on Broad Street, the Morris Building, and several adjacent structures also began burning. Fortunately the firemen were able to contain the fire in the upper stories of these buildings. When reinforcements from Atlanta arrived with their equipment at the Seaboard depot about 8 a.m., the fire was coming under control. The Atlanta chief relieved Athens's Chief McDorman, who had broken both wrists in a fall about 6 a.m.

By the evening of the twenty-fifth, only a few areas were still smouldering. The destruction was tremendous, but the hard work of the firemen and a good bit of luck had prevented an even wider tragedy. The ruins had hardly begun to cool before the downtown businessmen began rebuilding what had been destroyed. Photograph courtesy of University of Georgia Libraries Special Collections

"Our loss is close to a million dollars, but we will recover," said Moses Michael after the destruction of Michael Brothers Department Store in the great 1921 fire. The firm opened temporary facilities in the Southern Mutual Building within a few days and hired Neel Reid, a partner in the Atlanta architectural firm of Hentz, Reid, and Adler, to design a new store building. The rubble was cleared from the old site on Clayton Street, and work was begun on this handsome Renaissance Revival structure, which is perhaps Reid's most successful commercial building. This photograph was taken shortly after it was completed in 1922.

The Michael family operated the business there until 1953, when it was acquired by the Davison-Paxon Company. Davison's Department Store remained in the building until the completion of a new store in Georgia Square Mall. In the fall of 1981, the Michael family sold the building to a group of investors for renovation and redevelopment. This fine commercial building remains one of Athens's architectural landmarks. *Photograph courtesy of Mrs. J. B. Adams*

This display appeared in the window of the new Michael Brothers after its opening in 1922. Behind the manequins and merchandise on display can be seen some of the walnut interior fittings of the store which were removed by Davison's after they acquired the building in the 1950s. *Photograph courtesy of Mrs. J. B. Adams*

The proprietors of the American Cafe were photographed with some of their customers on January 30, 1914. The business was established about the turn of the century by Rich Huff and operated until about 1939. The first location, shown here, was on the east side of Jackson Street between Broad and Clayton.

The fire that destroyed Michael Brothers and many other buildings in the downtown in 1921 also burned the American Cafe. Huff then relocated on Broad Street east of Thomas, near the present Christian Hardware. On the left in the apron is Rich Huff, the owner. His brother Craig Huff, also in an apron, stands in the center of the photograph. *Photograph courtesy of Mildred Huff*

This interior view of the American Cafe was taken at the new location on Broad Street after the first business had been destroyed in 1921. The proprietor, Rich Huff, stands nearest the photographer on the right. Also behind the counter is Gus Huff. In the case on the left are pies and cakes, while cigars are displayed in the case on the right. Jars of candy and a gum machine are on top of the counter. Photograph courtesy of Mildred Huff

This photograph shows the north side of Clayton Street between Jackson and College as it appeared in the 1920s. The Southern Mutual Building, on the left, housed the Georgia National Bank, and later in the decade the C & S Bank, as well as Palmer & Sons Drugs. Fulton Federal Savings and Loan now leases this space.

The next building on the right is the Stern Building. At the time of this photograph, the Charles Stern & Company men's store occupied the building. Its successor firm, George Dean's, is still in this location. Next was the E. H. Dorsey clothing store, later Tony's Restaurant, now Rocky's.

The last building was originally a Victorian era hotel, but during the 1920s the Athens Shoe Company rented part of the space. Masada Leather Company now occupies that storefront. The rest of the ground floor, then and now, is used by McLellan's. The last building on the block, not visible in the photograph was the Davison-Nicholson Company department store, now remodeled as Foster's Jewelers. Photograph from the author's collection

S. H. Kress and Company opened a store at 155-157 East Clayton Street in 1915. It remained a part of the downtown scene for sixty-five years, finally closing in December 1980. This display of men's washable ties appeared in Kress's window during the 1920s. Photograph courtesy of Mrs. J. B. Adams

Mother Goose Bread was a familiar product to Athenians during the 1920s, and its colorful wrapper with drawings and nursery rhymes was particularly popular with children. It was produced by Skelton's Bakery, which grew rapidly into one of the largest in the state during that decade. The bakery, located on Washington Street between Lumpkin and Hull, burned in a spectacular fire in September 1922. By the following year, the business had been temporarily relocated to Barrow Street and was later moved to Prince Avenue. That last building is now part of the Coca-Cola complex.

The proprietor, James E. Skelton, is shown in this photograph standing beside one of his delivery trucks outside the bakery. Mrs. Skelton ran Skelton's Coffee Shoppe, which served light lunches and sold retail bakery goods at 193 East Clayton Street, next door to Patrick's Drugstore. The bakery was closed during the depression of the 1930s. Photograph courtesy of University of Georgia Libraries Special Collections

Benson's Bakery was to prove a more lasting commercial enterprise than the Skelton Bakery, becoming one of downtown Athens's institutions. The firm was founded in 1919 when W. H. Benson bought a small bakery and began to expand the operations. He started with two horses and wagons and an old truck. By the 1920s, the business began to prosper, and the firm entered in a parade the float (shown here), proudly proclaiming "Queen of All is Benson's Daisy Bread."

The bakery was originally located on Hancock Avenue between Hull and Pulaski streets, but later moved to its present site on the corner of Thomas and Washington. Benson's was the first bakery in the area to slice and wrap bread, and later pioneered the introduction of vitamin enriched bread. The aroma of fresh-baked bread from Benson's is one of the most familiar and pleasant smells in the downtown area. Photograph courtesy of Mrs. J. B. Adams

"For a quarter of a century, hotels here were a matter of shame to Athens, but happily that has now been changed," reported the Athens Banner in 1911, two years after the opening of the Georgian Hotel. It was, indeed, a far cry from the story-and-a-half hewn log house owned by John Cary that served as Athens's first hotel at the beginning of the nineteenth century.

The new hotel, which was designed by Atlanta architect T. Ten Eyck Brown and built at a cost of more than $200,000 opened on March 5, 1909, ushering in a new era in public accomodations for Athens. There were 100 rooms, all with running water and many with private baths. Several large rooms on the fifth floor (later converted to guest rooms) served as display rooms for traveling salesmen. There were dining rooms, a ballroom, a coffee shop, and a marble-lined lobby. "There are larger hotels in the South than the Georgian Hotel," said the Banner, "but nowhere can you find one that is more modern in its construction, nor more conveniently arranged."

It was operated as a hotel until January 1976, but in its later years much of the business went to the more modern motels that had been built around the city. Many of the residents were weekly or monthly guests. After 1977, much of the building remained vacant. Rehabilitation of the building for condominiums was begun in 1985.

In spite of its age, the building remains one of the most substantial and attractive in the downtown area. When this photograph was made in the 1920s, the Georgian was in its heyday. On the left in the photograph is the entrance to the Palm Garden Restaurant and on the right, at the curb, is A. H. Cook's bus. Photograph courtesy of Mrs. J. B. Adams

This photograph was taken during a social function in the early 1920s in the second floor ballroom of the Georgian Hotel. The room has a curved ceiling with lovely stained glass skylights, and the large windows and french doors make it a light, elegant space. Photograph courtesy of Mrs. J. B. Adams

The Palm Garden at the Georgian Hotel was very popular with Athenians during the 1920s. The restaurant served ice cream, soft drinks, and snacks, and was a favorite meeting place for women's organizations of the period. Also, the furniture was often moved out so that tea dances could be held.

Many that attended these dances have fond memories of them, but recall that their feet hurt after dancing all afternoon on the tile floors. The Palm Garden became Cecilia's Golden China restaurant in the early 1970s and now serves as the bar of Friends Restaurant. Photograph (circa 1920) courtesy of Mrs. J. B. Adams

Mr. A. H. Cook, a well-known local figure in the early part of the century, is shown in the photograph above standing beside the bus in which he transported patrons of the Georgian Hotel to and from the depots of the various railroad lines that served the city. Photograph courtesy of Athens Newspapers, Incorporated

In 1866 a number of Athens's leading citizens raised $100,000 to establish the National Bank of Athens in an effort to stimulate an economic recovery from the desolation of the Civil War. For years, the bank was located in the Gothic Revival building on the corner of Broad and Jackson streets. In 1959 the bank moved to its present location on the corner of Broad and Lumpkin. It is now Trust Company Bank.

This interior view shows how the National Bank of Athens appeared about 1920. The staff consisted of (left to right) Nan Ethridge, secretary; John White Morton, president; Evans Johnson, teller; Graves Stephenson, head collector and assistant cashier; J. Ovid Bird, assistant cashier; and A. S. Parker, cashier. W. W. Beacham, bookkeeper, was missing from the picture. Between the time this photograph was taken and the time the bank moved to new headquarters in 1959, the interior was remodeled. Since 1959 it has been again remodeled into two store spaces. Photograph courtesy of T. H. Milner, Jr.

The Palace Theatre first opened its doors on College Avenue about 1920 with "Major" Gidley as its major-domo. The original building, in the center of the photograph, narrowly escaped destruction in a fire, which completely gutted the Davenport Building (to its right in the photo) in October 1968. The fire, which started in the rear of Baxter's clothing store, was contained before it spread to the Palace and the Shackelford Building to the left. The old Palace was soon demolished and the present twin theater was erected on the site of both the original building and the Davenport Building.

During the 1920s, there were three movie theaters downtown: the Palace, the Strand (next to the Holman Building on Clayton Street) and the Elite, later named the Georgia Theatre (on the corner of Clayton and Lumpkin streets). Of the three original buildings, only the Georgia remains as a theater, but it is unoccupied. The Strand was substantially changed and the Palace destroyed for the present building. Photograph from the author's collection

On January 16, 1888, Athens's *New Opera House* opened its doors for its first performance: *Erma, the Elf*, starring Katie Putnam. The opening culminated the year-long efforts of Bailey Thomas and the Athens Opera House Association to bring a new and modern theater to the community. In the face of widespread skepticism, the company purchased the lot of Dr. R. M. Smith on Washington Street and in April 1887, contracted with E. B. McGinty and Company to build the opera house. The initial skepticism was, apparently, unfounded as the *Banner* soon reported that "our new opera house has been quite gay this week. Manager Crawford has found out that a good troup, and a first class theater will bring Athens people out every night in the week." For the next forty-five years, the theater was the principal center for live entertainment in the city. In 1906 the Michael brothers purchased the building and hired Chicago architect Frank Cox to draw plans for a $20,000 renovation. The interior was refurbished, the stage expanded, twelve new sets of scenery were painted, elaborate carpeting and red velvet curtains on brass rods were installed, and a new fireproof curtain decorated with a woodland scene was hung. It became, according to the *Banner*, "one of the coziest theatres in the country." It was rechristened the Colonial Theatre.

Over the years, the theatre was a showcase for local talent, a forum for religious and political speakers, and a stop for regional and national touring companies. Box parties, where local organizations would hire boxes and attend as a group, became popular social events. The building also provided a place for conferences, conventions, and commencements; and benefit performances were held by the U.D.C., the East Athens School, the Y.M.C.A., the Athens Woman's Club, the local fire department, and the Judia Jackson Industrial School, among others. Musical Performances included concerts by the glee clubs of the University of Georgia and other colleges. Minstrel shows were extremely popular, and some groups such as Black Patti returned several years in a row. The location of Athens along the main line of the Seaboard Railroad made it possible for the Colonial to attract big-name touring companies. W. S. Hart starred in *The Virginian* there in 1907, and in 1916, Sarah Bernhardt brought her series of Shakespeare plays to the house. In 1927 Will Rogers delighted the large crowds that came from all over the region to see his one-man show. The Montgomery Players broke all records by appearing for fourteen straight weeks in 1928. Contests, give-aways, benefits, prizes, and the use of local talent in the shows, contributed to their success. This photograph was taken during the record-breaking run. Two of the shows, *Dr. Jekyll and Mr. Hyde* and *Peggy of My Heart* were advertised on the billboards outside the theatre.

Vaudeville was never popular at the Colonial and flourished only during the years 1912 and 1916. Movies, on the other hand, proved to be a big draw, and ironically for a theatre designed for live performances, a movie became its biggest attraction. Amidst a publicity blitz, *The Birth of a Nation* opened in 1916 to standing-room-only crowds which came on special trains from communities in a hundred mile radius. Ticket sales were reported "absolutely unprecedented in show business here." Movies, however, contributed to the demise of the Colonial, as new theaters were constructed and traveling troups became scarce. The building also began to deteriorate and large parts of the plaster ceiling collapsed in 1928. Fortunately it was on a Sunday evening and no one was in the theater. Finally in September, 1832, city engineer Jack Beecham condemned the old building and it was taken down. The rear addition of McLellan's store now occupies the site. Photograph from the author's collection

The Holman Building, built in 1913, dominates this early 1920s view of Clayton Street at the intersection of Lumpkin. In 1914 the proprietor, W. S. Holman, advertised 168 offices for rent, complete with steam heat, hot and cold running water, and elevators. They were, he said, "considered to be the coolest offices in the state"; a definite selling point in the days before air conditioning. The ninth floor was designed to accomodate social functions—dances, meetings, and other gatherings. When the office building did not prove successful it was converted into the Holman Hotel, the Georgian's chief competitor for many years.

In the early 1960s the C & S Bank gutted and redesigned the interior and resurfaced the exterior for its principal Athens office. The building, which once again houses business and professional offices on the upper floors, was opened in April 1964. To the left of Holman in the photograph is the Strand Theatre. Cooper's Cafe adjoins the Strand in the commercial building on the far left.

At the right of the photo, across Lumpkin Street, is the Athens Empire Laundry. In the 1911 Athens Banner, the laundry's manager, Clare D. Heidler, touted the new "French Dry Cleaning Plant," which had been recently installed, adding that "the Athens Empire Laundry is clean, sanitary, and only healthy persons are employed." The corner location is now occupied by Abbott's Restaurant. Photograph courtesy of Mrs. J. B. Adams

A person who had not visited Athens since this photograph was taken in 1923 would have little trouble recognizing College Avenue today. There have been a few changes: the streetcar has long since disappeared, the Commercial Bank no longer exists, the chamber of commerce, the Post

Office and Western Union have found other quarters, and that favorite institution, Costa's, is just a memory. Some of the storefronts have been "modernized," but most of the buildings remain remarkably the same. In an effort to enhance the turn-of-the-century atmosphere, the city of Athens and the Athens Downtown Development Authority gave the streetscape a facelift in 1981, widening the sidewalks and planting trees and flowers. Photograph by Gates; courtesy of Isabel Wier McWilliams

The structure which dominates the skyline in the photograph of College Avenue on the previous page is the Southern Mutual Building. It was Athens's first "skyscraper" and is the best example in Northeast Georgia of the early twentieth century Commercial style of architecture. The building was erected in 1908 of brick-faced reinforced concrete at a cost of $225,000, replacing the company's earlier mansard-roofed headquarters building of 1876, which was moved to make way for the new ediface.

The company offices, which remain largely unchanged from their appearance in 1908, still have the rich oak furnishings, beveled glass, brass fixtures, and other has-beens of a more elegant period. This photograph could have been taken in 1910 rather than in 1980. The company remains an Athens tradition since moving to the city in 1848, the year after its founding. Photograph by Ellen Fitzgerald; courtesy of Athens Newspapers, Incorporated

"Costa's," said Dean William Tate,"—that was a magic word with us students in the 1920s, and with Athens people, too, and with alumni in their memories: over three decades of service!" Nearly everyone that visited the famous ice cream parlor in the Southern Mutual Building from 1908 until it closed about 1939 seems to have shared Dean Tate's enthusiasm. It was a social institution, and the place to go in Athens during the years it was open.

This photograph was taken shortly after the opening of Costa's on September 8, 1908. The Costa family standing behind the counter of their elaborate marble soda fountain are, from left to right: Mike John, Lea, Tony, Fred, Jim, Charlie, Jimmy Porter, Rosa, and Lawrence. Mirrors lined the walls and ceiling fans cooled the customers sitting at the tables.

The fountain delights, according to those who experienced them, were almost indescribable. You could have a fountain Coke for five cents, with a squirt of lemon, lime, or orange if you wished. Their chocolate milk made today's prepackaged concoction pale in comparison—a large glass of milk with an ounce of chocolate syrup, a scoop of ice cream plus a dash of whipped cream with a cherry on top—all for a dime. A huge banana split was only a quarter.

The cashier stood behind a glass showcase filled with candies of all descriptions. There was also a cigarette counter which served as a clearing house for thousands of athletic tickets. In their later years, Costa's added a restaurant, up a few steps to the rear of the ice cream parlor, where one could choose among their famous frozen fruit salads and other light meals. When Costa's finally closed its doors, Athens lost one of its great traditions. Photograph courtesy of Georgia Department of Archives and History

One of the factors contributing to the great success of the Costa family was the ice cream they sold. Originally made for their own soda fountain use, it became so popular that they erected a yellow brick building on Washington Street to manufacture it commercially. Their slogan for the ice cream was "Just a little bit better," and its popularity attests to the fact that it was.

The two Costa's cars, shown here in front of the ice cream factory, became almost symbols for the company. The building, which is still standing, now houses the Athens Police Department. Photograph courtesy of Gary Doster

Costa's was a particularly popular place to gather after University of Georgia football games to discuss the winning plays or analyze the disappointing defeats. One of the groups that met informally at Costa's was known as the Uptown Coaches, shown in this photograph at the entrance on College Avenue.

They are, seated from left to right: Speck Towns, Coach J. B. Whitworth, Harry Atwell, J. T. Kilpatrick, and Coach Bill Hartman (leaning against column). Standing in the rear, left to right, are: Tony Costa, Dr. Marion Hubert, and Dr. Leroy Edwards. Photograph courtesy of Nina Costa

This Historic American Buildings Survey photograph of the Franklin House was taken in 1936 when it was occupied by the Athens Hardware Company and a branch of the Dunlop Tire and Rubber Company. The building was constructed on the corner of Broad and Clayton streets about 1847 as an elegant hotel. Advertisements of the 1840s and 1850s indicate that it was popular with itinerant drummers and professional people, including daguerreotypists, music teachers, dancing instructors, French teachers, lawyers, and dentists.

Commercial spaces were located on the street level, while the guest rooms occupied the upper floors. Additions were made to the rear of the building in the 1850s. When the builder, William L. Mitchell, died in 1860, the property was sold for $16,300. It continued to be used as a hotel throughout the War Between the States, serving as home for a number of war refugees.

In 1865 the Childs-Nickerson Company opened a hardware store in the building. They changed their name to Athens Hardware Company in 1885 and continued to occupy the structure until 1972. During that period, part of the building was demolished, and the three-story building, seen at the far right of the photograph, was built. Photograph by L. D. Andrews, (August 13, 1963); from HABS, Library of Congress

This photograph of the Georgia Factory, one of Athens's major industrial plants in the nineteenth and early twentieth centuries, was taken during the early 1920s. The original textile factory on this site had been established in 1830 by John Johnson, Augustin S. Clayton, Abram Walker, John Nisbet, and William Dearing, and was probably the first major textile factory in Georgia.

The factory was purchased later in the century by John White, and it became the foundation of the extensive manufacturing, commercial, and banking interests of the White family. The community of Whitehall grew up around this factory and the later Whitehall Manufacturing Company, which was opened in 1895.

The original factory burned in 1892 and was replaced by the factory in the photograph the following year. The factory complex, now remodeled and extended, is occupied by Thomas Textiles, a clothing manufacturer. Photograph courtesy of Mrs. J. B. Adams

Drugstores in the 1930s dispensed not only medicines and sundries, but also sodas, ice cream, soft drinks, and a wide variety of fountain delights. They were popular gathering places for students and townspeople and competed enthusiastically for their patronage. This photograph provides a view of the interior of Patrick's Pharmacy in 1935.

Dr. J. K. Patrick, a graduate of the university's pharmacy school, operated this establishment for many years in the space now occupied by Rosenthal's Shoe Store on Clayton Street. A soda fountain provided refreshments, and Dr. Patrick was the first in Athens to sell pre-wrapped sandwiches, which were truly home-made, at his counter. Delivery boys would take soft drinks to many of the businesses around town.

The portraits on the walls were of the members of the 1935 University of Georgia football team and coaching staff. They were painted by local artist Jack E. Parr from photographs made in Arnett Studios. In the center of the poster on the rear balcony railing is the portrait of head coach Harry Mehre, which moved from side to side by an electric motor.

The artist, Jack Parr, later taught in Clarke County schools and organized the art program in the city's recreation department. On the rear counter is a small car, powered by a Briggs and Stratton engine, that was given away in a contest held by the store. Photograph courtesy of Jack E. Parr

In 1907 this Antebellum house became Athens's newest hospital through the efforts of Doctors J. P. Proctor and H. M. Fullilove. The house, which occupied the block bounded by Milledge, Hancock, Harris, and Meigs streets, had been built in 1855 by Sampson Harris and sold toward the end of the century to Bolling Stovall. The doctors purchased it from the Stovall family, renovated it completely, and opened it to their patients on April 17, 1907.

The hospital, named St. Mary's, had the first clinical x-ray machine and first ambulance (a one-horse vehicle) in Athens. When a new hospital was being constructed in 1918, the old house was moved to the rear of the lot near Harris Street.

When the Catholic Sisters took over the operation of the hospital this building was used as a convent. It was demolished in the early 1970s. The staff is shown seated on the front steps of the hospital. Photograph courtesy of University of Georgia Libraries Special Collections

One of the founders of St. Mary's Hospital, Dr. J. Peebles Proctor, was killed in this tragic accident on Jefferson Road on April 13, 1924. Dr. Proctor, who carried a collapsible operating table in his car, was on his way to Jefferson, Georgia, to perform an emergency operation. He was speeding along the narrow dirt Jefferson Road and ran off the bridge over the Seaboard Railroad tracks. The car plunged into the ravine, killing Proctor and a student nurse, Irene Day. Another nurse, Nellie Eberhardt, was injured but survived.

In this photograph, curious onlookers are inspecting the wreckage; and the convict road crew, in the striped prison garb, have come to repair the bridge railing. The site of the accident is at the present U. S. 78 bypass where Jefferson Road crosses the railroad tracks. Photograph courtesy of Mrs. J. B. Adams

In 1918 Doctors Fullilove and Proctor contracted with William W. Ferquerson to build this four-story brick faced, reinforced concrete building to replace the original St. Mary's Hospital. When completed the following year, it had doctors' offices, a staff dining room, a kitchen, an x-ray room, and a laboratory in the basement; and a check-in room, an emergency room, and several patient rooms on the first floor. On the upper floors were patient rooms and operating rooms.

The two doctors tended exclusively to their own patients until after Dr. Proctor's death, when it was then opened to any doctor who wished to practice there. The hospital was closed in 1937, two years after Dr. Fullilove's death. In 1938 it was purchased by the Missionary Sisters of the Most Sacred Heart of Jesus. The sisters renovated the hospital and installed new equipment after purchasing the building, and the hospital received the approval of the American College of Surgeons in 1940.

Two years later, a new wing known as St. Joseph's Hall was constructed between the main building and the convent. An additional wing was added in 1947, bringing the hospital's capacity to 100 beds. In 1966 a new 139 bed, $3.2 million hospital was completed and the old St. Mary's was closed. The property was sold in 1969, and the buildings were demolished in the early 1970s. Photograph courtesy of University of Georgia Libraries Special Collections

Athens General Hospital was organized by a group of local civic leaders in 1919, and two years later the new 100 bed hospital building was opened. Initially, twenty-four doctors practiced at the hospital. In 1924 Clarke County purchased the building and operated it through a board of trustees until September 1960, when the Hospital Authority of Clarke County was formed and took over control of the facilities. A major addition to the original building, begun in 1948 and completed in 1951, provided space for 100 beds, three operating rooms, several recovery rooms, an emergency department, and a delivery room. The price tag was $600,000.

A six-story addition was made in 1971-72, and older areas were renovated. Expansion continued during the 1970s and included the acquisition of additional property north of Cobb Street and west of Talmadge Drive. In 1980, Cobb Street was closed beyond King Avenue and the area was graded for parking. 1985 marked the beginning of an extensive new construction program, including the opening of an outpatient surgery center in the historic Talmadge House. This photograph, taken in 1926, shows the original Athens General before the many additions were made. Photograph by Gates; courtesy of University of Georgia Libraries Special Collections

During the 1920s, the Clarke County Anti-Tuberculosis Society erected this building as a T. B. sanitarium at a cost of $50,000. There were thirty beds, equally distributed between black and white patients. The society also employed a public health nurse to conduct a free tuberculosis screening clinic once a week and raised money to provide relief for the families of patients.

The building was later remodeled and converted for use as part of the Memorial Park facilities. It currently houses offices of the city Recreation and Parks Department. Photograph by Gates; courtesy of University of Georgia Libraries Special Collections

In 1915 Athens High School moved from its Childs Street building into the old Clarke County Courthouse which had been vacated the year before by county offices. The enlarged and renovated building had a capacity for 450 students, but only 264 were in attendance that first year. Programs quickly expanded, and by 1926 (when this photograph was taken), the school boasted a main building, an auditorium, a gymnasium and swimming pool, a manual training building, and a teachers' home.

Extra-curricular activities included band, orchestra, glee club, dramatic club, honor club, French club, literary societies, a newspaper, R.O.T.C., football, baseball, basketball, and track, all supported by an active P.T.A.

The school proudly reported that 80 percent of its graduates had attended higher institutions in the years 1923-1925, a record it enjoyed for many years. In 1939 a new brick gymnasium was constructed to provide more up-to-date facilities. A need for a new high school building became apparent, however, in the 1940s, and the present building was erected in 1951-52 on a twenty-six acre site west of Milledge Avenue. The old building was soon demolished. Finley Street was extended through the site to Prince Avenue and today Wendy's and Captain D's restaurants are located on part of the original campus. Photograph courtesy of University of Georgia Libraries Special Collections

This interior view of Mell Auditorium on the old campus of Athens High School was taken shortly after the completion of the structure in 1923. Part of the exterior may be seen to the right of the main building in the photograph of the high school, above.

It was named for Edward B. Mell, who served as principal of the high school for thirty-seven years. Although it was demolished in the 1970s, the memory of E. B. Mell and of this facility are perpetuated in the present Mell Auditorium at Clarke Central High School. Photograph courtesy of Mrs. J. B. Adams

The members of the 1925 Athens High School girls' basketball team lined up in front of Mell Auditorium for their photograph after winning the state championship without losing a single game. This formidable team repeated their performance the following year.

Members of the team are, from left to right: Kit Bowden, Laura Bradbury, Lucy Pound, Nell Slaughter, Martha Evans, Mildred Frierson, Rebecca Means, and Clyde Algood. Photograph courtesy of Lucy Pound Huggins

There were always dramas, plays, pageants, and performances of all kinds presented by the girls of Lucy Cobb Institute. These two photographs show the youngest and oldest girls demonstrating their theatrical talents.

This kindergarten group is shown rehearsing an operetta which was performed at commencement in 1927. The lone bumble bee is surrounded by a swarm of female butterflies. The butterflies are l-r: Ida Davison, Janet DuBose, Phyllis Jenkins, Catherine Davis, Elizabeth Lamkin, Louise Chandler, Emma Bowen, and Betty Crews. The bumble bee is Harrison Hiedler. Photograph courtesy of Georgia Department of Archives and History

In this photograph the older students are shown presenting one of Shakespeare's plays in the open area between the main school building and the two-story cottage at the rear of the Milledge Avenue campus. Many alumnae still recall their dramatic debuts in one of the Bard's great plays at Lucy Cobb. In a complete reversal of the practice in Shakespeare's time, all of the parts were played by women. Photograph courtesy of Mrs. J. B. Adams

The Publicity Committee of the Children of the Confederacy, organized under the sponsorship of Miss Millie Rutherford at Lucy Cobb Institute, is seen here advertising the sale of the Stone Mountain Memorial half-dollars, April 25, 1929.

Seated, left to right, are: Mary Alice Jester, Winifred Bowers, Laura Ann Phinizy, Pauline Hadaway, Mary Cobb Erwin, Nell Johnson, Lamar Lipscomb, Mary Lamar Erwin, Lucy Deupree Erwin, Martha Carter Storey, and Amelie Freeman. The driver is unidentified. *Photograph courtesy of University of Georgia Libraries Special Collections*

Fred A. Birchmore was photographed here about 1936 after his round-the-world bicycle trip. He rode his bicycle, named Bucephalus after the war horse of Alexander the Great, across North America, Asia, and Europe. Among his many adventures along the way was a solo ascent, sans cycle, of the Matterhorn. The blue steel, one-speed Reinhardt bicycle he rode is now a possession of the Smithsonian Institution.

Birchmore, an Athens native, earned a doctor of laws degree, but opted instead for a career in real estate. Still living in Athens, he is sought after as a public speaker and has participated in many community activities, serving as a Boy Scout leader, Girl Scout leader, tennis coach, and youth camp director.

In recent years he has hiked the Inca Trail in Peru, backpacked over the entire Appalachian Trail in 101 days, and retraced the European part of his bike trip with his son Danny. *Photograph courtesy of Georgia Department of Archives and History*

In 1903 Judia C. Jackson Harris founded the Model and Training School on four acres of land she donated on the old Danielsville Road north of Athens. Mrs. Harris, the second wife of Athens High and Industrial School principal Samuel F. Harris, was born in Athens and was educated at Atlanta University, Hampton, and Harvard. She returned to Athens to teach, soon becoming interested in the education of rural blacks. She began organizing the black tenant farmers into land clubs which would purchase farms from money they raised collectively. She sponsored agricultural fairs where people brought their pickles, cakes, and quilts, as well as livestock and other farm products.

Mrs. Harris also operated a summer cannery for local farmers and their families. The General Education Board of New York gave the money for the school in 1903, and the county provided the furnishings. When the school burned in 1926, Mrs. Harris mobilized her supporters to raise money for the new building (shown in the photograph), which was completed in 1929. It had four classrooms, a lobby, an office, and a library. The curriculum was a strenuous one, including algebra, Latin, and black history, and many of the school's graduates went on to college.

Mrs. Harris also had a love for plays and pageants, some of which were presented in the Moss Auditorium (later the Belk's store), the Morton Theatre, and the Colonial Theatre. Judia Harris retired from the school in 1950, six years before the school closed. Four years later she died at the age of eighty-seven, having made a major lasting contribution to black rural education in Georgia. Many of her students became educators and community leaders. Mrs. Harris may be seen in the photograph in the dark dress standing on the brick pier to the left of the entrance. Photograph courtesy of Helen Neal Joseph

This early aerial photograph shows the South Campus of the university as it appeared about 1923. Writing in that year, Dr. Andrew Soule, president of the State College of Agriculture, valued the physical plant, with sixteen buildings on more than 100 acres, at $1.5 million. The large building in the center of the photograph is Connor Hall (1908), the administration building for the college of agriculture. In front of Connor stands the Rock House (1844), originally the home of Governor Lumpkin. The open grassy slope in front and to the left of Connor Hall is now the site of the Science Center, the single largest expansion of university facilities in the history of the institution. The $12.5 million complex, housing chemistry, biological sciences, livestock and poultry sciences, food sciences, mathematics, geography, and geology, was dedicated on January 6, 1959, before all of the structures were completed.

The buildings at the far left of the photograph are the Veterinary Hospital (1910) and the Veterinary Medicine Building (1914). Directly behind Connor at right angles, obscured except for its roof, is Barrow Hall (1911-1916). Just to the right and behind Connor are the old greenhouses. Behind these can be seen the large amphitheatre which was used for outdoor theater performances and as a place for graduation ceremonies and other large gatherings until the Science Library and Graduate Studies Building was begun in the late 1960s.

To the right of the amphitheatre is Soule Hall (1919-1920), originally known as the Woman's Building. To the left is Hardman Hall (1918-1923), the animal husbandry building which contained an arena for livestock shows. Behind the amphitheatre, to the right, are the cavalry barns. In the far background, to the left of the road are the Sheep Building and Camp Wilkins (the roof of which is visible in the thick stand of trees). The open area behind Hardman Hall contains some of the experimental plots for testing new crops and agricultural methods. Photograph courtesy of Georgia Libraries Special Collections

The Veterinary Hospital, shown here during the 1920s, was erected to the east of Connor Hall in 1910. In 1914 a new veterinary medicine building was constructed adjacent to the hospital to, in part, provide a laboratory for production of hog cholera serum for Georgia farmers. When the State College of Agriculture was merged with the university during the 1932-33 reorganization of state colleges and universities, the veterinary medicine program was dropped.

The program was revived in 1946, and five years later the present building was completed on the site of the old Sheep Barn. The vet school today provides one of the nation's best veterinary medicine programs in its substantially expanded and modernized facilities. Photograph courtesy of University of Georgia Libraries Special Collections

The summer school short courses at the college of agriculture were popular with students during the 1920s. This class was photographed between Connor Hall and the old greenhouses. Soule Hall can be seen in the background.

The activities in the photograph were probably under the direction of Miss Laura Blackshear, who directed pageants and supervised dance classes as well as other recreational activities. The sight of her students doing "Here We Go Loop-de-Loop" was said to convulse even the most reserved spectator. Photograph courtesy of Mrs. J. B. Adams

By 1919 the university law school had outgrown its cramped quarters in Academic Building and additional space was required for its growing programs. The problem was solved by the purchase of the Athenaeum Club which stood opposite the campus on the northeast corner of Broad and Lumpkin streets. The building had been constructed in 1884 as a social club. The scope of the Athenaeum Club was broadened about 1899 into a business club when the organization merged with the Commercial Club of Athens. In 1901 there were 240 members.

The structure housed parlors, reception rooms, reading rooms, a billiard room, a gymnasium, and baths. Among those who served as president were Billups Phinizy, Moses Michael, and J. H. Rucker. By 1914 the Elks Club owned the building. The law school used the Athenaeum from 1919 until 1932 when Harold Hirsch Hall was completed on the campus, culminating an effort begun in 1927 to reorganize the school, expand the faculty, and provide up-to-date facilities and an adequate library.

The old building was later demolished, and the site is now used as a parking lot for the C & S Bank which bought the Holman Hotel (shown behind the Athenaeum in the photograph) in the 1960s, renovating it for their Athens headquarters. Photograph courtesy of University of Georgia Libraries Special Collections

Camp Wilkins was an important part of the summer program at the university in the 1920s and 1930s. In 1926, 662 Camp Wilkins boys and 430 Camp Wilkins girls were counted among the students of the college of agriculture. They came from all over the state to participate in agricultural short courses. The camp was located on the site of the present Agricultural Engineering Building.

The original Camp Wilkins dormitory was constructed with a donation from the Wilkins family of Athens and housed agricultural and forestry students during the regular terms. The facilities were very basic, not luxurious, and provided inexpensive housing for many hard-pressed students.

This photograph was taken some time between 1926 and 1932 and shows a group of Camp Wilkins girls cooking breakfast in the open air after returning from an early summer morning hike. Photograph courtesy of Georgia Department of Archives and History

This strange ensemble drawn up in front of the Georgian Hotel on Washington Street is part of a Sphinx initiation. The Sphinx is a secret society at the university, and membership in the organization is the highest honor a male student can achieve. Selection is based on academic and athletic performance, and other achievements. Each new member is given a number which is engraved on his gold sphinx pin.

Initiates, at the time this photograph was taken, had to dress up in outlandish costumes and appear about town. The members then joined the senior parade, in which they were often the most colorful and zany participants. The tradition of dressing in costume has been replaced by sewing a large white "S" on the back of the initiates' jackets. Photograph courtesy of Mrs. J. B. Adams

For many years, one of the social high points of the college year was Little Commencement, which was held in April on the weekend of the Tech-Georgia baseball game. In the days before coeducation, the college boys invited their hometown sweethearts to come to Athens for the weekend. A big band was imported for the festivities which included tea dances on Friday and Saturday afternoons, big dances on Friday and Saturday nights, and the "bawdy and spectacular senior parade" from downtown to Sanford Field on Saturday afternoon.

This photograph shows the participants in one senior parade on the Chapel steps before the beginning of the parade. Little Commencement was gradually replaced by homecoming festivities during football season in the fall, and the senior parade became a thing of the past. Photograph courtesy of University of Georgia Libraries Special Collections

The Octagon was a wooden building said to have been designed about 1914 or 1915 by Chancellor Barrow "like an umbrella, because you could get more that way under one roof" (Tate, Strolls). It stood to the east of the old Chancellor's House on the site of the present Main Library parking lot. It had a stage with a basketball court in front of it on the side opposite the main entrance. Bleachers were arranged around the other sides.

The building was open under the eaves for ventilation and a hard, blowing rain would sometimes come in. It was used only during warm weather. Dances, theatrical performances, and even high school commencements were held there for about twenty-five years until the wooden building had decayed beyond feasible repair and was demolished. Photograph courtesy of Anne and Branch Howe

This crowd was gathered at the Southern Railway depot on Hoyt Street in 1927 to greet the Georgia Bulldog football team returning from Yale after a 14-0 victory over the Elis. The Southern depot was a busy place in the 1920s, but by 1969 it was vacant, deserted, in a sea of kudzu behind a public housing project. Local restaurateur Lee Epting and partners obtained a lease on the property from the railroad and began the arduous task of rehabilitating the station and warehouse as a restaurant and entertainment complex. By 1972 the Station opened with a restaurant in a refurbished dining car, the Valdosta; a cabaret; several stores; and T. K. Harty's Saloon. The business thrived for a while and then slumped. Epting and partners sold to T. K. Harty, who was murdered shortly after taking over the operation. After a brief revival, there was another decline. The complex again stands empty. Photograph courtesy of Athens Newspapers, Incorporated

This photograph shows Sanford Stadium after its completion in 1929, looking from west to east across the famous playing field "between the hedges." In the background is the Central of Georgia Railroad track which was a favorite viewing-place for students until the east end of the stadium was enclosed in 1981.

The original seating capacity was about 33,000. The addition of the upper decks increased the total to about 58,000. Approximately 76,000 fans can now be accomodated with the east end addition and new bleachers in the west end. Photograph courtesy of University of Georgia Libraries Special Collections

As football became more popular during the 1920s, replacing baseball as the favorite intercollegiate sport, it became apparent that Sanford Field was not able to accommodate the fans who began to come from all parts of the state to Georgia games. Dean Steadman Sanford engineered the drive that culminated in a new stadium that would bear his name.

A plan was devised to finance the construction through a loan from the Atlanta and Lowry National Bank (now the Trust Company of Georgia) guaranteed by alumni and friends of the university, including many prominent Athenians. They agreed upon a site to the east of Sanford Field—a natural bowl-shaped depression along Tanyard Branch which had been used to grow plants for the campus and the botanical labs. Work was begun, using convict labor, in 1928 and was completed the following year. The cost was $237,000.

This photograph, looking north from Ag Hill, was taken during the early stages of construction. The concrete culvert in the foreground carries the waters of Tanyard Branch. In the upper left is the Antebellum Lucas House which was used for some years after the completion of the stadium as an athletic dorm. Photograph courtesy of University of Georgia Libraries Special Collections

Sanford Stadium was inaugurated by a game between Georgia and Yale on October 12, 1929. More than 30,000 people came by car and special train from all over the state to see the dedication ceremony and game, paying three dollars a ticket for the privilege. The hotels and restaurants were crowded to capacity. Athenians opened their homes to visitors, and local entrepreneurs set up food stands along Broad Street to help feed the hungry crowds. The Yale band, playing "Dixie," led the team from the railroad depot, through town, and to the stadium.

The ceremonies were opened by Chancellor Charles M. Snelling, who gave a welcoming address. Dean George Nettleton answered on behalf of Yale. Dr. Sanford was then presented a loving cup and $1,500 by the alumni in appreciation of his efforts to secure the new facility. Abraham Baldwin, a Yale graduate and first president of the Univerity of Georgia, was also honored in the ceremonies. Georgia entered the field the underdogs, but finished on top with a 15-0 victory. It was the "best defensive game of any Georgia 11 in recent years," according to the Pandora that year.

A blocked punt in the second quarter was recovered by Georgia's Vernon Smith for the first score of the game, which was followed by an extra point. In the third quarter the Yale quarterback was sacked behind his goal for a safety. Georgia's Smith caught a pass in the closing minute of the game for the final six points. The team went on to finish the season 6-4. This photograph shows the cover of the souvenir program for the game. Program courtesy of Carol Yoder

In 1938 President Franklin Delano Roosevelt came to the University of Georgia to receive an honorary doctor of laws degree. Roosevelt had visited Georgia for a number of years and had built the Little White House at Warm Springs in Meriwether County where he received treatment for polio.

During the early years of his administration, he was repeatedly attacked by Georgia Governor Eugene Talmadge, a staunch opponent of the New Deal. Roosevelt felt more at home on his visits to Georgia after the election of pro-New Dealer Eurith D. Rivers as governor in 1936.

This photograph shows, from left to right, Chancellor Steadman Sanford, Governor Rivers, and President Roosevelt at Sanford Stadium for the 1938 ceremony, where Roosevelt accepted his honorary degree and gave a brief speech. Roosevelt later went to Barnesville, Georgia, where he delivered a blistering attack on Georgia's Senator Walter F. George, who was running for re-election.

Although Roosevelt was popular with Georgians, they rejected his interference in state politics and re-elected Senator George by a good margin. Photograph courtesy of University of Georgia Libraries Special Collections

In 1928 Major A. T. Colley, an R.O.T.C. instructor, organized the first polo team at the university. The team used the cavalry horses which were stabled just north of the present Coliseum in an area of campus which was part of the college of agriculture's experimental farm. By 1931 Georgia fielded an eight man squad which played five games against two teams, Savannah and Fort McPherson. They won one game that year, beating Fort Mac 12-11.

Although they had only one victory, campus sportswriter Jimmy McIntyre wrote that "in all of the other games Georgia made their opponents realize they were playing a developing team." When horses disappeared from the military units about the time of World War II, so did polo on the university campus.

This photograph of the polo team was taken during the 1930s on the playing field near the present track. The houses along Lumpkin Street may be seen in the background. Photograph courtesy of University of Georgia Libraries Special Collections

In 1932 the General Assembly passed a plan for the reorganization of state colleges and universities under the control of a board of regents. As part of this reorganization, the State College of Agricultural and Mechanical Arts and the State Teachers' College (State Normal) were merged with the university, taking an equal place with other schools and colleges within the institution under the leadership of a dean. With the move of the State Teachers' College to the main campus, some use had to be found for the old normal school on Prince Avenue.

It became the Coordinate College for freshmen and sophomore girls. While the Prince Avenue location may have appeared to offer a "safe haven" away from the main campus for the girls, it proved to be inconvenient.

After World War II, the United States Navy acquired the property, moving its Supply Corps School to Athens in 1954. This photograph shows the old auditorium and the gates of the Coordinate College about 1933. The building was later demolished by the United States Navy. Photograph courtesy of Lucy Pound Huggins

This photograph was taken during a fashion show which was held about 1933 in Pound Auditorium at the Coordinate College. The outfits were provided by Michael Brothers Department Store and were modeled by university students.

Pound Auditorium is now used by the Navy School as a gymnasium and athletic building. Photograph by Arnett Studios; courtesy of Lucy Pound Huggins

William T. Peek was one of Athens's most colorful and popular figures during his long career as a traveling salesman, and his house on College Avenue near the Seaboard depot became a familiar city landmark. This photograph shows some of the garden sculpture—lions, urns, and a cannon, among others—that gave the place its distinctive character.

The owner, however, was no less colorful than his residence. Peek began his career as a traveling hardware salesman in 1891 when he was thirty years old and continued uninterrupted until the age of eighty-five. He soon developed his distinctive trademark, the slogan "Peek-A-Boo, I'll See You." He had cards printed with this one phrase and sent them ahead to his customers with the date of his visit written on the bottom.

In the early days he traveled by horse and buggy, staying in hotels along his way. He was able to visit his customers in a fifty mile radius from Athens about once every six months, taking orders and spinning stories. He claimed never to have lost a customer except by death or business failure. When the automobile came on the scene, Will Peek was the first "drummer" in Athens to use one, once making a record-breaking 100 mile round trip to Union Point in one day.

Peek's slogan became known by everyone, and he even received mail addressed "Peek-A-Boo, Athens, Georgia." He put it on everything: his stationery, his checks, in tile on the sidewalk in front of his house. When he neared eighty he even had his tombstone engraved with the message, "Peek-A-Boo, I'll See You."

At the age of eighty-five, Peek was forced by a heart attack to give up traveling, and he died three years later. His house is gone, and his familiar calling cards are no longer received by area hardware dealers, but one can still find his friendly slogan in Oconee Hill Cemetery. Photograph courtesy of University of Georgia Libraries Special Collections

This photograph was taken about 1925, just after the completion of the home of Mr. and Mrs. M. G. Michael on the northwest corner of Milledge and Woodlawn avenues. The house was later occupied by Mr. and Mrs. LeRoy Michael. The house was one of only four buildings in Athens designed by the noted Atlanta architect, Neel Reid.

The three other buildings by the firm of Hentz, Reid, and Adler are the Commerce-Journalism Building on the university campus, the Michael Brothers Department Store, and the White House (now Delta Tau Delta fraternity) on Prince Avenue. The landscaping of the Michael House, which can be seen in progress in the photograph, was done by Craig Orr of Athens, third from the left.

The house was remodeled beyond recognition by the Lamda Chi fraternity for a chapter house and dormitory. The building is now a two-story brick Neo-Greek Revival structure with a white columned portico. Photograph courtesy of Mrs. J. B. Adams

This photograph shows members of the Sphinx on College Avenue downtown lampooning Governor Eugene Talmadge for his interference with the internal affairs of the university which caused the loss of its accreditation. The affair, often referred to as the Cocking Case, was a deadly serious one with students, parents, faculty, and alumni and eventually caused Talmadge to lose the governorship.

Soon after taking office in 1941, Governor Talmadge apparently became convinced that communist and integrationist ideas were beginning to permeate the university system in Georgia. As evidence, he cited the accusations of Mrs. Sylla Hamilton, a former teacher in the practice school operated by the college of education, who had been fired during the reorganization of the college. She charged that Dean Walter D. Cocking had advocated mixing the races in the state's schools. In spite of a report by Regents' Chairman Sandy Beaver (a friend and supporter of Talmadge) clearing Cocking of the charges, the governor moved in a May 1941 meeting of the board of regents that Cocking be fired. The motion passed eight to four.

After the resignation in protest of University President Harmon Caldwell, a hearing was convened in Atlanta to reconsider the matter. This time the regents voted eight to seven to reinstate Cocking. The governor then sought and got another meeting in July. Between meetings he succeeded in replacing several regents who had opposed the ouster, and when the matter was again brought to the floor, Cocking was dismissed on a ten to five vote. The move to take over the board of regents was necessary, according to Talmadge, to remove "foreign professors trying to destroy the sacred traditions of the South." With Talmadge forces securely in control of the board, other university employees were soon dismissed and there followed a purge of "subversive" textbooks from the public schools of the state.

Reacting to these developments, the Southern Conference of Universities voted unanimously in October of 1941 to drop the university from membership in the organization, triggering a protest by university students who paraded through Athens until 3 a.m., burning Talmadge in effigy three times. In December, just days before Pearl Harbor, the Southern Association of Colleges and Secondary Schools revoked the accreditation of the university and the other state-supported colleges in Georgia, citing the unacceptable political interference in academic affairs.

A wave of protest swept the state. Virtually every newspaper opposed the actions of the governor; and Talmadge, who had underestimated public reaction to his policies, was defeated in his bid for re-election in 1942 by the young attorney general, Ellis Arnall. Under Arnall, the board of regents was reorganized and, to an extent, de-politicised. This action brought re-accreditation for the university and an end to the Cocking case. Photograph courtesy of University of Georgia Libraries Special Collections

Chapter Four
1941-1985

In the years 1941 to 1985, Athens grew dramatically, more than doubling its population from 20,650 to 42,549. The combined city-county population rose to 74,498, four times its total in 1900, as suburban developments spread into the surrounding countryside.

The year 1941 found the town and campus preoccupied with the Cocking affair, during which the university lost its accreditation because of political interference by the governor in the operation of the statewide university system. In the midst of this crisis, the nation was plunged into World War II. The war had an immediate effect on Athens—thousands of soldiers and sailors came to the university for training and major new facilities were constructed on campus to accommodate them. During the course of the conflict, many Athenians and university alumni (always considered as part of the extended Athens family) served their country with distinction. People on the home front rallied to support the war effort. The Ladies' Garden Club, the nation's first, once again set an example for the country by initiating a program to encourage vegetable and herb growing and the preservation of foods from those "victory gardens." Local residents recall summers of sweltering heat at the cannery on Boulevard where they put up fruits, vegetables, and meat for home use. Although rationing of food, fuel, and other vital commodities caused Athenians considerable inconvenience, the city shared in the general economic resurgence that the war brought about in Georgia, accomplishing more than all of the New Deal programs of the 1930s. Athens has continued to share in this renewed prosperity into the 1980s.

The G. I. Bill of Rights, passed by Congress in June 1944, brought a flood of veterans to the university after the war. Total enrollment in 1940 was 3,631, but by 1947 there were 7,846 students attending classes at the university, of which more than 4,300 were veterans. The additional students generated new funds which were used to expand programs and increase the number of faculty. Enrollment continued to grow dramatically in the post-war period, reaching over 24,000 in the early 1980s, a near seven-fold increase in forty years. The university campus, too, underwent a transformation; new buildings were erected to house expanded programs and old buildings were given new uses. Major new structures include: the science center complex, Gilbert Infirmary, Ilah Dunlap Little Library, the Veterinary School, Georgia Center for Continuing Education, the Coliseum, Visual Arts, Myers and Reed Halls, the high-rise dormitories on Baxter Street, Pharmacy School, Law School additions, the bookstore, the Psychology-Journalism complex, Graduate Studies building, and College of Education. There are now more than 200 buildings on the 581-acre main campus.

Academically, the university's reputation has vastly improved from the days when young Georgians were advised to go to a Northeastern or Midwestern university for a graduate education. Many university programs have achieved national recognition. The school's athletic teams have continued to enjoy the loyalty of Georgia fans. In 1940 a state guidebook reported that "many sports-loving Georgians regard the university as a mere adjunct to its football team." Perhaps the most memorable game (before the Bulldogs won the 1980 National Football Championship) was Georgia's victory over U.C.L.A. in the Rose Bowl on New Year's Day 1943, amid fears of a Japanese invasion of the West Coast.

During the past forty years, the university's student body has become more diverse, comprising a cross-section of Georgia's population, students from across the country, and a large group of international students. Campus educational, cultural, and social activities draw wide participation from the town as well as the university community. The town calendar closely tracks that of the university. Athens seems almost deserted during quarter breaks but comes alive again on the first day of the new term.

Other educational opportunities are also available in the Athens area. In 1949 the Christian College of

Declaring that the time had come for "Georgians to insist that political dictatorship shall no longer throttle and hamstring the operations of our state," Ellis Arnall declared his candidacy for governor in 1942 in a radio address over station WSB in Atlanta. He stumped the state in his effort to unseat Governor Eugene Talmadge and institute the reforms which would bring a return of accreditation to Georgia's institutions of higher learning. Arnall is seen in this photograph speaking to a large crowd gathered on Broad Street in front of the university arch.

No stranger to Athens, Arnall had attended the University of Georgia law school, serving as president of his class, the Pan-Hellenic Council, Phi Delta Phi, the Gridiron Club, the student body, and other campus organizations. After graduating first in his class, he practiced law in Newnan, served in the General Assembly, and was appointed to the post of attorney general, winning a term in his own right in 1940 without opposition. Removing the governor from state boards and commissions, including the board of regents, was only one plank in his reform platform, but it was the education issue which swept him into office with a 174,757 to 128,394 vote majority and an overwhelming county unit vote. To a large degree, Arnall succeeded in accomplishing his goals of reform: the chain gang was eliminated from the state penal system, the poll tax was abolished, the state debt was wiped out, and Georgia became the first state to allow eighteen-year-olds to vote. In reflecting on his term of office, Georgia historian E. Merton Coulter described Arnall as "the most dynamically constructive governor Georgia had had within the memory of its oldest inhabitants."

Arnall, the author of two best-selling books, The Shore Dimly Seen and What The People Want, was later president of the Independent Motion Picture Producers, served with distinction as director of the Office of Price Stabilization under President Truman, and has represented the United States in several international conferences. In 1966 Ellis Arnall again ran for governor, losing in the Democratic primary runoff to Lester Maddox. That was to be his last political campaign. Photograph courtesy of University of Georgia Libraries Special collections

Georgia opened to provide training for young men and women planning to go into the ministry or other religious work, and the Athens Area Vocational-Technical School, operated by the Clarke County School District, offers day, evening, and extension courses to students in a fourteen county area of Northeast Georgia. The United States Navy Supply Corps School, providing a comprehensive training program for all of the navy's supply officers, moved to Athens in 1954.

While the university remains Athens's largest employer, the community's industrial base has been broadened and strengthened by the location of new industries and the expansion of older industrial facilities. The development of Athena and Paradise Valley industrial parks along the north perimeter highway served as inducements for many companies to establish plants in Athens. Among the largest industrial employers are Central Soya, Certainteed, Coble Dairy, Gold Kist, General Time, The Kendall Company, DairyPak, Del Mar Products, DuPont, Reliance Electric, Westinghouse, and Wilkins Industries.

A good transportation system has helped foster continued industrial and commercial development. While railroad passenger service has disappeared, the rail lines still provide vital freight service. The major highways that converge on Athens provide access for the more than forty truck lines that serve the city, and the Athens Airport, which got its first paved runways during World War II, offers passenger and freight service.

On October 18, 1961, Athens entered a new era of commercial development with the opening of its first shopping center. Beechwood Shopping Center, with fourteen new stores, was built to serve the expanding suburban development on the city's west side. It was soon joined by Alps Center across the road and other shopping centers on the east and north sides including East Plaza, Georgetown and Homewood. In 1981, twenty years after Beechwood opened, the huge Georgia Square Mall was completed on the Atlanta Highway at the Perimeter, with four major department stores and nearly 100 smaller retail stores. These developments have brought about change in downtown Athens, the historic commercial center of the city. In the early 1960s the chamber of commerce advanced a $40 million revitalization plan that called for a pedestrian mall on Clayton Street, underground parking, and a huge auditorium-exhibit hall complex. If implemented, it would have caused the destruction of one of the city's most architecturally and historically significant blocks. Fortunately, the plan was not initiated, principally because of the tremendous cost, but it did stimulate thought and discussion of needed downtown improvements. A later downtown redevelopment program, sponsored by the city and downtown merchants groups, succeeded in improving the appearance of the area and creating a more inviting atmosphere for business, shopping, dining, and entertainment. Trees and flowers were planted, new lighting and benches were installed, overhead wires were put underground, and many distinctive and handsome turn-of-the-century buildings have been rehabilitated. Downtown Athens remains alive and well while adapting to the change brought about by the shopping centers and commercial strip development.

Many of Athens's historic buildings and neighborhoods have not fared so well. Beginning in 1965, a $5.5 million urban renewal project destroyed the old Lickskillet neighborhood north of Hancock Avenue, as buildings were razed and streets were rerouted. Even Prince and Milledge avenues suffered the loss of many classic homes for which Athens was so widely known. This rapid change helped galvanize interest in pre-

While Athens and the university were distracted by the Cocking Case, the Japanese attacked Pearl Harbor on December 7, 1941, propelling the United States into World War II. Most able-bodied men of military age were called into service, drastically affecting the University of Georgia. Total enrollment declined from 3,631 in 1940 to 1,836 in 1943-44. Many faculty members, too, were granted leaves of absence for military service or other war-related work.

Changes were made in academic requirements, with greater emphasis placed on science and mathematics. Students were also required to work throughout the term. Those called into service after half a quarter's satisfactory work were given full credit for the quarter, and seniors called before graduation received credit for their final quarter.

A Reserve Officers Training Corps had existed at the university for many years, and in 1940 a Civilian Pilot Training Service had been instituted. Other military training programs were soon added. In 1942 the Midland Radio School established a unit in Athens. The 250 men in the school were housed in the old Costa Building, which the university leased and renovated, and dining facilities were made available at Denmark Hall. In June of the same year, the navy established one of five United States pre-flight schools at the university.

In his 1942-43 annual report, Chancellor Sanford reported a total manpower contribution of 13,450 to the war effort: 772 R.O.T.C. graduates; 94 Civilian Pilot Training cadets; 31 Army Air Corps Enlisted Reserve; 328 in the army, navy, marines, and coast guard; 6,452 Navy Pre-Flight School trainees; 4,907 Army Signal Corps trainees; 190 Navy Officers Flying School students; 140 students in other navy programs; and 636 in specialized army programs.

The photograph shows three students examining a United States Army Air Corps enlistment poster. Photograph courtesy of University of Georgia Libraries Special Collections

serving the city's heritage. The Athens Historical Society, Athens-Clarke Heritage Foundation, Historic Cobbham Foundation, Joseph Henry Lumpkin Foundation, and Old Athens Cemetery Foundation were joined by area garden clubs and patriotic organizations in an effort to retain Athens's distinctive character. As a result of renewed community awareness, many historic structures have been restored, street trees have been planted, and older neighborhoods have begun to be rejuvenated. Neighborhood organizations have been formed in suburban neighborhoods as well as in historic districts in an effort to preserve and enhance the quality life that Athenians have enjoyed for 180 years. Identified in a national survey as one of the most pleasant places to live in the nation, Athens continues to attract new residents, including a large number of retirees. Tourists, too, are drawn to the area, contributing substantially to the local economy.

These efforts may be seen in the continually improving park system in Clarke County. Memorial Park, the city's first major park, was developed after World War II through the efforts of county and city governments and the Athens Junior Assembly. Since that time, parks and recreational facilities have been established throughout the community. The county's newest park, Sandy Creek, opened in the fall of 1981 north of the city near the Sandy Creek Nature Center. The many local visual and performing arts groups also provide an important contribution to the cultural life of Athens. So many groups and individuals participate in arts activities, in fact, that gallery and performing spaces are inadequate to meet the demand. Schools, too, are an important community concern. Sixteen public and three private schools provide educational opportunities to the county's youngsters.

In an effort to foster greater commitment to community leadership and responsibility in both public and private sectors, the Athens Area Chamber of Commerce facilitated the formation in 1982 of Leadership Athens, a program in which up-and-coming leaders learn more about the community and potential for guiding its future.

In 1985, both town and gown joined to celebrate the bicentennial of the event that shaped their common destinies, the creation of the University of Georgia. As Athenians look toward the completion of their city's second century, they have much to be proud of in their past and can view the future with the same optimism and enthusiasm that characterized their forebears.

The United States Navy Pre-Flight School formally opened at the university on July 4, 1942 under the command of Captain C. E. Smith. There was an immediate and dramatic impact on both town and campus brought about by the rapid influx of thousands of military trainees. Headquarters was established at Baldwin Hall, and other buildings were turned over to the navy for its exclusive use—Woodruff Hall, the physical education building, Lucas House, the Faculty Club, the Agronomy Barn, Memorial Hall, the girls' cafeteria, and six dormitories.

Even these facilities proved inadequate for the massive training program, so the university and the navy launched a construction program which left a permanent imprint on the campus. Candler Hall and Old College were completely remodeled on the interior; two new dormitories were built; an addition was made to Memorial Hall to provide larger gymnasium facilities; a new track and playing fields were constructed; and Stegeman Hall was erected. A large part of the cost of these improvements was borne by the navy, and after the war the buildings reverted to the university.

This 1942 aerial photograph shows navy cadets in formation on the drill field spelling out NAVY. Photograph courtesy of University of Georgia Libraries Special Collections

Filling stations became one of the most visible symbols of the automobile age to be imposed on the face of American cities. Early stations drew their inspiration from traditional architectural sources and reflected the eclecticism of early twentieth century styles. This building, in a modified Tudor Revival style replete with half-timbering, stood for many years on one of Athens's busiest and most visible intersections, the corner of Broad and Lumpkin streets.

Built on the site of the Reverend Matthew Henderson's nineteenth century gardens, this structure fell to the wrecker's ball (a fate it shared with most of its contemporaries) when the First National Bank erected its main downtown office here in 1958-59. The signpost on the corner directs motorists toward nearby towns along U. S. routes 29 and 129. These highways are presently routed around the downtown area on the Athens Perimeter. Photograph courtesy of T. H. Milner, Sr.

In this 1945 photograph, a G Club initiate (in the center with a sheet protecting his jersey) tries to catch eggs, dropped from the second story of the Q-Room, in his mouth. The G Club consisted of football team members who had won letters. Officers in 1945 were Charles Eaves, Mike Castronis, Billy Rutland, and George Jernigan. Other members included Bill Chanko, Morris Janko, Reid Mosley, Carlse Phillips, and Charles Smith, according to the Pandora.

The Q-Room was for years an all-male institution, located on the east side of College Avenue between Broad and Clayton. It was, according to Dean William Tate, "the major hangout for male college students, with a soda fountain at the front, then a deep room with many tables, each with a good light above, with racks of balls. From early morning to late at night the clicking of those balls made a steady hum."

Betting on the games was, he said, fairly common, but there was little drinking. Seniors who were regulars might qualify for the highly prized Q-Room Diplomas, with formally worded references to attendance and performance and a knowledge of angles and tangents. Photograph courtesy of University of Georgia Libraries Special Collections

During the 1940s, Founder's Memorial Garden on the University of Georgia campus began to take shape. Planning for the garden had begun in 1939 when the Garden Club of Georgia voted to join the university's Department of Landscape Architecture in constructing a series of gardens adjacent to the department's buildings as a memorial to the founders of the Ladies' Garden Club of Athens.

Organized in 1891, the Athens club was recognized by the National Council of State Garden Clubs as the first such organization in America. The garden was designed and built during the 1940s under the direction of Hubert B. Owens, head of the landscape department and later dean of the School of Environmental Design. Below the boxwood garden area shown in the photograph is a large sunken formal garden with statuary and a sunken pool surrounded by a serpentine brick wall. There are, additionally, many varieties of trees and shrubs in the informal areas of the garden surrounding the 1857 university professor's house, now state headquarters for the Garden Club of Georgia.

The gardens have been carefully cared for and the house has been restored and furnished as a house museum. Both are open to the public. Photograph courtesy of University of Georgia Office of Public Relations

On May 1, 1948, radio station WRFC began broadcasting from temporary studios at its transmitter site on Lake Road, becoming the chief competitor of WGAU, which had been founded ten years earlier to fill the void left by the move of pioneering station WTFI to Atlanta. WRFC soon moved into studios on Lumpkin Street, where it remained until the station acquired the 1910 Hardeman-Sams House on Milledge Avenue in 1964. Offices and studios still occupy the renovated house, which is located in the Dearing Historic District, listed in the National Register of Historic Places.

The performers shown here, broadcasting live over WRFC, are Pee Wee and Peggy Pruett, a brother and sister act. They were one of the pioneer groups on this radio station and appeared all over Northeast Georgia. Their recorded tune, "Paper of Pins," reached the top of WRFC Hillbilly Hit Parade in the early 1950s. Their sons, first cousins Stan Pruett and Tony Pritchett, also entertained in the Athens area during the 1970s. Photograph courtesy of Athens Newspapers, Incorporated

The Susan Medical Center opened its doors in 1946 to provide the black residents of Northeast Georgia with its first maternity hospital. Dr. Andrew Jones (fourth from right), built the hospital with donations he and others collected locally and from around the country. The center was named for Dr. Jones's mother, Susan Jones. After Dr. Jones's death in 1952, the hospital was purchased by Dr. D. R. Green who continued to operate the facility as a hospital until 1964. From 1964 until his death in 1980, Dr. Green used the building as a medical office. The Susan Building now houses the law firm of Thurmond, Thurmond, Miller, and Rucker who have carefully restored the building. They have also retained and display many original photographs and documents that chronicle its history as an important part of the black community.

The photograph shows members of the Northeast Georgia Medical Society in front of the Susan Medical Center during one of the society's regular meetings about 1947. This group of black doctors met on the third Sunday of each month to hear special medical lecturers. Those in the photograph are, from left to right: Dr. Gilbert, Royston; Dr. Raymond Carter, Atlanta; Dr. Funderburg, Monticello; Dr. Butler, Gainesville; Dr. Rembert Jones, Elberton; Dr. Harry Nash, Atlanta; Dr. Andrew Jones, Athens; Dr. D. R. Green, Athens; Dr. Sessom, Washington; Dr. Lawrence, Greensboro. Photograph courtesy of Michael Thurmond

The Athens Junior Assembly was organized in 1935 as a community service organization patterned on the Junior League model. The founders were Elizabeth Hall Cumming, Eugenia Blount Friend, and Marie McHatton Hanson. On October 28, 1978, the organization became the 243rd Junior League in America and was officially incorporated as the Junior League of Athens, Georgia. The purpose of the organization is to promote volunteerism and develop the potential of members to serve the community.

Over the years, members have supported many important projects including a number of health clinics and were instrumental in organizing the Recording for the Blind. In 1968, the group undertook the restoration and maintenance of the Taylor-Grady House, which it uses as its headquarters, opens on public occasions, and rents for private functions.

In 1940, the Assembly held its first follies to raise money to fund children's clinics. Since that time, many thousands of dollars have been raised for similar projects by the follies. The circus was the theme of the 1949 follies. Nearly 3,000 Athenians attended the event which raised $3,600 for the Simon Michael Clinics. There was a midway, the show included a special performance by the YMCA Tumblers, Louis Griffith sang "My Wild Irish Rose," and the Cowgirl Rockettes, shown in the photograph, performed to the delight and amusement of the audience. Members of the Cowgirl Rockettes are, left to right, front row: Mug Welch, Joann Maupin, Karen Carithers, Margarett Gunn Wilson, Fay Welch, Betsy McCaskill, Flossie Gerdine; middle: Mary Simpson Barth, Peggy Allen, Mickey Martin, Jeanne Benson, Emmie Middlebrooks; back: Grace Stephens, Joan Butler, Sidney Jones, and Kitty Trussell. Photograph courtesy of Junior League of Athens

The Poss name is recognized all over Georgia by frequent visitors to Athens and many who have never set foot in the city. For many years, Poss' has been synonymous with barbecue. R. E. Poss began making hash on Saturday afternoons in his backyard on Boulevard. His neighbors pursuaded him to market his popular product, and he had no trouble selling all he could make in his ten gallon iron stew pot.

Poss soon opened a barbecue restaurant on the Atlanta Highway, shown here during the 1940s, which was popular with students and townspeople and which became a regular stop for alumni returning to Athens for football games and other athletic events over a period of forty years. This landmark establishment (which had been enlarged and modernized) was demolished for the construction of the new Richway Store.

The Poss family still caters large parties at nearby Poss' Lakeview and provides food and drink to the spectators at University of Georgia athletic events. Other Poss products include Brunswick Stew, Southern Hash, Beef Stew, Chili with Beans, Camp Stew, and Hot Dog Chili, among others, and are found on grocery store shelves around the Southeast. Photograph courtesy of University of Georgia Libraries Special Collections

On May 24, 1954, a strange event occurred on the University of Georgia campus which has since been the subject of newspaper and magazine articles, films, and legend. During the afternoon of that day, a giant metal abstract expressionist sculpture of a horse was placed in Reed Quadrangle. Constructed of three-inch thick steel plates by Chicago sculptor Abott Pattison, a visting professor at the university, the "Iron Horse" was soon the center of a storm of protest.

That evening and night as many as 500 students gathered around the horse; threw paint on it, drew graffiti on it; and placed an old mattress, tires, and a couple of bushels of horse manure under it; set it on fire; and marched around it with torches, chanting, "Burn the horse." The fire department had to be called twice. "The men trying to destroy it," said one art professor, "acted as if they were afraid of it." The next morning, while the mattress was still smouldering, the art faculty met and voiced support for the artist. However, amid threats that the sculpture would be dynamited, President O. C. Aderhold ordered it removed.

C. M. Thompson, an employee of the university's physical plant, had loaded it onto a flatbed truck and transported it to his Madison County farm by 5 p.m. on May 25th. Back on campus the Chi Phi's constructed a wooden parody with a $5,000 price tag which was dubbed the "Modern Mule." After some time, the iron horse was moved about 30 miles south of Athens to a Greene County farm owned by retired university professor L. C. Curtis. The horse remains there today, in a field visible from Georgia Highway 15 just north of the bridge over the Oconee River at Skull Shoals.

The events of May, 1954 were the subject of a film by Bill Van der Kloot of Atlanta entitled "The Iron Horse." The film won a gold medal at the Chicago film festival (Van der Kloot had the sculptor, Pattison, accept for him) and has been shown all over the world. The photograph shows the horse in its Greene County field where it is often visited by college students, travelers, picnickers, and photographers. Photograph by Don Nelson; courtesy of the Athens Observer

Alfred H. Holbrook (left) and Lamar Dodd (right) were responsible for founding the Georgia Museum of Art on the university campus. Holbrook, a wealthy lawyer, came to the university in 1945 to study art under Dodd. Dodd was instrumental in persuading Holbrook to stay, and a 1948 exhibition of Holbrook's personal collection inaugurated the museum.

Holbrook's gift of 100 paintings by American artists, covering a 100-year period, was designated the Eva Underhill Holbrook Collection, a memorial to his first wife. Holbrook served as curator of the growing museum collections until his retirement in 1969 at age 95. He held the title Director Emeritus until his death in 1974, six months before his 100th birthday.

Lamar Dodd has achieved international recognition as an artist, teacher, and administrator. His works are in private collections and museums, including the Metropolitan, Whitney, Pennsylvania Academy of Fine Arts, and High Museum in Atlanta. He is widely recognized for his artistic impressions of the NASA space program over a 20-year period. Since his retirement as department and division head, he has executed an ambitious and powerful series of paintings on open-heart surgery. LaGrange College, in Dodd's home town, has named its new arts center for him.

The museum originally occupied part of the university library, but expanded to fill the entire building, which was remodeled after the library moved its present facility in 1953. The Georgia Museum of Art has been designated the official state museum by the Georgia General Assembly. Collections have expanded to such an extent that only five percent may be exhibited at one time. Groundbreaking for a new museum designed by architect Edward Larabee Barnes is set for fall, 1986. Photograph courtesy of University of Georgia Libraries Special Collections

For many residents of the state, their first (and often repeated) contact with the University of Georgia has been through the Georgia Center for Continuing Education. Nearly 1.5 million persons have participated in degree and non-degree programs sponsored by the Georgia Center.

The $2.5 million Georgia Center building, designed by architects Stevens & Wilkinson of Atlanta, was hailed as the first "contemporary" building on the campus when construction was begun in 1955, and it received the Progressive Architecture Citation as the best design of the year for an educational facility. The building, and the landscaped grounds designed by nationally known landscape architect Thomas Church, are located on the corner of Lumpkin and Carlton streets on south campus.

The building houses conference rooms, guest rooms, dining rooms, offices, and broadcast facilities. The center was made possible by $3 million in construction and program grants from the W. K. Kellogg Foundation. In 1984, the Foundation donated an additional $8.5 million which, when matched with a $5.4 million allocation from the state, provided the wherewithall for an ambitious expansion of facilities and programs which will make the Center one of the largest university-based continuing education facilities in the world. Photograph from the author's collection

Athens's economy got a boost in 1954 when General Time opened a 110,000 square foot, $2.5 million plant on the Newton Bridge Road. The first clocks to come off the assembly line were the Westclox Bantam and the Seth Thomas Cathay models. It took, according to a brochure produced by the company for its opening, 382 different operations to make an electric clock, and all of these were performed at the Athens plant.

This photograph, taken shortly after the opening of the factory, shows the clocks being assembled. In 1963 General Time opened a second plant on Hillcrest and Brookwood Drive to manufacture electric automobile clocks. The second plant has since been closed, but plant number one has expanded and modernized and it continues to produce fine timepieces. Photograph courtesy of Athens Newspapers, Incorporated

Athens and the University of Georgia were in the national spotlight during January 1961 when the first black students were admitted to the university, striking a blow against segregated public education in Georgia. In 1960 two black Atlantans, Charlayne Hunter and Hamilton Holmes, applied for admission as transfer students to the university but were turned down. The two students then filed suit against the university claiming that they were being denied admission on the basis of their race.

On January 6, 1961, Judge W. A. Bootle of the Federal District Court for the Middle District of Georgia, ruled in the plaintiffs' favor and ordered them admitted immediately for the winter term. Three days later, on January 9, Holmes and Hunter arrived to register for classes.

This photograph shows the two surrounded by reporters, students, and curious onlookers as they passed through the university arch on their way to registration. The first three days on campus were relatively uneventful for Holmes and Hunter, except for the cold stares, occasional catcalls, and groups of students and reporters that followed them around. The situation changed dramatically, however, following the Georgia-Georgia Tech basketball game when a demonstration in front of Miss Hunter's dormitory turned into a serious disturbance.

The two students were taken to Atlanta for their safety, but they returned to campus the following week after many university faculty members signed a resolution calling for their return and Governor Ernest Vandiver guaranteed that order would be maintained. Holmes and Hunter remained at the university until their graduation two-and-a-half years later. AP Wirephoto; courtesy of Associated Press and Athens Newspapers, Incorporated

A critical situation faced the University of Georgia on the night of January 11, 1961, when a large, unruly crowd gathered in front of Myers Hall where Charlayne Hunter had been assigned a room. Police and university officials rushed to the scene as rocks and bottles began crashing thorugh the dormitory's windows. The police finally brought the crowd under control after battling the rioters with tear gas, but it was the cool, controlled actions of one man that was largely responsible for preventing disaster that night—Dean William Tate.

When he arrived at Myers, he began walking through the crowd checking student ID cards and calmly talking with those gathered in front of the dormitory. He retained his composure in the face of the hostile strangers, although he was hit by a tear gas cannister and a rock, and received a black eye when coming to the assistance of a besieged policeman. "He saved the University and the city of Athens from terrible trouble that night," said Police Chief Hardy. "Without him, the situation would have developed into a much worse one."

Other Southern universities were not so fortunate. Russell H. Barrett in Integration at Ole Miss *asserts that the tragedy in Oxford might have been averted if there had been the human element present, the equivalent of Dean Tate. This photograph of Dean Tate and Chief Hardy was taken on Broad Street during those fateful weeks. Photograph courtesy of the* Atlanta Constitution *and the* Atlanta Journal

Charlayne Hunter and Hamilton Holmes received their diplomas from the University of Georgia during commencement exercises in 1963. Holmes went on to receive a medical degree and is now a doctor at Emory University Hospital. Miss Hunter, now Charlayne Hunter-Galt, entered the field of journalism, writing for the New Yorker *magazine and the* New York Times *before becoming a reporter on the* MacNeil/Lehrer Report, *a nightly news analysis program on public television. AP Wirephoto; courtesy of Associated Press and Athens Newspapers, Incorporated*

Just four months after the integration of the university, the nation's new attorney general, Robert Kennedy, came to Athens to deliver his first formal address since assuming office. The occasion of his speech was the tenth annual observance of Law Day, and his opening remarks set the tone of his speech: "Respect for the law—in essence that is the meaning of Law Day—and every day must be Law Day or else our society will collapse."

The civil rights statutes would be enforced by the Kennedy Administration, he assured the audience, along with the anti-trust laws, the laws against kidnapping and robbing federal banks, and all other federal laws. The Attorney General also commended Georgia students and faculty for their restraint during the crisis in January, saying, "When your moment of truth came, the voices crying 'force' were overridden by the voices pleading for reason. . . . You are the wave of the future—not those who cry panic. For the country's future you will and must prevail." The graduation of Charlayne Hunter and Hamilton Holmes from the university would, he said, send a clear message to third world countries that America stands for justice at home as well as abroad.

At the conclusion of his speech, Kennedy received a standing ovation from the audience. The photograph shows the Attorney General at his airport arrival aboard the Caroline. Photograph courtesy of University of Georgia Libraries Special Collections

The University of Georgia Coliseum, built on South Campus in 1961-64, was designed to meet several needs: to provide a place for agricultural exhibitions; to serve as a hall for large concerts, banquets, and assemblies; to house the athletic department and an arena for basketball and other indoor sports. The basketball facilities, with a crowd capacity of over eleven thousand, are a far cry from those at the old Athens Y.M.C.A. where Georgia's first games were played, and a considerable improvement over the old Octagon, the small gym in Memorial Hall, and Woodruff Hall, where games were played over the years. A new era for Georgia basketball began on February 22, 1964 when the inaugural game was played against Georgia Tech in the new building.

Designed by the architectural firm of Cooper-Barrett-Skinner-Woodbury and Cooper of Atlanta, the building cost over four million dollars. The roof is supported on two diagonal parabolic arches spanning 384 feet between fan-shaped columns and buttresses. During construction, one dare-devil pilot flew his small plane through the massive arches, and later, spiked iron fences had to be placed across the arches at the roofline to keep motorcyclists from riding to the top and down the other side.

While many appreciate its practical aspects, not everyone has praised its aesthetics. One critic, according to Dean Tate, said it was "as ugly as a pregnant oyster." Psychics predicted it would soon collapse, killing thousands, but 1984 marked the Coliseum's 20th birthday. This photograph was made in 1963 while the building was still under construction. Photograph courtesy of Charles Rowland

Governor Lester Maddox (1967-1971) was photographed riding backwards on a bicycle in front of Athens High School on a visit to the city during his term of office. The Atlanta businessman, who had dropped out of school in the tenth grade to help support his family and who later achieved national notoriety for refusing to integrate his restaurant, the Pickrick, was elected governor in 1966, his first political office.

Defeating five opponents in the Democratic primary, he faced wealthy Republican Howard "Bo" Callaway in the general election. Although Callaway garnered more popular votes than Maddox, he failed to achieve a majority because of write-in votes for former Governor Ellis Arnall. The General Assembly, which was overwhelmingly Democratic, decided the election in favor of Maddox. In Clarke County, Callaway had won with 5,934 votes to Maddox's 3,477. Nearly 2,000 write-in votes were cast in the county for Arnall (as well as a few votes for State Senator Jimmy Carter, Colonel Sanders, Vince Dooley, and "Roadrunner").

Maddox surprised many of his critics during his term as governor, which was noted for its openness and honesty. He showed a strong interest in education and prison reform and appointed more blacks to office than any of his predecessors. Maddox was elected lieutenant governor in 1970, was defeated for a second term as governor in 1974 by George Busbee, and ran unsuccessfully for the presidency against his old antagonist, Jimmy Carter, on the American Independent Party ticket in 1976.

The Athens High School building, in the background of the photograph, was dedicated on September 10, 1952. In 1970, the year Maddox left office, the school was desegregated, merging with Burney-Harris, the black high school. Renamed Clarke Central, the school continues to serve county students. Photograph courtesy of Athens Newspapers, Incorporated

Athens is familiar to people throughout the country who buy and enjoy a local product, Benson's Old Home Fruit Cake. The cakes, produced by a division of Benson's Bakery, have been sold through civic organizations and by university students during many holiday seasons. A number of students have, in fact, won scholarships provided by the company as a reward for their sales efforts.

Edsel Benson, head of the bakery firm, stands in front of a map showing the distribution of his famous fruit cakes in this photograph. The cakes are produced at Benson's Old Home Kitchens plant in Bogart. Photograph courtesy of University of Georgia Libraries Special Collections

At her death in 1939, Ilah Dunlap Little, wife of Atlanta attorney John D. Little, left $400,000 for the construction of a new library on the university campus. The will specified that the new building was to be erected on the site of the old Chancellor's House, facing Old College across the south quadrangle. Other provisions required that the building be designed with columns.

Construction was delayed until 1950 because the Little gift was not sufficient to defray the cost of the library as designed by the architect, Alfred M. Githens of New York. The additional money was provided by the University System Building Authority after its creation in 1949, and the building was finally completed in 1953 at a cost of $1,938,932. In less than twenty years the library was overcrowded and the facilities were taxed to their limits. The opening of the Science Library on South Campus eased the space problem, but it was not until the 1970s that a major addition, larger than the original library, provided adequate facilities.

The original building today houses Special Collections and University Archives. The new addition houses the Richard B. Russell Library, containing the papers of the late United States senator and graduate of the university. This photograph of the library's main facade was taken during the 1960s. A latin inscription in the entablature is the motto of the university and translates as: "...to teach and to inquire into the nature of things." Photograph from the author's collection

In October 1969, students had organized a Vietnam Moratorium and invited Jeanette Rankin, veteran feminist and opponent of war, to speak to their rally. The Montana congresswoman, who had voted against American involvement in both world wars, spoke to the 1,500 students, professors, and staff out of a long and deep personal commitment and in a language they could understand.

Rankin had established her second home in Georgia in 1924, first in Clarke County and later in Oconee County three miles west of Watkinsville. Writing in 1958, two years before his election as president, John F. Kennedy characterized her as "one of the truly courageous women in American History."

From a self-imposed retirement from public speaking of almost twenty years, Rankin emerged from her Oconee County retreat to take an active part in the anti-Vietnam movement, the new feminist movement, and the effort to bring about a more democratic electoral system.

After her death in California on May 18, 1973 at the age of ninety-two, her Georgia friends held a memorial tribute at the Oconee County elementary school just a short distance from her Georgia home. The photograph shows Jeanette Rankin speaking to the Vietnam Moratorium on the campus in 1969. Photograph courtesy of Athens Newspapers, Incorporated

During the late 1960s, University of Georgia students joined thousands of their fellow students at colleges around the nation in protesting United States involvement in the Vietnam War. Demonstrations, meetings, and marches were common sights on the Georgia campus. In 1968, protestors painted anti-war and pro-Cuban slogans on the military building on campus. During one long night of protest in 1970, students marched on Academic Building and the home of the university president on Prince Avenue. As in the integration crisis almost a decade before, the presence and personal persuasion of Dean William Tate helped keep the situation under control. Rather than checking ID cards, this time Dean Tate donned "love beads" and sat in the middle of the crowd. Photograph courtesy of University of Georgia Libraries special collections

During the 1960s, urban renewal was remaking the face of downtown Athens, and the Brumby House was slated to come under the wrecker's ball. This threat to Athens's oldest house was the impetus for the formation of the Athens-Clarke Heritage Foundation. The foundation sought a way to save the historic structure, finally succeeding in moving it from its original location on Hancock Avenue to a new site on the re-routed Dougherty Street several hundred feet away. This photograph shows the house being moved (during a University of Georgia football game!) in October, 1967. For four years it sat derelict and forlorn in its weed-choked lot, assailed by critics as a hopeless folly. Photograph courtesy of Athens Newspapers, Incorporated

When Bowdre Phinizy, who owned the Athens Herald, purchased the Athens Banner in 1921, the Banner office was located at the site of the present A & A Bakery, while the Herald facilities were at the corner of Washington and Lumpkin streets. Earl B. Braswell was appointed publisher of the renamed Athens Banner-Herald and guided the paper until 1965. During his tenure, the newspaper moved its offices to the building in the photograph, which was located on Hancock Avenue between Thomas and Jackson.

In July 1965, after Phinizy's death, the Banner-Herald was sold to Southeastern Newspapers Corporation of Augusta and Savannah for $1.7 million. The following year, after the Hancock Avenue headquarters was slated for demolition by urban renewal, the paper moved to its present offices on East Clayton Street, later rechristened Press Place along the block in front of the newspaper office. The new facility had previously been C. A. Trussell Ford and later Christian Hardware.

In 1967 the Banner-Herald acquired the Athens Daily News, which had begun in 1965 by taking over the operation of the weekly Athens Advertiser. The two papers, under the direction of publisher Robert Chambers since 1972, remain the only dailies in the city. In 1982 the Banner marked its 150th year of publication in Athens. Photograph courtesy of Athens Newspapers, Incorporated

Several years elapsed between the time the Brumby House was moved and funds could be raised for its restoration. However, the house was finally restored in 1972 with the assistance of a grant from the United States Department of Housing and Urban Development, city funds, and private contributions. In the interest of returning the house to its original appearance (and because of a lack of funds to do more), additions made over the years were stripped away. The portico, rear porch, and shed room were reconstructed, and the house was refurbished according to the plans of architect Wilmer Heery.

Upon completion of the restoration, the Athens-Clarke Heritage Foundation furnished the house with period furniture through the generosity of several donors and deeded the house to the city of Athens. The foundation now leases the house from the city and it is operated as the Athens Welcome Center by the Athens Area Chamber of Commerce, the foundation, and the city.

Over 15,000 visitors come to the Church-Waddel-Brumby House each year, and it has become one of Georgia's most popular historic house museums. The photograph shows the house as it appeared in 1973 after completion of the restoration. The lot has since been landscaped and an herb garden added through a generous gift from the original investors in Athens History Village. Photograph courtesy of Athens Newspapers, Incorporated

In 1974, seven years after the Brumby House was moved from the site, the Robert G. Stephens Federal Building was completed on Hancock Avenue between Jackson and Thomas streets. The building houses the state offices of the Agricultural Stabilization and Conservation Service, the Farmers Home Administration, and the Soil Conservation Service, as well as local offices of the Internal Revenue Service, the Social Security Administration, and other federal agencies. It is named for retired Georgia Tenth District Congressman Robert G. Stephens. Photograph by Hal Brooks; courtesy of Athens Newspapers, Incorporated

Athens native Laura Hutchins Paddock, better known to her fans as "Aunt Lollipop," entertained children all over the Eastern Seaboard with her stories and puppet shows. A graduate of Lucy Cobb Institute, she developed a proficiency at storytelling, first to her own children and later to the kindergarten students she taught, and made her radio debut in 1940 on local radio station WGAU. About the same time, she became fascinated with puppets during an art course at the University of Georgia.

When her husband's career took them to Boston and Baltimore, and finally to retirement in Florida, Laura Paddock continued to pursue a career in puppetry and storytelling in schools, libraries, on radio, and television. She appeared regularly in a variety show on television station WBZ in Boston, where the producer dubbed her "Aunt Lollipop," the name by which she was known to the thousands of children she entertained.

After returning to her family home on Dearing Street in Athens in 1966, she had her own show on WGTV, the university's educational television station, and continued to entertain for parties and benefits until her death in 1979. In the photograph, Aunt Lollipop and her favorite puppet, Pedro (a guitar-playing monkey), are seen doing what they liked to do best, entertaining a group of captivated youngsters. Photograph courtesy of Athens Newspapers, Incorporated

Many Athenians were awakened from their sleep by a loud explosion at 11:25 p.m. on July 17, 1970. The blast occurred when three Texaco gasoline storage tanks on Hull Street near the old Southern Railroad depot blew up, sending flames some 500 feet into the air. A driver transferring gas from a truck to one of the tanks was seriously burned, but survived.

The Texaco explosion also shattered plate glass windows in the downtown area, forcing merchants to spend much of the night and the following day sweeping up glass and boarding up their show windows. The young lady in the photograph is examining the damage to a store on Clayton Street.

Bethel Church Homes, a number of houses on Pulaski Street, and several university buildings suffered damage from the blast. Some fifty people were injured, but no one was killed. Glass was shattered as far away as the Visual Arts Building on campus and the President's House on Prince Avenue. Photograph by Steve Deal; courtesy of Athens Newspapers, Incorporated

One month after his defeat by Lester Maddox in the 1966 gubenatorial primary, State Senator Jimmy Carter of Plains began his second campaign for Georgia's highest state office. Exhibiting the tireless determination which would eventually win him the presidency, Carter shook an estimated 600,000 hands and made some 1,800 speeches. He developed a superb grass-roots political organization to combat the popularity of his chief opponent, former Governor Carl Sanders, who was endorsed by most of the state's newspapers and politicians.

Carter won the primary and runoff against Sanders and handily defeated Republican Hal Suit in the general election. In Clarke County, Sanders beat Carter by 635 votes in the primary, but lost to him by 72 votes in the runoff. It was a different story, however, in the general election. Clarke was one of only six counties to give the Republican a majority— 7,244 for Suit and only 6,422 for Carter.

During his term in office, Carter pushed through a reorganization of the executive branch, strove to end racial discrimination in state government, and sponsored a number of measures to protect Georgia's natural resources, but he failed to get meaningful property tax relief or consumer legislation.

On December 12, 1974, the governor announced that he was a candidate for the presidency. The public reaction was one of disbelief and ridicule. On January 21, 1976, he was inaugurated as the thirty-ninth president of the United States. Carter paid a brief "whistle-stop" visit to Athens during his unsuccessful 1980 re-election campaign. When the votes were counted in November, the citizens of Clarke County gave Carter 10,519 votes, Ronald Reagan 8,094, and John Anderson 1,060.

In the photograph, Carter is shown shaking hands on Clayton Street during the 1970 governor's race. Behind Carter in the center of the photo is Athens City Councilman Dwain Chambers; at the far right is C. W. Crawford. Photograph courtesy of Athens Newspapers, Incorporated

After more than a decade during which the city and the University of Georgia lost many of their historic landmarks, the tide began to turn during the early 1970s. By 1972 the University Chapel, one of the area's most significant structures, was beginning to suffer damage as the old stucco on the exterior cracked and deteriorated. The university soon began a restoration program for the venerable building.

In this photograph, Willie Dunn (left) and W. F. Adams of the university physical plant, are seen removing the old stucco from one of the fluted columns prior to restuccoing. Photograph courtesy of Athens Newspapers, Incorporated

The old Federal Building (1905-06) which originally housed the Post Office and the Federal Courthouse, was the subject of the first major commercial adaptive re-use project in the downtown area. The elegant brick and stone structure was threatened with destruction when federal offices moved out and early downtown revitalization plans called for a parking lot on the site.

Instead, the First American Bank and Trust Company acquired it in 1971, renovating the basement and first floor for its headquarters while reserving the upper two floors for future development. The building's distinctive architectural features were retained, following the plans of architect Wilmer Heery, Sr., and a concrete parking deck was built unobtrusively into the slope behind the structure.

The bank, founded by J. H. Hubert in 1927 as a private banking company, was originally located in the Colonial Hotel building on College Avenue. In 1949, a year after moving to the corner of Washington and College across from the present location, the bank received a state charter and became the Hubert State Bank.

The present investors acquired the bank in 1962, changing its name to First American Bank and Trust. This photograph shows the exterior of the bank after the completion of the restoration work in 1973. Photograph courtesy of Athens Newspapers, Incorporated

This first floor interior view of the First American Bank after its renovation shows the main banking room. The arches once framed the post office windows in the old facility. Photograph courtesy of Athens Newspapers, Incorporated

In the spring of 1973, Athens reeled under the fury of two successive tornadoes. On March 31, several twisters swept across Georgia doing an estimated $100 million in damage and leaving nearly 5,000 persons homeless in ten counties. Athens was one of the areas hardest hit, suffering one fatality and widespread property destruction along U. S. 78 West, the North Bypass, and Georgia 106. Over 100 trailers were destroyed in three trailer parks, and homes were damaged or destroyed in the Forest Heights, Prince Avenue, and Boulevard areas.

Clean-up from the first tornado had not yet been completed when a second storm hit the city on May 28, following almost the same path as the earlier twister. Slamming first into the previously damaged Holiday Estates and Forest Heights areas, the tornado struck Knottingham subdivision and heavily damaged the married housing apartments at the Navy School on Prince Avenue. Boulevard was once again ravaged as ancient trees fell and houses lost their roofs. The Pulaski and Tibbits streets neighborhood was hit before the twister passed out of the city, striking the edge of East Athens.

The damage was staggering. The $1 million Oglethorpe Elementary School was totally destroyed; a gaping hole was torn in the rear of the Y.M.C.A. building on Hawthorne; trees blocked many of the city's streets; local hospitals were kept busy treating the injured; and the fire department answered sixteen calls, two of which were major fires. A death occurred when a liquor store on Prince Avenue collapsed.

Although the debris has long since been cleared away and many damaged buildings have been repaired or replaced, scars still remain on the landscape and local residents cannot forget that incredible spring. This photograph shows some of the devastation caused by the May 28 tornado at the corner of Boulevard and Satula Avenue. Photograph by Larry White; courtesy of Athens Newspapers, Incorporated

In early 1974, one of Athens's most venerable landmarks, the Franklin House, was threatened with destruction when the owners let a demolition contract on the building. Plans called for the valuable corner lot to be cleared and the land sold for new commercial development.

Reacting quickly to the situation, the Athens-Clarke Heritage Foundation organized a drive to raise the money to purchase the land and the demolition contract which had been let. In two hectic weeks, the foundation put together a "patchwork quilt" of financial resources totaling $75,000 which included individual contributions, guaranteed loans, and a $5,000 grant provided by Governor Jimmy Carter from his emergency fund. Local efforts included a "money taxi" run by foundation trustees and friends who picked up donations all over town. The demolition contractor even donated the money he had been paid when the foundation bought his contract.

After purchasing the building, the foundation applied for and received a $30,000 National Park Service grant through the Georgia Department of Natural Resources to stabilize the deteriorating structure. Local businessman Hugh Fowler bought the Franklin House in December 1977. Fowler removed two rear wings from the building and in 1981 began restoration of the facade. Completion of exterior work is slated for 1985.

In an effort to rally support to save the building in 1974, foundation trustee Jeanné Downs and her grandchildren posed for this photograph in a second floor doorway. The scene, something of a cross between Barbara Fritchie and Grant Wood's American Gothic, drew wide attention for the project. Photograph by Walker Montgomery; courtesy of Athens Newspapers, Incorporated

Dean Rusk became the Samuel Sibley Professor of International Law at the University of Georgia in 1970 after a distinguished career in public service. A native of Cherokee County, Georgia, Rusk graduated from Boys' High School in Atlanta before going on to Davidson College and St. John's College, Oxford. After teaching at Mills College in California, he went to work for the government, in military intelligence and in the State Department under Dean Acheson.

John F. Kennedy appointed him secretary of state in 1961, a position he held as well in the Johnson Administration. In 1969, the board of regents confirmed his appointment to the Georgia faculty in a nine to four vote, even though he was opposed by Governor Lester Maddox as being too far left and an "internationalist."

Since his appointment, Rusk has organized an outstanding program in international and comparative law at the university, and in 1977 the Rusk Center was opened in historic Philosophical Hall. His wit, charm, and vast knowledge of international affairs have made him a popular speaker throughout the state, and he is always in great demand.

Although accustomed to speaking with the world's leaders, Rusk appears quite at home fielding questions from students in Mrs. Dorothy Keach's gifted classes from Gaines, Winterville, and Whitehead Road schools. Photograph courtesy of Athens Newspapers, Incorporated

At his death in September 1980, Dean William Tate was one of Georgia's best known and best loved men. He served the university for more than fifty years as an undergraduate, graduate, teacher, assistant dean, dean of men, and dean emeritus. A native of Calhoun, Georgia, Tate came to Athens as a freshman in the fall of 1920.

As a student he achieved almost every academic honor open to him. He was a track star and was active in many extracurricular activities including Phi Kappa literary society and Delta Tau Delta fraternity. He married an Athenian, Susan Frances Barrow, granddaughter of Chancellor Barrow, and after an absence of seven years, during which he was head of the English Department at McCallie School in Chattanooga, returned to Athens to stay.

As dean of men, Tate had the reputation of a stern disciplinarian, but his rapport with the students was remarkable. He cared for all of them individually, and they knew it. "He saved the careers of many young men by straightening them out when someone else might have thrown them out of school," said former congressman and fellow teacher Robert G. Stephens. The dean, however, had no patience with any student who would not make an effort. "Teaching a student who won't try," he said, "is like going hunting and having to tote the dog."

His ability to control potentially explosive situations—protests of the Cocking affair in 1941, the integration riots in 1961, the women students' rebellion in 1968, and the Vietnam protests of 1970—is legendary.

Tate had a remarkable memory for names, places, and events. He was a raconteur extraordinaire who could keep an audience entertained for hours with his stories of the North Georgia mountains and his tales of Athens's history. His Strolls Around Athens, a collections of columns from the Athens Observer, is a lasting personal memoir of the city and university he loved.

Even after his retirement in 1971 ("statutory senility" he called it), Bill Tate remained active in university affairs, chastising the administration when he felt they were wrong, defending his university against unjustified attacks. He would do anything within reason for the university. Mrs. Tate felt he had gone beyond that point when he agreed to pop out of a cake during the university's 190th birthday celebration in 1975. "Well at least," the dean told her, "I had my clothes on."

Always active, Dean Tate never stopped learning, growing, and contributing to his community. He continued writing his weekly newspaper column from the hospital until the week before he died on his seventy-seventh birthday. He left an enduring mark on the university and the Athens community and will be long remembered. *Photograph by Larry White; courtesy of Athens Newspapers, Incorporated*

In the early spring of 1974, the "streaking" craze swept across the country and, of course, found enthusiasts in the Athens area. Streakers would take off their clothes and dash nude down streets, through classrooms and meetings, and across the university campus. There were streakers in cars, on motorcycles, and even parachuting from airplanes. In March, hundreds, perhaps thousands of students ran naked across the Gillis Bridge from Myers Hall to Reed Quadrangle in what was billed as the world's greatest streak. University officials and city police regarded the goings-on with a great deal of patience, and the fad soon disappeared.

During the streaking craze, Dean William Tate recalled two streaking incidents that had occurred while he was a student in the early 1920s. One Chi Phi won twenty dollars for streaking downtown, but a second boy was frightened during his dash by two fraternity brothers dressed as policemen. An hour later, Dean Tate received a call from a lady on Dearing Street asking him to come pick up a naked student hiding in her shrubbery.

Not all streakers moved across town with great speed. The photographer caught this fellow on crutches leisurely "streaking" on campus. Photograph by John Toon, The Athens Observer; courtesy of photographer

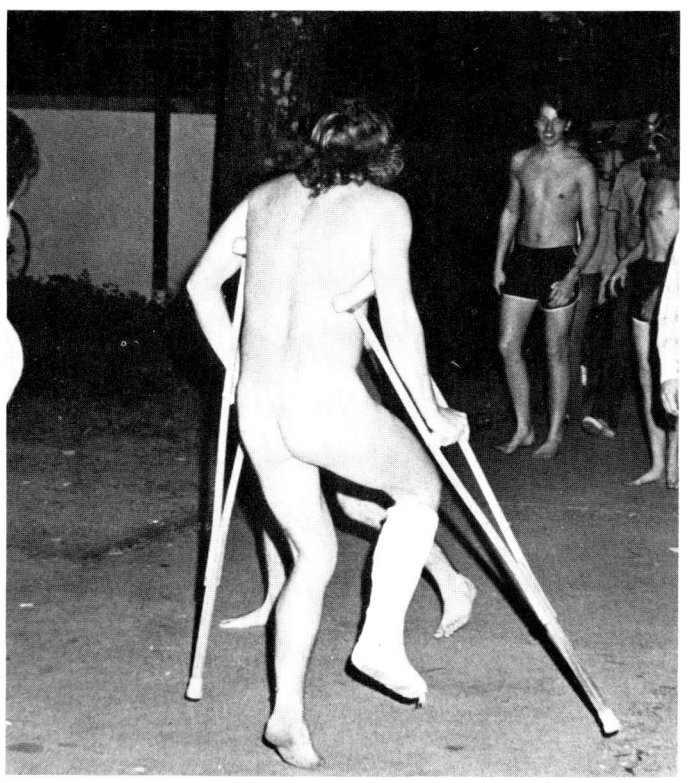

In February 1977, a colorful chapter in Athens's history went up in smoke as the Athens Fire Department set a practice fire at Effie's, the city's most notorious "house of ill repute." No one can remember a time when the houses on Elm Street were not open for business. Effie Matthews, the most infamous madam, lived and worked in the house at 175 Elm, but her reputation and name spread to the nearby "houses." Although Effie died in the mid-1960s, her legendary presence lived on. In 1972, District Attorney Harry Gordon campaigned on a pledge to rid Athens of Effie's, and the houses were soon raided and closed. The contents of the three houses were sold at auction in the summer of 1974. The fire in 1977 brought an end to Effie's story.

Dean Tate once said that students were "exuberant in their loyalties" to institutions, and Effie's was one of them. Although the operations were periodically shut down, they seem to have caused little trouble in the community. Policemen, however, were caught in a dilemma—there were demands from the community to wipe out vice, but Effie's had become a landmark, and raids often brought outcries from those who favored a live-and-let-live policy. Photograph by David Hennings; courtesy of Athens Newspapers, Incorporated

Effie's may be gone, but it is not forgotten. Actually, it is not entirely gone. After the fire cooled, a local entrepreneur, Hoyt Ray, cleaned and numbered the bricks and sold each of them with a plaque certifying that the purchaser owned "a piece of Old Athens." Photograph courtesy of Athens Newspapers, Incorporated

Athens's first decorator showhouse was held in the spring of 1977 in the elaborate Cheney House on Milledge Avenue, one of the city's few remaining Queen Anne mansions. The event, which was so successful it had to be extended an extra week, raised money for the Historic Cobbham Foundation and demonstrated the possibilities of the house, which was then on the market.

The 1893 house had been saved from destruction in 1971 when the Athens-Clarke Heritage Foundation took an option on the property, selling it to a young couple for restoration. After the house had changed hands several times, it was again threatened in 1977. Both foundations offered an option on the property, but it was sold to a young lawyer who completed its restoration. The building now houses J.T. Interiors.

The Cheney House is also the scene of a well-known Athens legend. Two sisters, Frances and Maud Cheney, were living in the house when a neighbor's cat came over to have her kittens. Maud cared for them and loved them, and when the cat went home, Maud kept the kittens in spite of the neighbor's demand for their return. The dispute finally went to court, where the judge ruled against Miss Cheney. When she still refused to return the kittens, and cursed the judge, she was sentenced to jail for contempt of court. Whether she actually served her sentence, no one knows, but it is said that she sat on the steps of the jail denouncing the sheriff who told her to spend her sentence at home.

The photograph shows a group of volunteers helping to get the house ready for the 1977 decorator showhouse. Photograph by Karakin Goekjian; courtesy of Athens Newspapers, Incorporated

In April 1977, a group of Cobbham residents became involved in a protest over the decision of Prince Avenue Baptist Church to demolish a Victorian house on the corner of Hill and Church streets for a parking lot. Neighborhood residents were uneasy because this demolition marked a further expansion of the church, which already owned virtually the entire block bounded by Hill, Church, Cobb, and Harris, and part of the block to the east. Residents and preservationists feared continued destruction of the irreplaceable houses in the historic district.

In the church's view, their religious mission required the additional parking spaces for a growing congregation. "If God didn't want us to have this house for the church, we couldn't have gotten it," said one church member. "So the fact we got it means that it's all right with God." The neighborhood group was careful not to criticize the church's evangelical effort but urged the congregation to consider alternatives to further destruction.

In two separate protest marches, the first protest the city had seen in some time, sign-carrying demonstrators paraded in front of the church. Church members offered ice water to the marchers and put the service on loudspeakers. There were strained feelings on both sides, but representatives did meet to discuss their concerns. The church members remained firm in their resolution to do whatever was needed to support their programs, and the Victorian house was torn down. However, no additional homes have been destroyed for parking. Several renovated structures are currently in use by the church.

This photograph shows a group of demonstrators marching in front of the house which sparked the protest and which was then being demolished. Photograph by John Toon, The Athens Observer; courtesy of the photographer

Prince Charles, heir to the British throne, received a warm welcome from more than 50,000 fans when he attended the Georgia-Kentucky game in October 1977. "I don't believe I've ever seen such enthusiastically friendly people," the prince told University President Fred Davison as they walked the length of the field at Sanford Stadium.

Charles stopped to talk with two pretty majorettes and met the coaches, Vince Dooley and Fran Curci. Georgia player Jeff Lewis presented him with an autographed football. He also managed to upstage rock star James Brown, who was performing in the halftime show. The conservatively dressed prince remarked to Athens Mayor Upshaw Bentley that he felt rather somber in the sea of red at the game. To remedy the situation, the university presented him with a red blazer and red T-shirt.

After the third quarter, His Highness was escorted to the Athens Airport where he greeted a group of fans gathered at the fence, and then he bid farewell to the Classic City. The photograph shows Prince Charles and Davison walking between the hedges in Sanford Stadium. Photograph by Stewart Simonton; courtesy of Athens Newspapers, Incorporated

The Upson House, one of Athens's finest Greek Revival mansions, still stands on Prince Avenue because of the interest of the Upson family and the foresight and community consciousness of the city's oldest banking institution. Built in 1847 by Dr. Marcus A. Franklin, the house was purchased in 1855 by Stephen Upson who installed inlaid parquet floors, silver hardware, and other elegant decorative features.

In 1974 the Upson descendants sold the property, which had been recorded by the Historic American Buildings Survey and listed in the National Register of Historic Places, to the First National Bank with the stipulation that the house not be destroyed. The bank completely restored the building, refurbished its elegant details, and added a rear wing for a vault and drive-in window.

The design by Group Five Architects of Atlanta won wide acclaim. "You may be withdrawing your last $20," wrote Conoly Hester in the Banner-Herald, "but you'll feel like a millionaire as you walk in the doors." The first public function held in the restored house was a meeting of the Athens-Clarke Heritage Foundation in January 1980, where the group presented its preservation award to bank president T. H. Milner. The project has been an unqualified success. The photograph was taken at ceremonies marking the beginning of work on the project. Photograph by Richard Fowlkes; courtesy of Athens Newspapers, Incorporated

After forty-five years in business on Athens's busiest corner, the Varsity restaurant closed on December 20, 1978. The Varsity had been established by Frank Gordy as a branch of his original fast food restaurant on the corner of North Avenue and Spring Street in Atlanta, near Georgia Tech.

The Varsities became famous, and Gordy became a millionaire. In the early days, the restaurant was a males-only establishment. Ladies, however, could enjoy Varsity sandwiches and drinks in their cars, until downtown congestion forced an end to curb service. In 1963 a second Varsity was opened on Broad Street at Milledge, and Athenians can still satisfy a craving for a hamburger, rings, and a frosted orange at the newer facility.

The downtown restaurant was finally closed, according to Gordy, because of downtown parking problems, yet that Broad Street corner across from the university arch has the busiest foot traffic in town. Others attributed the restaurant's failure to bad management after the retirement of L. P. Suddath, manager from 1932 to 1975.

The photograph shows the Varsity as it looked at the time of its closing in 1978. The building it occupied, the old Colonial Hotel, has been remodeled as the College Square Building, with restaurants and shops on the first floor and offices above. Photograph by Bob Simonton; courtesy of Athens Newspapers, Incorporated

Dean William Tate, a long-time customer of the varsity, is shown eating the last hamburger served at the downtown location. Photograph by John Toon; courtesy of the Athens Observer

Dean William Tate (at right) is shown delivering the principal address to the groups assembled for the 1978 homecoming at Lucy Cobb. Photograph by John Toon, The Athens Observer; courtesy of the photographer

In July, 1978 the Friends of Lucy Cobb and Seney-Stovall joined the Historic Cobbham Foundation in a homecoming under the huge magnolias in front of the Lucy Cobb Institute. The Friends were organized the previous May to draw attention to the need for restoration of the main buildings of the historic campus and to act as a fund-raising organization for that purpose.

After Lucy Cobb closed during the Great Depression, the university accepted the property from the trustees of the school with the understanding that it be kept up. The campus was used over the years by a number of university programs, but the structures gradually deteriorated. The top floor of the main building finally had to be removed, and the chapel was boarded up after suffering extensive water damage. The future of these historic structures looked bleak.

Finally, in response to the urging of the two non-profit groups and a number of alumni, the university applied for and received a $50,000 matching federal grant for the restoration of the exterior of the Seney-Stovall Chapel. The work on the chapel was completed in early 1981. A second grant was received for major structural and engineering work in the interior, with matching funds being raised by the Friends of Lucy Cobb.

In late fall, 1984 Lucy Cobb Institute received an early Christmas present from the U.S. Congress—a special $3.5 million grant to restore the campus to serve as the home of the Carl Vinson Institute of Government. The Institute, named after the Georgia Congressman who served longer than any other member of the U.S. House of Representatives, will consolidate its many research and service activities there. U.S. Senator Mack Mattingly, a strong supporter of historic preservation, spearheaded an effort supported by Senator Sam Nunn and Congressman Doug Barnard to raise funds for the project. Institute Director Melvin Hill has coordinated the efforts to return this Athens landmark to a use that will benefit all Georgians.

The photograph above shows the Seney-Stovall Chapel after the completion of exterior restoration. *Photograph courtesy of the University of Georgia Office of Public Relations*

Ellis Merton Coulter, one of the University of Georgia's most popular and well-known professors, left a lasting mark in his chosen field of southern and Georgia history and on the 10,000 students he taught during his long career. Born in North Carolina in 1890, Coulter came to Athens as an associate professor of history in 1919. He became a full professor in 1923 and served as department head from 1941 until his retirement as emeritus professor in 1958. Coulter published some forty books and over 100 articles and edited the Georgia Historical Quarterly for fifty years (1924-1974). His most widely read book, Georgia: a Short History, sold over 25,000 copies. College Life in the Old South, about the University of Georgia, has remained one of his most popular works. Always accessible to students, faculty, alumni, and visitors alike, Coulter was a familiar figure on campus, working in his cluttered office in Phi Kappa Hall nearly every day until his death shortly before his 91st birthday. The photograph below shows Dr. Coulter as so many people remember him, seated at his desk, surrounded by books and papers, working on yet another manuscript. Photograph courtesy of University of Georgia Office of Public Relations

All of Athens seemed to be stage-struck in the fall of 1980 as the cast and crew of "Breaking Away," a prime time television show, began filming on location in Athens. The show was based on a highly acclaimed feature film of the same name set in Bloomington, Indiana. The Athens area was chosen because of similarities to Bloomington and the considerably milder climate.

The stars included Shaun Cassidy, who played Dave Stohler, a recent high school graduate and bicycling enthusiast; Vincent Gardenia and Barbara Barrie, as his parents; and Jackie Earl Haley, Thom Bray, and Tom Wiggen, as his friends. The professional cast and crew were supplemented with local talent and university drama students. The producers, in fact, gave $7,000 to the university for scholarships.

When the season began, Athenians gathered around their sets to see familiar faces and locations around the area. The show was cancelled after the first of the year, in spite of good reviews, because of low ratings.

Although some residents were inconvenienced by the filming, the community showed the visitors typical Southern hospitality and got to know the interesting personalities. Vince Gardenia and local restaurateur Bob Russo even collaborated on a benefit for Italian earthquake victims. The photograph shows the crew filming an episode outside Fire Hall No. 2. Photograph from the author's collection

Vince Gardenia (left) and Shaun Cassidy rehearse a scene for "Breaking Away." Photograph courtesy of University of Georgia Office of Public Relations.

Actress Barbara Barrie receives the attention of a makeup man during filming on location in Athens. Photograph courtesy of University of Georgia Office of Public Relations

The University of Georgia Botanical Garden, which was only an idea shared by Dr. Francis Johnstone, members of the Garden Club of Georgia, and a few others in 1968, now comprises 293 acres representing a broad cross-section of Georgia's piedmont. Five miles of hiking trails traverse old agricultural fields, upland forests, gorge-like ravines, slopes, a flood plain, and scenic river frontage along the Middle Oconee River. Special gardens include displays of herbs, roses, azaleas, camellias, magnolias, dogwood, and a wide variety of native plants and wildflowers. A perennial garden is ablaze with color from May until November. Programs at the garden include short courses and nature walks as well as art exhibits and concerts.

Two striking buildings designed by Atlanta architect Peter Norris and made possible by generous grants from the Callaway Foundation of LaGrange enhance the garden's programs. The award-winning Callaway Building, completed in 1975, is administrative center for the garden. The visitor center/conservatory complex shown in the photograph, was completed in 1985. The $3 million center has exhibit space, a mini-theatre, classrooms, offices, a tea room, gift shop, and a 10,000 square-foot "great room" or conservatory with a glass roof that soars 64 feet above the ground level. The conservatory houses displays of tropical and semi-tropical plants and is also used for social gatherings and concerts.

Each year over 40,000 people visit the garden, which has been designated by the Georgia General Assembly as the official State Botanical Garden. Photograph by L. David Dwinell; courtesy of the photographer

For nearly a decade the Sandy Creek Nature Center has been an educational and recreational resource for the citizens of Clarke County, both youngsters and adults. Groups of school children take regular field trips to the center (located just off U.S. 441 north of the Perimeter) for nature walks or special programs in geology, entomology, or nature crafts.

Originally funded by private contributions and appropriations from city and county governments and the Clarke County Board of Education, the center offically became a part of the county government in 1981. In addition to the professional staff, trained volunteers take groups on trail walks, help with maintenance, and assist with special programs which have covered such topics as weaving, natural dyes, and healing with herbs.

An annual nature photography contest, "Snake Day," and a Halloween haunted woods have been popular events. A log house was moved to the center in 1981 from the Palmetto Community in Oglethorpe County to provide an example of the type of structure the early settlers built and lived in. The center's programs have been further enhanced by the development of the adjacent Sandy Creek Park. The photograph shows a group of school children on a nature walk. Photograph courtesy of the Sandy Creek Nature Center

When the Athens Fire Department closed Fire Hall No. 2 on Prince Avenue in 1979, preservationists feared that the elegant two-story building at the intersection of Hill and Prince would be lost. Built in 1901 on the former site of a black volunteer fire company's headquarters, the fire hall was the first facility constructed by the city fire department, which had used downtown volunteer company facilities since its organization in 1891.

In November 1979, however, the city council agreed to lease the local landmark to the Athens-Clarke Heritage Foundation. The city made exterior repairs, repointing and painting, while the foundation completely renovated the interior at a cost of $30,000. Original details were repaired and refinished, or reproduced, and new lighting and mechanical systems were installed. Meanwhile, foundation business was conducted in the dust, rubble, and noise of construction.

Mayor Lauren Coile cut the ribbon and officially opened the restored building in the spring of 1981. The fire hall now serves as headquarters and educational center for the foundation. Changing exhibits on preservation and history are displayed on the first floor, and the upstairs space is used as an office, library, meeting space, and workshop. Other local organizations, too, use the facilities for meeting and work. Photograph by Dennis O'Kain; courtesy of the Athens-Clarke Heritage Foundation

In April 1981, the Athens Young Women's Christian Organization celebrated its seventy-fifth anniversary by breaking ground for a new building on Research Drive east of the city. Programs and facilities for local women have grown dramatically since sixty women met to organize the Athens Y.W.C.A. on May 1, 1906.

Early facilities were located over Williamson's Grocery on Clayton Street and later in the Moss Building. In 1910 the "Y" moved to the Bessie Mell Industrial Home in order to provide a boarding house for women. After that building was sold the following year, the organization acquired the Stevens Thomas House at Hancock and Pulaski. A modern gymnasium and swimming pool, erected on the corner lot in 1913, has served several generations of Athens women. Expanding programs forced the "Y" to seek a new location, and a fund-raising campaign made possible the acquisition of the Research Drive property and an adjoining former day-care center. The photograph was taken during ground breaking ceremonies in 1981. Photograph by William B. Winburn; courtesy of Athens Newspapers, Incorporated

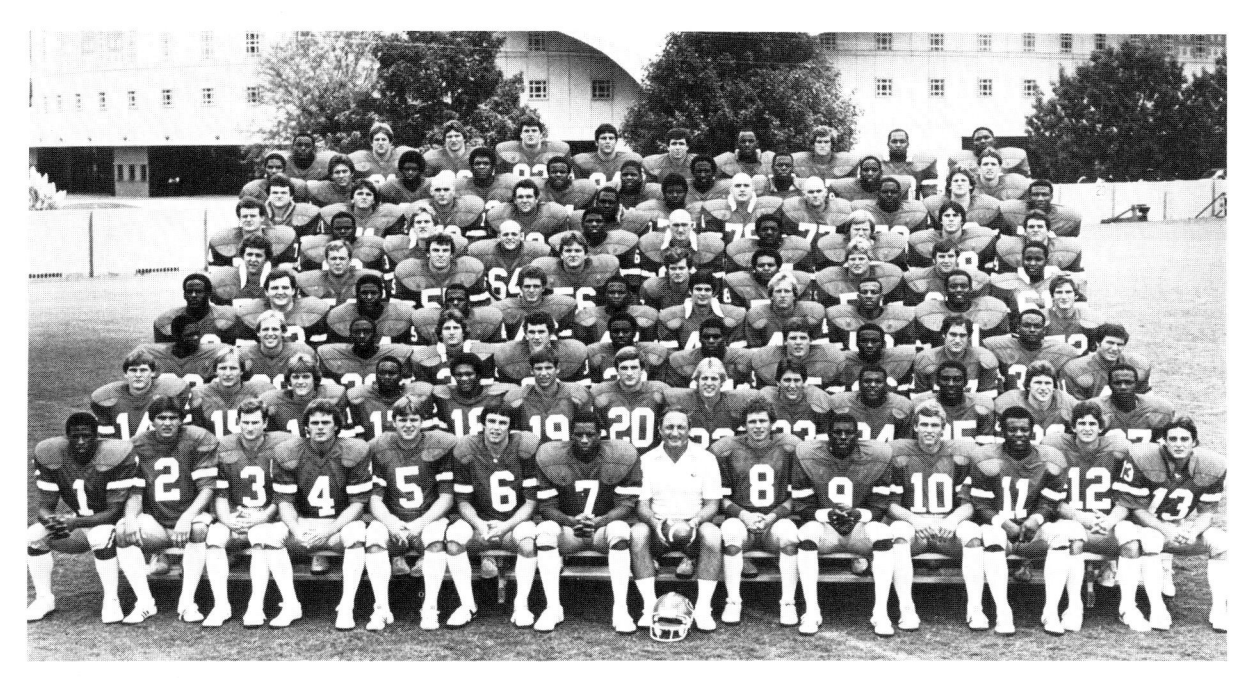

When the 1980 pre-season polls were issued, Georgia was ranked from 6th (Playboy) to 20th (UPI). Before the season was over, the team, which finished 6-5 in 1979, would astound the prognosticators and delight their fans. The season began with a spectacular 16-15 come-from-behind win over Tennessee in Knoxville and concluded with a 17-10 victory against Notre Dame in the Sugar Bowl and the Bulldog's first national championship.

In the process, they beat Texas A&M (42-0), Clemson (20-16), TCU (34-3), Ole Miss (28-21), Vanderbilt (41-0), Kentucky (27-0), South Carolina (13-10), Florida (26-21), Auburn (31-21), and Georgia Tech (38-20), finishing the season as the only undefeated major college team in the nation.

A number of the outstanding players won regional or national honors: Scott Woerner, Rex Robinson, Jeff Hipp, Tim Morrison, Nat Hudson, Eddie Weaver, Jimmy Paine, and Buck Belue. Throughout the season, however, the nation's eyes were fixed on freshman superstar Herschel Walker from Johnson County, Georgia, who (incredibly for a freshman) finished third in balloting for the Heisman Trophy. He won the Heisman during the 1982 season.

Walker's spectacular running inspired the entire team to an all-out championship effort. The entire Bulldog team is shown seated for a group photograph in front of the Coliseum. Head football coach Vince Dooley, named 1980 Coach of the Year, is seated in the center of the first row. Photograph courtesy of University of Georgia Sports Information Office

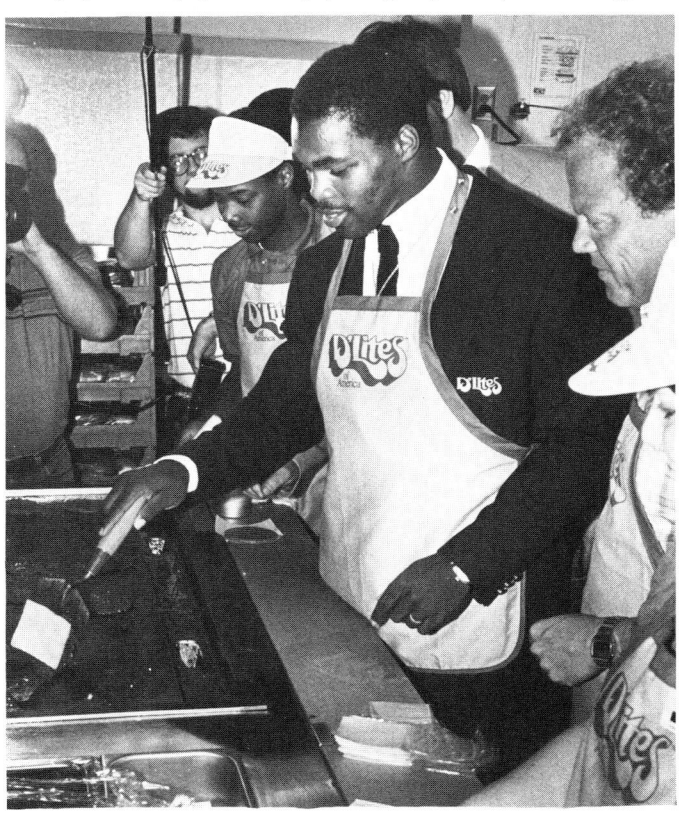

During the spring of his Junior year, Herschel Walker signed a multi-million dollar contract with the New Jersey Generals of the new United States Football League and left Athens amid a controversy as to whether he should have played another year at Georgia before turning professional. Walker and his wife often return to Athens, however, and he has invested some of his earnings in a local enterprise. Walker purchased a franchise for D'Lites, a fast food chain featuring lower calorie items.

On April 24, 1984, Walker opened in Athens the first of 14 restaurants to which he has the rights in Georgia and Tennessee. Ironically, one of D'Lites's features is a lower-calorie high-fiber sandwich bun developed by the University of Tennessee, the school against which freshman Walker launched his spectacular career as a running back, leading the Bulldogs to a one-point victory against the Volunteers in Knoxville at the opening of the 1980 football season.

The photograph shows Herschel Walker demonstrating how its done at D'Lites to John Patrick (right) of television's "P.M. Magazine." Photograph by Wingate Downs, courtesy of Athens Newspapers, Incorporated

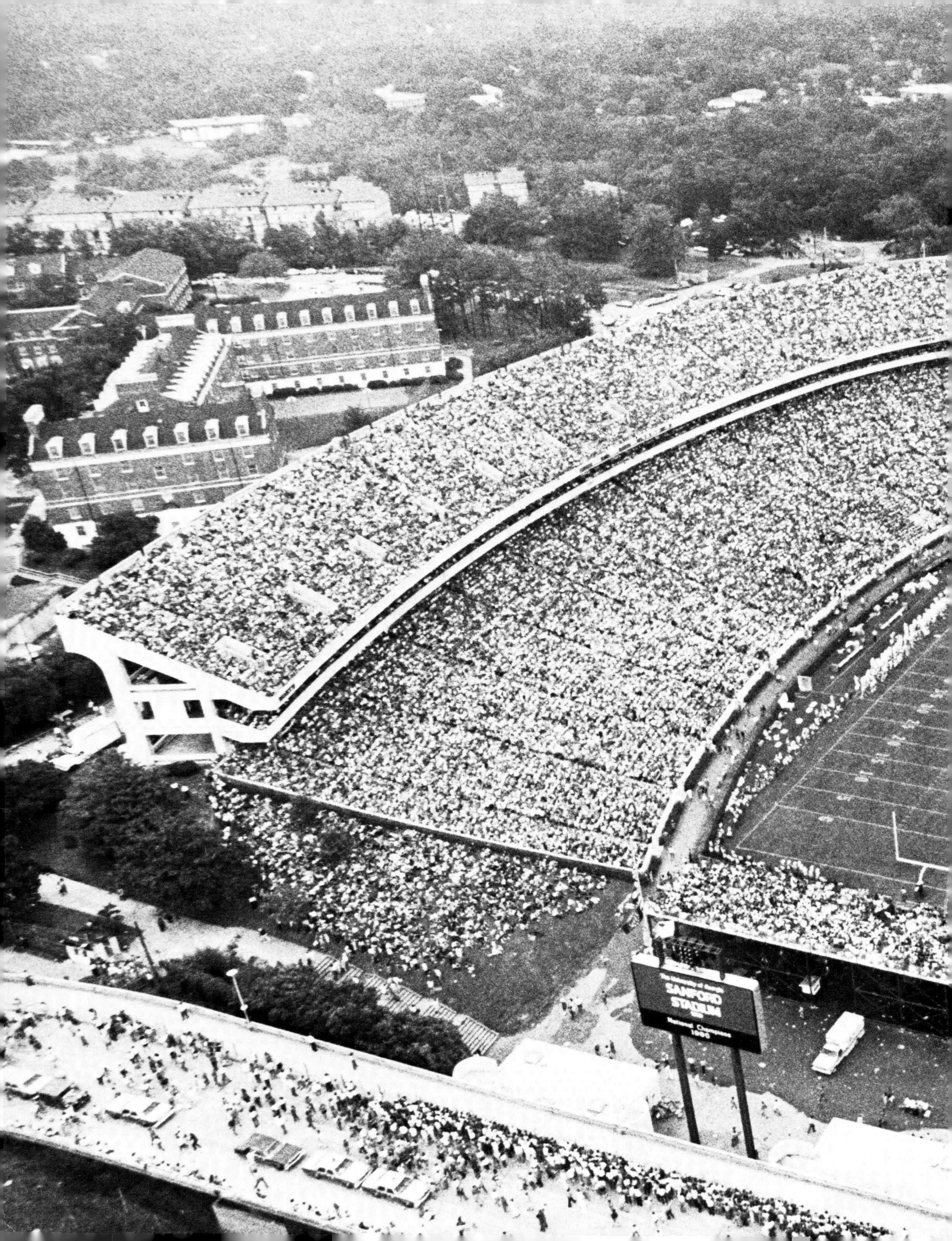
SANFORD
STADIUM

On the first Saturday in September 1981, 79,600 football fans filled Sanford Stadium to see the Georgia Bulldogs embarrass the Tennessee Volunteers by defeating them 44-0 in the first game played in the expanded stadium (shown here). The Marvin M. Black Company of Atlanta, contractor for the $7,999,000 rehabilitation project, had finished installing the seats in the new east end addition only days before the game.

Other parts of the structure, including some restrooms, concession stands, and one ramp, remained incomplete, but that did not dampen the enthusiasm of fans who were lucky enough to have seats in the expanded stadium for the battle between the hedges. Only fourteen years before, in the summer of 1967, the capacity of the stadium had been increased to over 58,000 by the addition of the upper decks, and in 1980 the field was given a new playing surface—a natural grass super turf with special drainage and watering systems.

The 1981 addition made Sanford Stadium, now fifty-two years old, one of the largest and most modern college stadiums in the Southeast. Photograph by Cynthia Downs; courtesy of Athens Newspapers, Incorporated

At 9:30 a.m. on February 11, 1981, a new chapter in the commercial history of Athens began with the opening of Georgia Square Mall on the Atlanta Highway west of the city. Designed to serve a multi-county area of Northeast Georgia, the enclosed shopping mall contains over ninety stores, including four major department stores, with a total of 850,000 square feet of space on two levels.

It is, according to CBL Associates, the developer, one of the largest malls in the state, only slightly smaller than Atlanta's Cumberland or Lenox Square. The total investment by the developer and individual stores is approximately $20 million. The complex employs over 2,000 workers. Photograph by William Winburn; courtesy of Athens Newspapers, Incorporated

For almost thirty years the United States Navy Supply Corps School has been part of the Athens community with facilities for training supply officers on the historic State Normal School campus on Prince Avenue. The present Navy Supply Corps system dates from 1934, when the secretary of the navy established the school at the Navy Yard in Philadelphia. Until moving to Athens, the nomadic school was operated at nine different locations.

The university sold the old facility, which it had used as an adjunct campus for freshmen and sophomore women, for $450,000 in 1953. The new school was commissioned on January 15, 1954. Since taking over the property, the navy has erected new structures for classrooms, officers quarters, and a wide variety of other facilities while demolishing a number of venerable campus buildings.

Seven historic structures remain today, however, on the landscaped grounds shaded by huge trees. The old Carnegie Library houses the Supply Corps Museum, which is open to the public. Winnie Davis Hall, a gift from the U.D.C. in memory of Confederate President Jefferson Davis's daughter, is used as headquarters.

Over 18,000 officers have been trained at the school in Athens, and it is a favorite post for faculty members. In addition to the basic 24-26 week course and a number of special courses, the school also trains two classes of foreign officers each year.

In July 1981 a recent class of supply officers assembled in the courtyard in front of Winnie Davis Hall for graduation exercises. Photograph by William B. Winburn; courtesy of Athens Newspapers, Incorporated

The Morton Theatre, a 1910 black vaudeville theater on Washington Street, received a reprieve and new hope for re-use as the community's performing arts center when the Morton Corporation purchased the building on September 24, 1981.

The Morton Building, a four-story structure which housed commercial enterprises on the first floor with the theater and professional offices above, was built by black entrepreneur Monroe B. "Pink" Morton at the center of the turn-of-the-century black commercial district. The theater saw performances by many jazz era greats—Bessie Smith, Louis Armstrong, Duke Ellington, Butterbeans and Susie, Blind Willie McTell—before being turned into a movie theater in the 1930s.

It also served as a showcase for local talent and as a place for community activities until it was closed after a small fire in the projection booth in the mid-1950s. Interest in restoring Athens's only remaining early theater began in the early 1970s, receiving a boost when the building was listed in the National Register of Historic Places in 1979.

A design study funded by the National Endowment for the Arts demonstrated that the theater could be restored for use by the many performing arts organizations in the county that currently have no suitable permanent facility. The project got off the ground with a $27,000 grant from the Georgia Department of Natural Resources, with $37,000 matching money coming from Community Development Block Grant funds allocated by the city. At one point, the matching funds were withdrawn by the mayor but were restored by the city council.

The Morton Corporation succeeded in raising money for minor repairs, but major rehabilitation funds were not forthcoming. The future of this significant building remains in doubt. Photographs of interior and exterior by James R. Lockhart; courtesy of the Georgia Department of Natural Resources

The photograph above shows College Avenue as it appeared during the several months of construction prior to the opening of College Square. Although merchants and shoppers were inconvenienced for a time, the project seems to have been more than worth the trouble. Photograph by Hal Brooks; courtesy of Athens Newspapers, Incorporated

On November 12, 1981, the Classic City Band played old fashioned tunes, and ladies in turn-of-the-century costumes strolled along the sidewalks as dedication ceremonies were held for College Square, a $200,000 project which provided a facelift for College Avenue between Broad and Clayton streets. Funds for the redevelopment were provided by the city council from the sale of an old parking garage on Broad Street.

In the meantime, merchants were rehabilitating their stores, and investors were snapping up available older buildings, confounding the prophets of doom who had predicted the demise of the downtown in the wake of the opening of Georgia Square Mall on the Atlanta Highway.

"These are the good old days for Downtown," said Mayor Lauren Coile (right foreground) at the dedication ceremonies. His sentiments were echoed by University President Fred Davison and officials of the Athens Downtown Development Authority and the Downtown Council.

The College Avenue improvements were designed to enhance the turn-of-the-century character of the downtown and encourage pedestrian traffic in the area. The sidewalks were widened, planters and period lighting were installed, and park benches were provided. Eighteen trees were planted to commemorate significant events in the city's history, and kiosks were erected to provide information on community activities.

After 180 years, downtown Athens is still a bustling and interesting place, and the College Square project represents another effort to make it a more liveable and attractive one. Photograph of ribbon cutting courtesy of Athens Newspapers, Incorporated

Downtown Athens hosts a number of activities throughout the year that make doing business there a pleasure. Open-air concerts, exhibitions, festivals, gala events complete with costumes, and the annual Twilight Criterium bicycle race all contribute to the lively atmosphere. The photographs on this page are, clockwise from the top left: the Stilt Man advertising a local restaurant, photograph by Wingate Downs; the "Notable Exceptions" barbershop quartet, photograph by Ellen Fitzgerald; the Chocolate Shop and two shoppers in Victorian Era costume, photograph by Hal Brooks; and a downtown festival, photograph by Wingate Downs; courtesy of Athens Newspapers, Incorporated

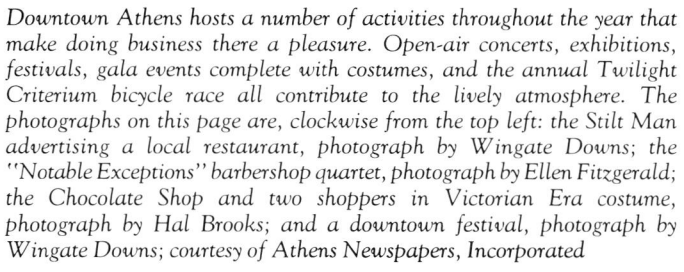

The Intercollegiate Tennis Coaches Association (ITCA) Collegiate Hall of Fame was dedicated on the University of Georgia Campus on May 16, 1984. The two men most responsible for the new facility, Kenny Rogers, a recording industry superstar (center, above), and Dan Magill, the winningest college tennis coach in history (right, above) are shown at the conclusion of a celebrity doubles tournament held at Henry Feild Stadium to mark the opening of the new $200,000 facility.

Magill, long-time sports information officer for the University of Georgia and the nation's most colorful and entertaining tennis coach, quietly built one of the finest college tennis programs in the country at a school that is known widely for football. It is also due largely to his efforts that Georgia has been in the national spotlight for the past decade as host for the NCAA tennis championships. Those efforts were rewarded in 1985 when the Bulldogs were crowned national champions for the first time and Georgia player Mikael Pernfors won his second NCAA singles championship, playing his teammate George Bezecny in the finals.

An interest in tennis brought Kenny Rogers in contact with Magill, but it was his marriage to former Athenian Marianne Gordon (above, left, holding their son Christopher) that brought Rogers to Northeast Georgia. Beginning her career as a songwriter and model, Gordon has been a regular on the long-running television show "Hee-Haw." It was through her work on that show that she met country music star Rogers. Together they bought a large parcel of land northeast of Athens that had been part of the postbellum plantation of James Monroe Smith. They built a house, developed a horse farm, and restored three historic brick barns that had been part of the old Smith plantation, christening their property "Beaverdam Farms." In addition to their contributions to the Collegiate Tennis Hall of Fame, the Rogers's have shown themselves to be good citizens through their support of other community efforts such as YWCO and 4-H. Photograph by Ellen Fitzgerald; courtesy of Athens Newspapers

Almost forty New Wave bands have come out of Athens since the B-52's attracted worldwide attention with their hit single "Rock Lobster." "It was Liverpool in '63, San Francisco in '65, Detroit and Motown in '67, New York in the '70's, but it's Athens, Georgia, now," declared Dan Matthews, editor of Tasty World, a local rock magazine, in an interview with the Washington Post. The Post ran a widely-circulated article on the Athens phenomenon in August, 1984 entitled "O Little Town of Rock 'n' Roll."

Athens has given rise to groups with names like Pylon, REM (for Rapid Eye Movement), Go Van Go, Dreams so Real, Wheel of Cheese, Rack of Spam, Art in the Dark, Oh-Ok, Love Tractor, Buzz of Delight, Kilkenny Cats, and Banned 37 (named for its place on the list of bands). As Post writer Art Harris described it, the bands "form, split and reincarnate like ambitious amoebas," performing in at least four local clubs.

Dressed in Salvation Army Thrift Store clothing, the band members, for the most part, eschew the blue hair and safety-pinned ears of the "punk" crowd. "No image is the image," for most performers.

All of this activity has attracted the attention of record company executives who will listen to almost any tape that comes from the Classic City. "It's a big help if you can say you're from Athens," according to one musician. "It will get you in the door." Many aspiring New Wave musicians are drawn to Athens and the University of Georgia for this reason. What else makes Athens alluring to aspiring rock stars? "You've got the intellectual movement of a city with small town quiet and it's cheap," said another musician. For whatever reasons, Athens has left its mark on the contemporary music scene. The photograph above, which accompanied the Washington Post article, shows the band Go Van Go performing at Athens's 40 Watt Club. Photograph by Don Nelson; courtesy of the Athens Observer

On October 1, 1984, representatives of colleges, universities, and learned societies from throughout the United States and around the world joined University of Georgia faculty members in a colorful procession which opened a huge academic convocation in the Coliseum, the first major event of the university's bicentennial celebration.

A number of distinguished Georgians joined university officials on the rostrum. Among them was Governor Joe Frank Harris (to the left of the podium in the photograph), one of 22 University of Georgia graduates to hold the state's highest office. The keynote address was delivered by George Bush, Vice President of the United States (standing).

During the ceremonies, five internationally renowned faculty members, Lamar Dodd, Glenn Burton, Norman Giles, Eugene Odum, and Dean Rusk were presented with sterling silver medallions in honor of their accomplishments. Participants also heard the world premier performance of a three-movement symphonic suite written for the occasion by Pulitzer Prize winning composer Karel Husa, who conducted its first public performance by the 77-piece University Festival Orchestra.

The months that followed the convocation were filled with many special events. Founders' Week was celebrated January 21-27, 1985, midway through the 16-month celebration. Activities included a lecture by Yale University President A. Bartlett Giamatti, a concert by the Atlanta Symphony Orchestra, a first-day-of-issue ceremony for the Abraham Baldwin stamp, a student bicentennial birthday party at the Tate Center with a cake large enough to feed 2,000, and a gala Founders's Day dinner at the Coliseum.

Two new histories were offered by the University of Georgia Press, A Pictorial History of the University of Georgia by F. N. Boney and The University of Georgia: A Bicentennial History, 1785-1985 by Thomas G. Dyer. Many visitors viewed two major exhibits, "The Rising Hope of Our Land, The University of Georgia, 1785-1985" and "Georgia's Legacy: History Charted Through the Arts."

Special commemorative vehicle license plates were issued by the state to thousands of motorists, a bicentennial medal was struck, and all mail leaving Athens bore a bicentennial postmark.

On April 27, 1985, a gigantic exposition was held on campus during Alumni Weekend. Classrooms, laboratories, libraries, and other facilities were opened for concerts, exhibits, lectures, and sporting events. Graduates at the 1985 commencement ceremonies in June were presented with special diplomas. The celebration concluded in October, 1985 with the Sunbelt Agricultural Exposition in Moultrie and the first International Congress of Plant Molecular Biology in Savannah. Photograph courtesy of University of Georgia Office of Public Relations.

A special flag was raised at the end of graduation ceremonies in Sanford Stadium on June 9, 1984 to mark the beginning of the University of Georgia's bicentennial observance. The flag flew on campus throughout the succeeding sixteen months, during which hundreds of events were held to celebrate the university's 200th birthday. Photograph courtesy of University of Georgia Office of Public Relations

William Thompson, an art professor who has been a sculptor and teacher for over 25 years, was commissioned to create a medallion for the university's bicentennial celebration. The medallion, which was designed to resemble an ancient coin, was cast in two forms, bronze and silver. The obverse features a tree, symbolizing the age and growth of the university, the branches of which represent the institution's three-part mission: teaching, research, and service. Two campus landmarks, the chapel and arch, are shown among the branches. On the reverse, the sun bursts through clouds to shine on the chapel, symbolic of pride in the institution's past and faith in its future. Photograph courtesy of Athens Newspapers, Incorporated

The United States Postal Service joined in commemorating the 200th anniversary of state-supported higher education in America by issuing a seven-cent postage stamp with a portrait of Abraham Baldwin, founding father of the University of Georgia. The artist, Richard Sparks of Norwalk, Connecticut, executed the drawing from a portrait of Baldwin which hangs at the university. The stamp is part of the Postal Service's Great American Series and was issued at a first-day ceremony held on January 25, 1985. The official first-day envelopes featured a four-color design incorporating two campus landmarks, the chapel and arch, by professor emeritus Lamar Dodd. The stamp is red on a white background. Photograph courtesy of Athens Newspapers, Incorporated

On the evening of May 18, 1985 the City of Athens and the Bicentennial Community Events Committee sponsored a "Night in Old Athens," a community celebration of the university's 200th birthday. Guides in period costume welcomed guests to the old north campus and conducted tours of the historic buildings. Musicians and dancers performed for the visitors as they strolled through the grounds and viewed the decorative arts exhibition at the Georgia Museum of Art. An elaborate dinner was served under the trees in front of Old College. Diners were entertained by the Georgia Woodwind Quintet, and a fireworks display concluded the gala evening. Photograph courtesy of University of Georgia Office of Public Relations

At commencement ceremonies in June 1981, Sheriff Jerry Massey continued a tradition begun at the university's first commencement in 1804. In that year, the Clarke County sheriff was asked to lead the ten students to the brush arbor in front of the rising walls of Old College and to keep order during the ceremony.

Custom requires that the sheriff wear a long coat, hat, and red sash. He must also carry an unsheathed saber (to protect the students from attack by Indians, according to local tradition). Photograph by Ellen Fitzgerald; courtesy of Athens Newspapers, Incorporated

Visitors to the university campus calling on the president are directed to the historic Lustrat House. One of several professors's houses built on campus during the nineteenth century, this structure bears the name of Professor Joseph Lustrat, whose family occupied the dwelling from 1904 until 1927. Lustrat came to the university from France and was head of the Department of Romance Languages. The appearance of the solid two-story brick edifice built in 1847 gives no hint that it has been moved. It originally occupied the site of the Peabody Library (now the Georgia Museum of Art) and was rolled to its present location when that building was begun in 1903. At the time, it was occupied by the family of popular English professor Charles Morris who, according to Tom Reed, was angered by the move and vacated the premises. Before being converted into an office for the president, the building served as a house museum, displaying the furniture of Ilah Dunlap Little, benefactor of the university library. Photograph courtesy of University of Georgia Office of Public Relations

The unusual house shown in the photograph was once the home of Thomas R. R. Cobb and his wife Marion McHenry Lumpkin. It is said to have been given to them after their marriage in 1844 by her father, Joseph Henry Lumpkin, who lived in the Greek Revival mansion next door. The original part of the house was built by either Charles McKinley or Jesse Robinson in 1830. Thomas Cobb's papers indicate that the two distinctive octagonal wings were added to the house in 1852. The house was later occupied by the A. M. Dobbses, the Col. R. S. Taylor family, and Lambda Chi Alpha fraternity. It was owned for many years by St. Joseph's Catholic Church which used it as a parish house, rectory, and office.

In 1985, after a new school was constructed behind the house, the church sought proposals from individuals and groups interested in moving the structure. In spite of the efforts of the United Daughters of the Confederacy, the Heritage Foundation, and others to find a way to keep the house in Athens, it was given to Stone Mountain Memorial State Park. Although the structure may have been physically "saved," its relocation to a recreational park away from all historical associations represented a major loss for the community. The photograph shows the house just prior to its move. *Photograph by Paul Efland; courtesy of Athens Newspapers, Incorporated*

Athenians have discovered that it is possible to damage the historic significance, integrity, and ambiance of a structure without demolishing it or moving it from its original location when its setting is dramatically altered. The Lehmann-Bancroft House, described by A. L. Hull in Annals as "a little bandbox of a place," resembles a small Greek temple with its slender Doric columns and gable pediment, the only one of its era in Athens. Built in 1834 by William Lehmann, the house was once surrounded by considerable acreage. Lehmann, a German Lutheran who was educated in Bonn, Germany, came to the university in 1831 to teach Latin, Greek, French, Italian, and Spanish. James Bancroft bought the house from Lehmann in 1845, and the property was long known as the Bancroft farm.

In recent years the house was owned by the Land family until acquired by a speculator who began restoration but sold the property for development. As the photograph shows, the large old trees which shaded the spacious lot at 392 South Pope Street were cut down, the lawn was paved, and apartments were constructed along one side of the lot. The house, which was itself divided into apartments, now sits forlornly amid a sea of asphalt, automobiles, and trash receptacles. *Photograph by William B. Winburn; courtesy of Athens Newspapers, Incorporated*

While many Athens landmarks are gone, many survive to lend grace, charm, and a sense of place and history to the community. The impressive Greek Revival mansion in the adjacent photograph and those structures shown on this and following pages are examples of buildings that have been preserved or restored by individuals and institutions that value their heritage. This house, located at 425 Hill Street, is still occupied by descendants of the original owners, Governor Howell Cobb and his wife Mary Ann Lamar. Mrs. Cobb's brother, John B. Lamar, contracted with Washington C. Yoakim for the construction of the house in September, 1849. The house cost $3,200 to build and originally occupied the entire block. Recalling his visits to the house during the early 1870s when Mrs. Cobb was still living, Sylvanus Morris wrote in Strolls, "Nothing is more pleasant than the recollection of the hospitality of that home." The same hospitality can be found today in the house which has been preserved and refurbished by Mr. and Mrs. Milton Leathers III. Photograph by Bill Bedgood; courtesy of the Athens-Clarke Heritage Foundation

Ross Crane, the New Jersey-born builder of many of Athens's finest Antebellum structures, built this house for his own residence in the 1840s. Constructed of load-bearing brick, the walls vary in thickness from 16 to 24 inches. Prominently sited on Pulaski Street at the western terminus of Washington, the grounds retain much of their 19th century ambiance, with huge magnolias and one of the city's oldest boxwood gardens, in spite of the encroachment of the downtown commercial district and hard years of use by a fraternity. The house has undergone a number of alterations since its construction, including the addition of two side wings during the 1930s. Used as an Elks lodge in the 1920s and purchased by Sigma Alpha Epsilon fraternity in 1929 for a dormitory and chapter house, it had deteriorated significantly by the late 1970s. Alumni mounted a successful fund drive to refurbish the structure which continues to serve the Georgia Beta Chapter as its fraternity house. The property is listed in the National Register of Historic Places. Photograph by Dan McClure; courtesy of the photographer

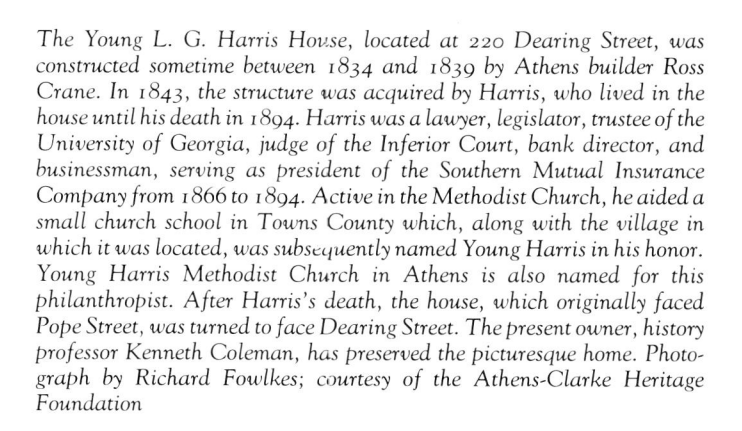

The Young L. G. Harris House, located at 220 Dearing Street, was constructed sometime between 1834 and 1839 by Athens builder Ross Crane. In 1843, the structure was acquired by Harris, who lived in the house until his death in 1894. Harris was a lawyer, legislator, trustee of the University of Georgia, judge of the Inferior Court, bank director, and businessman, serving as president of the Southern Mutual Insurance Company from 1866 to 1894. Active in the Methodist Church, he aided a small church school in Towns County which, along with the village in which it was located, was subsequently named Young Harris in his honor. Young Harris Methodist Church in Athens is also named for this philanthropist. After Harris's death, the house, which originally faced Pope Street, was turned to face Dearing Street. The present owner, history professor Kenneth Coleman, has preserved the picturesque home. Photograph by Richard Fowlkes; courtesy of the Athens-Clarke Heritage Foundation

The Meeker-Barrow House, built in 1857, is a fine example of the Italianate style which was popular in Athens during the late 1850s. The formal gardens were laid out by Fruitlands Nurseries of Augusta in the mid-nineteenth century and have been maintained over the years in the original plan. According to A. L. Hull, John A. Meeker, son of the house's builder, was the first local man to engage in scientific farming during the postbellum period, developing a farm "equipped with latest machinery and conducted on modern and Northern lines." When the university trustees decided to landscape the campus, John Meeker was engaged to do the work, and P. J. A. Berckmans of Fruitlands Nurseries contributed many of the shrubs and plants. In 1937, the property was acquired by the James Barrow family, who have carefully preserved the historic character of the property. Photograph by Richard Fowlkes; courtesy of the Athens-Clarke Heritage Foundation

The First African Methodist Episcopal Church is one of Athens's most intact historic churches and houses the city's oldest black congregation. Organized as Pierce's Chapel in 1866, the congregation met in a structure near the Oconee River until 1916 when plans for the present church were drawn by architect L.H. Persley of Macon. The builder, R.F. Walker of Athens, took almost a year to finish the high-style structure which features such details as round-headed stained glass windows and a hammerbeamed ceiling. During the 1960s the congregation successfully resisted efforts by the urban renewal program to relocate them and demolish their church, although their parsonage was acquired and torn down in 1969. In 1973 an educational building was constructed adjacent to the church. On March 10, 1980 the First AME Church was listed in the National Register of Historic Places, and a planning grant was awarded to the congregation by the Georgia Department of Natural Resources. The subsequent restoration of the structure has been a major accomplishment for the membership and has ensured the preservation of an important community landmark. Photograph by James Lockhart; courtesy of Georgia Department of Natural Resources

Tradition has it that Thomas Wray purchased an 1825 student dining hall during the 1840s and built the Doric-columned front section seen in the photograph. After the Civil War, the house was acquired by John W. Nicholson, a business partner and brother-in-law of William S. Grady, father of Henry W. Grady. Mrs. Grady and Mrs. Nicholson were sisters. Grady and Nicholson built Athens's first gas works in the 1850s. The house passed to John Nicholson's son, Madison Nicholson, who was living in the house at the turn of the century.

The house remained in the Nicholson family until acquired by the Christian College of Georgia. The college has preserved this large and impressive Greek Revival mansion. One of the interesting features of the house is a secret stair which provides an unsuspected outside entrance and exit. *Photograph by Dan McClure; courtesy of the photographer*

In 1892, Charles Alexander Scudder and his wife bought a small cottage on Milledge Avenue and transformed it into the striking two-story Victorian structure shown in the photograph. Scudder was a prominent jeweler whose parents had come to Athens in the 1840s or 1850s from Princeton, New Jersey. The house remained in the Scudder family until 1963. It became rental property and was later leased to Tau Kappa Epsilon and Sigma Pi fraternities. In 1981, the property was purchased by Mr. and Mrs. Ward Lewis who spent a year restoring the structure before taking up residence there.

Behind the main house is a picturesque carriage house which was also restored by the Lewises. Many Athenians remember the art exhibitions given in the carriage house each year for the students of Nina Scudder. The restored and re-landscaped property commands a prominent location on the northwest corner of Milledge Avenue and Baxter Street. *Photograph courtesy of Athens-Clarke Heritage Foundation*

BIBLIOGRAPHY

In preparing the manuscript, the author consulted the extensive collections of the University of Georgia Libraries Special Collections; various issues of local newspapers, including the *Athens Banner-Herald Athens Daily News, Athens Observer*, and the *Red and Black*; the *Pandora* and *Alumni Record*; and the following:

Art Work of North Central Georgia. Chicago: Gravure Illustration Company, 1919.

Athens, Georgia, Home of the University of Georgia, 1801-1951. Athens: Mayor and Council of the City of Athens, 1951.

Boney, F. N. *A Pictorial History of the University of Georgia*. Athens: The University of Georgia, Press, 1984.

Brooks, Robert Preston. *The University of Georgia Under Sixteen Administrations, 1785-1955*. Athens: The University of Georgia Press, 1956.

Coleman, Kenneth, general editor. *A History of Georgia*. Athens: The University of Georgia Press, 1977.

Cooney, Loraine M., compiler. *Garden History of Georgia, 1733-1933*, edited by Hattie C. Rainwater. Atlanta: Garden Club of Georgia, 1976.

Coulter, Ellis Merton. *College Life in the Old South*. Athens: The University of Georgia Press, 1951.

Cumming, Mary G. *Georgia Railroad and Banking Company, 1833-1945*. Augusta, Ga: Walton Publishing Co., 1945.

Dyer, Thomas G. *The University of Georgia, A Bicentennial History, 1785-1985*. Athens: The University of Georgia Press, 1985.

English, John W., and Rob Williams. *When Men Were Boys, An Informal Portrait of Dean William Tate*. Lakemont, Georgia: Cobble House Books, 1984.

Georgia, A Guide to Its Towns and Countryside, compiled by the Federal Writers' Project, Work Projects Administration. Athens: The University of Georgia Press, 1940.

Hajos, Albin. *Hajos' Athens Georgia, Photo-Gravures*. Athens: the author, 1900.

Hartshorn, W. N., editor. *An Era of Progress and Promise, 1863-1910*. Boston: The Priscilla Publishing Co., 1910.

History of Athens and Clarke County. Athens: H. J. Rowe, 1923.

Hull, Augustus Longstreet. *Annals of Athens, Georgia, 1801-1901*. Athens: Banner Job Office, 1906; republished with index, Danielsville, Ga: Heritage Papers, 1978.

Hynds, Ernest C. *Antebellum Athens and Clarke County*. Athens: The University of Georgia Press, 1974.

Mell, Edward Baker. *Reminiscences of Athens, Georgia, About 1880 to 1890*, edited by Jones M. Drewry. Athens: 1964.

Morris, Sylvanus. *Strolls About Athens in the Early Seventies*, facsimile reprint of the 1912 edition. Athens: Athens Historical Society, 1969.

Muir, John. *A Thousand Mile Walk to the Gulf*. New York: Houghton Mifflin Co., 1916.

Papers of the Athens Historical Society, Volume II., edited by Patricia Irvin Cooper, et al. Athens: the society, 1979.

Reed, Thomas W. *"Uncle Tom" Reed's Memoir of the University of Georgia*, edited with an introduction by Ray Mathis. Athens: University of Georgia Libraries, 1974.

Sell, E. S. *History of the State Normal School, Athens, Georgia*. Athens: 1923.

Steed, Hal. *Georgia: Unfinished State*. New York: Alfred A. Knopp, 1942.

Stegeman, John F. *These Men She Gave*. Athens: The University of Georgia Press, 1964.

Strahan, Charles Morton. *Clarke County, Georgia, and the City of Athens*. Athens: the author, 1893.

Tate, William. *Strolls Around Athens*. Athens: The Observer Press, 1975.

Thurmond, Michael. *A Story Untold*. Athens: Clarke County School District, 1978.

Tuck, Henry C. *Four Years at the University of Georgia, 1877-1881*. Athens: the author, 1938.

Wood, Maud Talmage. *Once Apunce A Time*. Athens: the author, 1977.

Index

A
Ackerman, Alfred 36
Adams, W. F. 175
Aderhold, O. C. 166
Alfriend, Alfred H. 53, 55
Algood, Clyde 147
Allen, Peggy 165
Alpha Delta Pi Sorority House
  (see Hamilton House)
Alpha Gamma Delta Sorority House
  (see Thomas-Carithers House)
Alpha Tau Omega Fraternity 56
American Cafe 131, 132
American Legion of Honor 48
American State Bank 88
Anderson, Henry C. 116
Arch, University of Georgia 41, 90
Arnall, Ellis G. 158, 160
Ashe, William C. 39
Ashford, Alexander Woodson 38
Athena Industrial Park 160
Athenaeum Club 151
Athens Area Vocational-Technical
  School 160
Athens Banner staff 90
Athens Banner-Herald Building 173
Athens Baptist Church
  (see First Baptist Church)
Athens, city of
  1804 map 16
  1866 view 53
  1874 map 59
  1909 bird's eye view 106, 107
Athens-Clarke Heritage
  Foundation 36, 162, 173, 177, 181,
  188, 201
Athens Coca-Cola Bottling Company
  Hancock Avenue building 115
  Washington Street building 114
Athens Cotton and Wool Factory 34
Athens Empire Laundry 138
Athens Factory
  (see Athens Manufacturing Company)
Athens Fruit Company 118
Athens Gas Light Company 14
Athens General Hospital 145
Athens Guards 44
Athens Hardware Company 142
Athens High and Industrial
  School 121, 123
Athens High School 68, 72
  Childs Street building 121
  Girls basketball team 147
  Mell Auditorium 146
  Milledge Avenue campus 171
  Prince Avenue campus 146
  Red Cross chapter, 1918 124
Athens Historical Society 26, 162
Athens Hotel 33
Athens Industrial Home
  (see Bessie Mell Industrial Home)
Athens Junior Assembly 165
Athens Manufacturing Company
  27, 34, 35, 51
Athens Park and Improvement
  Company 77
Athens Railway and Electric Company
  47, 114
Athens Savings Bank 88
Athens Street Railway stock
  certificate 68
Athens Woman's Club 31, 101
Atwell, Harry 141
"Aunt Lollipop"
  (see Paddock, Laura Hutchins)
Augusta Chronicle
  University of Georgia founded 12

B
Bacon, Mary 63
Baldwin, Abraham 10, 11, 199
Balloon ascent 94
Bancroft, George 53, 55
Bancroft, James 201
Bank of Athens 13
  banknotes 34, 47
Bank of the State of Georgia 13, 26
Barnett, J. W. 102
Barnett, Samuel W. 53, 55
Barrie, Barbara 186
Barrow, David C. 82, 84, 108, 110
Barrow, James 203
Barth, Mary Simpson 165
Baumgarten, P. H. 21
Baxter, Sarah Cobb 28
Beacham, W. W. 136
Beaver, Sandy 158

Beechwood Shopping Center 160
Beene, Horace 53
Bell Telephone
  (see Southern Bell Telephone)
Benson, Edsel 171
Benson, Jeanne 165
Benson, W. H. 133
Benson's Bakery 171
  Parade float 133
Berckmans, P.J.A. 203
Bernard, H. R. 30
Bernstein Brothers 113
Bernstein's Furniture 101
Bessie Mell Industrial Home 67, 101
Bethune, J. H. 53
Billups, John 17, 37
Birchmore, Fred 148
Bird, J. Ovid 136
Bishop, John 32
Blackshear, Laura 150
Bloomfield, Robert L. 34, 51, 77
Bloomfield Street scene 77
Bludwine Company
  advertisement 116
  bottling plan 116-117
  delivery wagon 116-117
  (see also Budwine)
Bobbin Mill 52
Boggs, William E. 81, 86
Boulevard area 77
Bowden, Kit 147
Bowen, Emma 147
Bowers, Winifred 148
Bradbury, Laura 147
Bradford and Shaw 30
Bradley Foundation 37
Bradshaw, Mrs. W. F. 37
Bradwell, Samuel D. 111
Brand, Charles H. 113
Branson, Eugene C. 111
Braswell, Earl B. 173
Breaking Away 186
Brittain, Henry L. 38
Broad Street, c. 1885 view 68
Broun, William 36
Brown, A. Ten Eyck 113, 134
Brown, Aaron 121
Brown, John 14
Brown, Reverend John H. 66, 67
Brown, Julius L. 53
Brown, L. C. 115
Brown, Captain Samuel, Assembly
  Room 20
Brownson, Nathan 11
Brumby, Ann Wallis 98
Bryan, William Jennings 93
Buckingham, James Silk 13
Budwine Company
  (see Bludwine Company)
Budwine Boy and Dog 117
Burke, Moselle Lyndon 71
Burke, Thomas Alexander 71
Burney, Mrs. A. H. 121
Burton, Glenn 198
Bush, George 198
Butler, Joan 165

C
C & S Bank 138
Caldwell, Elizabeth 121
Caldwell, Harmon 158
Calvin, George W., store 87
Camak House 26
Camak, James 26, 27, 35
Camak, Thomas U. 45
Camak's Company 45
Carithers, James Y. 73, 79
Carithers, Karen 165
Carlton, H. H. 70, 71, 93
Carlton, Helen 70
Carlton, James 20, 25
Carlton, Olivia 70
Carlton, W. A. 53
Carlton-Mandeville House 25
Carnival of 1900 94, 95
Carr, William 34
Carroll, Benjamin R. 41
Carr's Hill 27
Carter, Jimmy 175
Cary, John 16
Casey, J. H. 53
Cassidy, Shaun 186
"Cat-Alley" 33
Center Hill School 15
Central Hotel 33
Central of Georgia Railroad 48, 99,
  110
Central Presbyterian Church 76
Chambers, Dwain 175

Chandler, Louise 147
Chapel, University 21, 80, 175
  Chapel painting 21
Charbonnier, L. H. 39, 41, 53,
  58, 68, 80
Charles, Prince of Wales 182
Chase, Albon 90
Check Factory 51
  (see also Athens Manufacturing
  Company)
Cheney House 181
Cheney, Maud 181
Chi Phi Fraternity 56
Chicopee Mills 51
Childs, Asaph K. 25, 31, 36, 37
Childs, A. K., House 37
Childs, Frances Ingle 37
Childs Street School
  (see Athens High School)
Christian Church
  (see First Christian Church)
Christian College of Georgia 159, 204
Christmas party 120
Christy, John 58, 90
Church, Alonzo 13, 15, 24, 36, 173
Church, Alonzo III 36
Church silver service 36
Church, Sarah J. Trippe 36
Church, Thomas 166
Church-Waddel-Brumby House 24, 173
Citizen's Pharmacy 130
City Hall 91, 102, 103
  (see also Town Hall and Market House)
Civic League 130
Clark, Louis S. 122
Clarke County Anti-Tuberculosis
  Society 146
Clark County Courthouse
  Prince Avenue 47, 68
  Washington Street 113
Clark, Elijah 13
Clarke Rifles 44
Clayton, Augustin S. 34, 142
Clayton Street, views 99, 130, 132, 138
"Cloverhurst" 70, 71
Cloverhurst Country Club 101, 130
Cobb, Andrew J. 86
Cobb Governor Howell 16, 43, 50, 202
Cobb, Judge Howell 28
Cobb, Howell, House 202
Cobb, John A. 12, 38
Cobb, Lucy 40
Cobb, Mary Ann Lamar 50, 202
Cobb, Sarah Rootes 38
Cobb, Thomas R. R. 15, 16, 35, 40, 42,
  43, 44, 85, 92, 201
Cobbham 12, 182
  (see also Historic Cobbham
  Foundation)
Coca-Cola
  (see Athens Coca-Cola Bottling
  Company)
Cocking, Walter D. 158
Cofer, H. L. 38
Cohen, M. G. & J. 80
Coile, Lauren 194
Coleman, Kenneth 202
Coliseum University 170
College Avenue, views 88, 90, 91, 103,
  138-139, 194
College Square 194
Colley, A. T. 154
Colonial Hotel 33, 90, 184
Colonial Theatre 139
Commercial Hotel 33, 90
Compton, Martha Lumpkin 109
Congregation Children of Israel 92
Confederate Constitution 44
Confederate Memorial Day 48
Confederate Monument 46, 57
Confederate postmaster provisional
  stamp 45
Connor Hall 110
Connor, J. J. 110
Cook, A. H. 134, 135
Cook and Brother Armory 43, 51
Cooke, George 21, 27
Cook's Company 41
Cooper-Barrett-Skinner-Woodbury and
  Cooper 170
Cooper's Cafe 138-139
Costa, Anthony 118
Costa Building 141
Costa family 140
Costa, Joseph 116-117
Costa, Tony 141
Costa's 101, 140, 141
Cotton 105
Coulter, E. M. 22, 185

Covered bridge 85
Cox, Frank 137
Crane, Ross 20, 25, 30, 202
Crane, Ross, House 202
Crawford, Annie 64
Crawford, C. W. 175
Crawford, Mrs. E. A., School 48
  Students 64
Crawford, Reese 53
Crawford, Thomas 45
Crews, Betty 147
Cumming, Elizabeth Hall 165
Cummings, Mr. 121
Curtis, C. M. 166

D
Daughters of the American
  Revolution 101
Davenport Building 136
Davis, Catherine 147
Davis, Madison 46
Davis, Winnie 70
Davison, Mrs. Alexander H. 120
Davison, Fred 182, 194
Davison, Ida 147
Davison-Paxon Company 131
Day, Irene 144
Dearing, Eugenia Hamilton 39
Dearing, William 27, 34, 68, 142
De Fontaine, Felix G. 44
Demosthenian Hall 18, 80
Demosthenian Literary Society 18, 28
Dennis, William L. 53, 55
Denny Motor Company 130
DeRenne, Mrs. George Wymberley
  Jones 44
Deupree Block 130
Dispensary, Athens 86, 87
  gin bottle
D'Lites 189
Dobbins-Jones-Long House 30
Dobbs, A. M. 201
Dodd, Lamar 167, 198, 199
Dorsey Company 101, 113
Dorsey, E. H. clothing store 132
Double-barrell cannon 28, 46
Dougherty, Charles 91
Downs, Jeanne 177
DuBose, Charles 53
Dubose, Janet 147
Dudley, A. G. 51
Dunlop Tire and Rubber Company 142
Dunn, Willie 175
Durden's Music Store 101

E
Easley, Daniel 11, 14, 23, 105
Eberhardt, Nellie 144
Edwards, Leroy 141
Edwards Mills office 114
Effie's 180
Elite Theatre 136
Elks' Club 151
Emmanuel Episcopal Church 26, 53, 92
Epps, Ben 100, 104
Erwin, Andrew C. 119, 130
Erwin, Lucy Dupree 148
Erwin, Mary Cobb 148
Erwin, Mary Lamar 148
Ethridge, Nan 136
Evans, Martha 147
Everleila Sanitorium 32
Explosion, 1970
  (see Texaco)

F
Federal Building
  College Avenue 176
  Hancock Avenue 174
Felton, W. H. 81
Ficketts Jewelry Building 119
Field, Robert 14
Filling station, Broad and Lumpkin 163
Finley, Robert 14
Fire companies, volunteer 13, 52, 87
Fire Hall No. 1 97, 118
Fire Hall No. 2 97, 186, 188
First A.M.E. Church 203
First American Bank and Trust
  Company 176
First Baptist Church 25, 92
First Christian Church 92
First Methodist Church 14, 53, 92, 120
First National Bank of Athens 163, 183
  (see also National Bank of Athens)
First Presbyterian Church 19, 53, 92
Fitts, E. B. & Company 110
Fleming, Alice Thomas 72
Fleming, J. H. 72

Fleming, J. H., House 72
Fleming, T., and Sons 89
Forbes, W. T. 129
Franklin College
 (see University of Georgia)
Franklin House 33, 105, 142, 177
Franklin, Marcus A. 183
Freeman, Amelie 148
Friend, Eugenia Blount 165
Friends of Lucy Cobb/Seney-
 Stovall 60
Frierson, Mildred 147
Frobos, Walter 21
Fruitlands Nurseries 203
Fullilove, H. M. 144-145

G

Gainesville Midland Railroad 99
Garden Club of Georgia
 Founders' Memorial Garden 164
Gardenia, Vince 186
General Time 168
Georgia, Carolina and Northern
 Railroad 85
Georgia Express 12
Georgia Factory 142
Georgia Museum of Art 167
Georgia Railroad 12, 26, 27
Georgia Railroad Bank 13, 26, 34
 Banknote 27
Georgia Railroad Depot 25
Georgia Square Mall 192
Georgia Theatre 136
Georgia Troopers 44
Georgian Hotel 134, 135, 151
 Palm Garden 134, 135
Gerdine, Flossie 165
Gerdine, Susan Golding 25
Giles, Norman 198
Gilleland, John 46
Gilmer Hall 41
Githens, Alfred M. 172
Go Van Go 197
Goetchius, George 53
Golding-Gerdine House 25
Golding, Thomas 25
Goodman, Charlie 53
Goodrich, L. F. 102
Gordon, Marianne 196
Goss, Isham H. 32
Grady, Anne Gartrell 54
Grady, Henry W. 53, 54, 55, 56
Grady, Mattie 54
Grady, William S. 54, 204
Grady, William S. House 54
Grant, John Thomas 37
Green, D. R. 165
Green, Lewis 58
Griffeth, Frank 104
Griffeth Implement Company 104
Griffeth, William 104
Griffith, Louis 165
Gross, Bishop 92
Grove School 24, 148, 63

H

Haddaway, Pauline 148
Hamilton, Emily 56
Hamilton, Ethel 56
Hamilton House 57
Hamilton, James S. 39, 56, 57
Hamilton, Natalie 56
Hamilton, Rebecca Crawford 56
Hamilton, Sarah 39, 56
Hamilton, Sylla 158
Hamilton, Thomas N. 22, 39
Hancock Avenue view 114
Hancock Hotel 33
Hanson, Marie McHatton 165
Hardin, General 23
Hardin, Mary 23
Hardin, Mary, Home 23
Hardy, Chief 169
Harris, E.D. 114
Harris, E. D., Drugstore 114
Harris, E. G. 79
Harris, Judia C. Jackson 148-149
Harris, Joe Frank 198
Harris, Sampson 144
Harris, Samuel F. 121
Harris, Sarah H. 24
Harris, W. H. 114
Harris, Young L. G. 85, 202
Harris, Young L. G., House 202
Hartman, Bill 141
Hayes, Hiram 25
Hazelhurst, Louise 56
Hebrew Benevolent Association 101
Heery, Wilmer 176
Heidler, Clare D. 138

Hiedler, Harrison 147
Henderson, Reverend Matthew 53, 163
Herrington, S. M. 91
Herrington House 91
Herty, Charles Holmes 82
Hety Field 80, 82
Highland Guards 44
Hill, Benjamin Harvey 37
Hill, Caroline Holt 37
Hill, Walter B. 48, 56, 97
Hillsman, Patty 121
Hillyer, Junius 85
Hillyer, Mr. 53
Hillyer, Rebecca 38
Historic Cobbham Foundation 162, 181, 185
Hodgson, A. H. 34
Hodgson, Asbury H. 74-75
Hodgson, Bill 82
Hodgson Brothers 30, 84
Hodgson, Edward R. 23, 30, 45, 57
Hodgson, Elizabeth Preston 23
Hodgson, Frederick Grady 94
Hodgson, Harry 108
Hodgson, Hugh 23
Hodgson, Joseph M. 70
Hodgson, R. B. 53
Hodgson, Rob 45
Hodgson, Sally Paine 74-75
Hodgson, Will 45
Hodgson, W. V. P. 30
Holbrook, Alfred H. 167
Hollis, P. B. 53
Holman Building 138
Holman, W. S. 79, 138
Holmes, Hamilton 168, 169, 170
Home School 30, 31, 48, 64
Hope Fire Company 52
Hubert, J. H. 176
Hubert, Marion 141
Hubert State Bank
 (see First American Bank and Trust)
Huff, Craig 131
Huff, Gus 132
Huff, Rich 131, 132
Huger, Arthur 28
Huggins, H. T. 88-89
Huggins, J. H. 89
Huggins, John I. 91
Huggins' Store 88-89
Hull, Asbury 16, 21, 30, 43
Hull, Augustus Longstreet 55, 81
Hull, Reverend Hope 21
Hull, John Hope 30
Hull-Morton-Snelling House 30
Hull, William Hope 40, 42
Hulme, George Henry 73
Hunnicutt, Deupree 36, 88
Hunnicutt, John A. 88
Hunter, Charlayne 168, 169, 170
Hunter, B. T. 41
Husa, Karel 198

I

"Iron Horse" 166

J

Jackson, Davenport 53
Jackson, Howell 53
Jackson Street Cemetery 14
Jackson, W. H. 69
Jackson, Walter E. 113
Jenkins, Phyllis 147
Jennings, Jefferson 16, 43
Jeruel Academy 48, 66, 67, 97
Jeruel Baptist Institute
 (see Jeruel Academy)
Jester, Mary Alice 148
Johnson, Evans 136
Johnson Guards 44
Johnson, John 142
Johnson, Macon C. 86
Johnson, Nell 148
Johnston, Richard Malcolm 28
Jones, Andrew 165
Jones, Edward E. 85
Jones, Louis 53
Jones, Sidney 165
Jones, Susan 165
Jones, William L. 30, 53
Junior Ladies' Garden Club 69
Junior League 54, 165

K

Kellogg, W. K., Foundation 167
Kennedy, Robert 170
Keno, Joe 33
Kilpatrick, J. T. 141
King, John P. 27

Knights of the Golden Eagle 48
Knox Institute 48, 97, 122, 123
 Carnegie Hall 123
Kress, S. H., store window 133

L

Lackland, John 28
Ladies' Garden Club 101, 159
Ladies' Memorial Association 57
Lamkin, Elizabeth 147
Lane-Hodgson 23
Lane, Sterling 23
Lanier Hotel 33
Lampkin, Lewis J. 39
Lawson, Hugh 11
Leadership Athens 162
Leathers, L. M., Company 113
Leathers, Milton 202
LeConte, John 36
LeConte, Joseph 36
Lehman-Bancroft House 201
Lehman, William 201
Lester Hall 84
Leverett, Ella 120
Lewis, Ward 204
Library, University of Georgia
 First library 41, 80
 Second library 109
 Ilah Dunlap Little Library 172
Lipscomb, Andrew A. 15, 57, 53
Lipscomb, Lamar 148
Lipscomb, Mary Ann 38, 62
Lipscomb Volunteers 44
Little-Cleckler Construction
 Company 113
Little, Ilah Dunlap 172, 200
Long, A. B. 29
Long, Crawford W. 28, 29, 30, 126
Long, Crawford W., House 29
"Long, Tom" 29
Lowe and Company 87
Lucas, F. W. 24, 80
Lucas House 24, 153
Lucy Cobb Institute 15, 40, 43, 48, 60, 61, 97, 185
 Alumni Hall 60, 61
 Children of the Confederacy 148
 Margaret Hall 60
 Kindergarten Operetta 147
 Parade floats 63, 100
 Seney-Stovall Chapel 60, 61, 185
 Shakespeare play 147
Lumpkin, E. K. 84
Lumpkin, Hotel 33
Lumpkin, Joseph Henry 22, 31, 42, 43, 201
Lumpkin, Joseph Henry, Foundation 31, 162
Lumpkin, Joseph Henry, House 31, 64
Lumpkin, Marion 207
Lumpkin, W. W. 41
Lumpkin, Wilson 16, 109
Lumpkin, Wilson, House 109
Lumpkin's Battery 44
Lustrat, Joseph 200
Lustrat House 200
Lyle-Hunicutt House 36
Lyle, James R. 36
Lyndon, Edward S. 71
Lyndon, Mary 98
Lyons, C. H., Sr. 66

M

Macon and Northern Railroad 110
Maddox, Claude 80
Maddox, Lester 171
Magill, Dan 196
Malcom, A. L. 99
Mallison Braided Cord Company
 Office 114
Mandeville family 25
Market Street School
 (see Washington Street School)
Martin, J. W. 30
Martin, Mickey 165
Masons 48
Massey, Jerry 200
Matthews, Effie 180
Maupin, Joann 165
Max Joseph Building 130
McCaskill, Betsy 165
McCay, Charles 36
McClesky, L. L. 53
McGinty, E. B. and Company 137
McGinty, M.B. 58
McGregor Company 89, 115
McGregor, D. W. 115
McKibben, N. V. 53
McLaren, E. H. 53

McLellan's store 132
McWhorter, Hamilton 71
Means, Rebecca 147
Meeker, John A. 203
Meeker-Barrow House 203
Mehre, Harry 143
Meigs, Josiah 10, 11, 14, 16, 18
Meldrim, Peter W. 53
Mell Auditorium
 (see Athens High School)
Mell, Benjamin 45
Mell, Bessie Rutherford 67
Mell, Edward Baker 65, 121, 146
Mell House 39
Mell, John D. 39
Mell, Patrick H. 45, 53, 84
Mell Rifles 44-45
Mell, T.S. 88
Memorial Hall 127
Memorial Park 146, 162
Methodist Church
 (see First Methodist Church)
Michael, Annie 106
Michael Brothers Department Store 113
 Old building, Clayton and Jackson 87
 Before fire of 1921 130
 New store, 1922 131
Michael, Emma 106
Michael houses, Prince Avenue 106-107
Michael, LeRoy 156-157
Michael, M. G., House, Milledge
 Avenue 156-157
Michael, Moina 112, 126
 Stamp 126
Michael, Moses G. 87, 88, 106, 151
Michael, Simon 87, 106
Middlebrooks, Emmie 165
Milledge, John 11, 12, 14
Mims, W. R. 53
Missionary Sisters of the Most Sacred
 Heart of Jesus 145
Mitchell, A. L. 53
Mitchell, Robert, Furniture Company 70
Mitchell, William L. 142
Mitchell, William P. 53
Model and Training School 148, 149
Moore College 47, 49, 58
Moore, Richard D. 49, 58, 85
Morris Building 130
Morris, Charles 200
Morris, Sylvanus 84
Morton Corporation 193
Morton family 30
Morton, John White 136
Morton, Monroe Bowers "Pink" 76, 193
Morton, Monroe Bowers, House 76
Morton Theatre 76, 100, 193
Moss, Julia P. 63
Moss, R. L. 25
Moss, William Lorenzo 25
Moss-Side 25
Mother Goose Bread truck 133
Muir, John 47
Myers, H. P. 53
Myers, Moses 92

N

National Bank of Athens, 36, 68, 88, 136
 (see also First National Bank of Athens)
Nelson, George, Company 167
Nesbit, John 90
Nevitt, John W., House 69
New Wave Music 197
New College 13, 14, 20
New Opera House 48, 137
Newton, Elizer L. 33
Newton House 33
Newton, John H. 22
Nicholson, John W. 204
Nicholson, Madison 204
Nicholson, Minor 63
Nickerson, Reuben 37
Nisbet, John 34, 142
Normaltown 98
Norris, Peter 187
Northeast Georgia Medical Society 165

O

Oconee Hill Cemetery 14, 35, 97
Oconee Rangers 44
Octagon 152
Odum, Eugene 198
O'Farrell, James 90
Old Athens Cemetery Foundation 162
Old College 11, 17
"Old Tub"
 (see Green, Lewis)
Oliver, Charles 29

Orr, Craig 157
Orr Drugs 84
Ostrich 101

P
Paddock, Laura Hutchins 174
Palace Theatre 136
Paper mill 43
Paradise Valley Industrial Park 160
Parker, A. S. 136
Parks, William 53
Parr, Jack E. 143
Patrick, J. K. 143
Patrick's Pharmacy 101, *143*
Pattison, Abott 166
Payne, John Howard 23
Peabody, George Foster 97, *108*, *109*
Pearson, H. C., Jr., "Pop" 129
Peek, William T. 156
Peek, William T., House 156
"Peek-A-Boo" 156
Persley, L. H. 203
Phi Kappa Hall 22
Phi Kappa Literary Society 18, 22
Phi Mu Sorority House
 (see Phinizy-Segrest House)
Philosophical Hall 19
Phinizy, Barrett 63
Phinizy, Billups 72, 151
Phinizy, Billups, House *72*
Phinizy, Bowdre 53, *172*
Phinizy, C. H. 88
Phinizy, Ferdinand 16
Phinizy, Mrs. Ferdinand 39
Phinizy, Laura Ann *148*
Phinizy-Segrest House *39*
Pierce's Chapel 203
Police Department, city of
 Athens 47, *100*
"Polly" 65
"Poppy Lady"
 (see Michael, Moina)
Poss, R. E. 166
Poss' Barbecue 166
Pound, Jere M. 111
Pound, Lucy *147*
Powder Magazine 12
Pratt, Daniel 21
President's House, University of
 Georgia *37*
Prince Avenue Baptist Church 182
Princeton Factory 26
Proctor, J. P. 144-145
Progressive Era 76
Pruett, Pee Wee 164
Pruett, Peggy 164

Q
Q Room *163*

R
Rankin, Jeanette *171*
Reaves, Rufus K. 49
Reaves, Rufus K., House *49*
Reed House 19
Reese, Anderson 90
Reid, Neel 131, 156
Richardson Alfred 46
Richardson, Mrs. George 20
Richardson House
 (see New College)
Ritch's Company 44
Rivers, Eurith D. 154
Rock College 41, 48
Rock House *109*
Rockwell, Norman 117
Rogers, Christopher 196
Rogers, Kenny 196
Rolfe, L. M. 104
Roosevelt, Franklin Delano 154
Rowe, H. J. 90, *119*
Royal Arcanum 48
Rucker-Hodgson House *70*
Rucker, J. H. 70, 151
Rucker, J. P. 53
Rusk, Dean *178*, 198
Russell, R. A. 53
Rutherford, Laura Cobb 38, 40, 62
Rutherford, Mildred Lewis 38, 60, 61, 62
Rutherford, Mildred Lewis, House *62*
Rutherford, Williams 38, 53, 62, 85

S
Saint Joseph's Catholic Church 92, 201
Saint Mary's Hospital
 First hospital, Milledge Avenue *144*
 Second hospital, Milledge Avenue *145*
Samaritan Building 100, 114
Sandy Creek Nature Center 162, *187*
Sanford Field 98, *110*
Sanford Stadium 98, *153*, *190-191*
Sanford, Steadman V. 110, *154*
Schevenell, Len 94
Schevenell, Richard 94
Scudder, A. M. 15
Scudder, Charles A. 204
Scudder, Nina 204
Scudder House 204
Scudder Jewelry Company 119
Seaboard Railroad 48
 depot *85*
 trestle *85*
Segrest, Mrs. R. T. 39
Seney, George I. 60-61
Shackelford Building 84
Shehee, Mrs. W. E. 36
Sigma Alpha Epsilon Fraternity
 House *202*
Skelton, James E. *133*
Skelton's Bakery *133*
Slaughter, Nell *147*
Sledge, James 90
Smith, Annie 28
Smith, Hoke 22
Smith, Jennie 21
Smith, W. C. 53
Smith, W. P. 30
Snodgrass, Mr. 68, 78
Snelling, Charles M. 30
Sosnowski, Callie 31, 48
Sosnowski, Sophie 31, 48, *64*
Southern Banner 16, 90
 (see also *Athens Banner*)
Southern Bell Telephone
 Company 47, *119*
Southern Cultivator 26
Southern Manufacturing Company 77
Southern Mutual Insurance
 Company 13, 34, 202
 1876 building *89*
 1908 building *132*, *138*, *140*
Southern Ry. 48
 Depot *152*
Southern Watchman 16, 58, 90
Speer, Eustace, House 22, *46*
Stanley, Thomas 92
State College of Agriculture and
 Mechanical Arts 47
State Normal School 41, 48, 192
 Bird's eye view *111*
 Canning club *111*
 Domestic science department *112*
 Parade float *113*
 Students *111*
 YWCA *112*
Stegeman Hall 110
Stegeman, Herman 98
Stephens, Alexander 28
Stephens, Grace 165
Stephenson, Graves 136
Stern Building *132*
Sterm, Meyer 88
Stevens & Wilkinson 167
Stevens, William Bacon 92
Stillwell, W. R. 20
Storey, Martha Carter *148*
Stovall, Bolling 144
Stovall, Nellie 61
Strahan, Charles Morton 28, 99, 113
Strahan House 28
Strand Theatre 100, 136, *138*
"Streaking" 180
Streetcar Barn *78-79*
Summey House
 (see Old College)

T
Taft, William Howard 72
Tallulah Falls *93*
Talmadge Building 119
Talmadge, Eugene 158
Tate, William 61, *169*, *179*, *184*, *185*
Taylor-Grady House *54*, 165
Taylor, R. S. 201
Taylor, Robert 54
Texaco gasoline tank explosion 174
Thomas, Bailey 136
Thomas-Carithers House *73*
Thomas, George 86
Thomas, Mrs. George Dudley 72
Thomas, Stevens 16, 32, 34

Thomas, Stevens, House *32*, *33*
Thomas Street view *105*
Thomas, W. Bailey 53
Thomas, W. W. 53, *55*, 59, 61, 72, 73, 74
Thompson, Blanche 114
Thompson, C. M. 165
Thompson, William 199
Thunderbolts 44
Thurmond House 38
Thurmond, Samuel P. 38
Thurmond, Thurmond, Miller &
 Rucker 165
Toombs Oak *21*
Toombs, Robert 21, 53
Tornado damage, 1973 *177*
Town Hall and Market House 13, 28, 53
Towns, Lena H. 74
Towns, Speck *141*
Treanor House 38
Treanor, Kate McKinley 38
Tree That Owns Itself *69*
Troup Artillery 43, 44
Trussell, C. A. *118*
Trussell Ford *118*
Trussell, Kitty 165
Tuberculosis Sanitarium 146
Tuck, Henry 86
Twiggs, John 11

U
Union Baptist Institute
 (see Jeruel Academy)
Union Hall 100
Union bus terminal 99
United Confederate Veterans
 Cobb-Deloney Camp *103*
United Daughters of the
 Confederacy 48, 101
United States Navy Supply Corps
 School 41, 155, 160, 192
University High School 41, 43
University of Georgia
 Admission of Women 98
 Baseball 82
 Bicentennial Celebration 198-199
 Bicentennial flag *198*
 Bicentennial medallion *199*
 Boat crew *82*
 Botanical Garden *187*
 Camp Wilkins *151*
 Carl Vinson Institute of
  Government 60, 185
 Class of 1868 53
 Cocking Affair 158, 159
 Commencement *198*, *200*
 Commencement ball
  invitation *20-21*
 Coordinate campus 41, 155
 Field day, 1893 *80*
 Football team, 1895 *81*
 Football team, 1935 *143*
 Football team, 1980 *189*
 Forest Resources, School of 74
 Founder's Memorial Garden *164*
 4-H Cooperative Dormitory 30
 G Club *163*
 Georgia Center for Continuing
  Education 167
 Integration 168-169
 ITCA Collegiate Hall of Fame 196
 Lacrosse team *82*
 Law school 42, 151
 Military Building *172*
 Military companies 80
 Museum 41
 Navy Pre-Flight School 162
 North Campus *83*
 Pharmacy School 20
 Physical Plant 51
 Polo team 154
 President's House *37*
 Pushball *110*
 Rose Bowl game 159
 Senior parade *124-125*, *152*
 Small Business Development
  Center 51
 Student Army Training Corps *123*
 Students playing cards *84*
 Students with WWII poster *161*
 South Campus *149*
 Sphinx Society 151, 158
 Summer School 150
 Thalian Dramatic Club 83
 Vietnam war demonstrations *172*
 View of campus from *Gleason's
  Magazine* *23*

World War II 161-162
United Daughters of the
 Confederacy 201
Upson House *183*
Upson, Stephen 183, *185*

V
Van der Kloot, Bill 166
Varsity Restaurant *184*
Venable, Charles 36
Venable, James 28
Veterinary Hospital 150

W
WCTU 101
WGAU 101
WRFC 164
WTFI 101
Waddel Hall
 (see Philosphical Hall)
Waddel, Moses 12, 19, 24, 92
Waddell, James P. 53
Walker, Abraham 34
Walker, Abram 142
Walker, Herschel *189*
Walker, Major 22
Walker, R. F. 203
Walton, George 11
Ware, Edward R. 71
Ware-Lyndon House *71*
Washington Street School 65
 First 10th grade *120*
Welch, Faye 165
Welch, John W. 93
Welch, Mug 165
Welch, William Pinckney 72
Welch, William Pinckney, House *72*
Welch, Margaretta White 72
West, Henry S. 113
Westlake Country Club 101
Wheat and Oat Fair, 1901 96, *99*, *100*
White, George 12
White, H. C. 39
White Hall *74*, *75*
White, James 37
White, John R. 74, 99, 135, 142
Whitehall 142
Whitehall Manufacturing
 Company 142
White's Company 44
Whitman, H. 53
Whitworth, J. B. *141*
Wilbanks, John 77
Wilbanks, Minnie Power 77
Wilkins, S. B. *115*
Williams, William 27
Wilson, H. N. 30
Wilson, Margaret Gunn 165
Wilson, S. F. 53
Winnie Davis Hall *194*
Wray-Nicholson House 204
Wray, Thomas 204
Wright, Mrs. E. A. 60
Wyche, Mrs. 121

Y
YMCA 48, 127
 Camp at Tallulah Falls *129*
 First building *85*
 Second building *128*
YWCA 32, 67, 101
 Summer camp at Tallulah Falls *129*
YWCO 188
 (see also YWCA)
Yancy, Hamilton 53
Ye Garden Restaurant 101
Young, E. B. 53

Z
Zebenee, Joseph
 (see Keno, Joe)